BETTER TOGETHER

The Collected Wisdom of Modern Dog Trainers

Edited by Ken Ramirez

Better Together
The Collected Wisdom of Modern Dog Trainers

Karen Pryor Clicker Training
Sunshine Books, Inc.
49 River Street, Suite 3
Waltham, MA 02453 USA
U. S. (Toll Free) 1-800-472-5425
781-398-0754

www.clickertraining.com

For information about special discounts for multiple-copy purchase, please contact Karen Pryor Clicker Training sales:
U. S. (Toll Free) 1-800-472-5425 or 781-398-0754 or
wholesale@clickertraining.com

© 2017 by Sunshine Books, Inc.

Cover/book design: Lindsay Peternell

All rights reserved, including the right to reproduce this book or portions thereof in any form whatsoever.

First edition published 2017

Printed in the United States of America

ISBN-10: 1-890948-50-0
ISBN-13: 978-1-890948-50-4

Library of Congress Control Number: 2016963618

BETTER TOGETHER

The Collected Wisdom of Modern Dog Trainers

Table of Contents

Introduction 1

Chapter 1: Clicker Principles 7
Does Your Dog Require a Leader? If So, What Kind? 8
by Aidan Bindoff

Operant Conditioning vs. Clicker Training 12
by Kellie Snider

Are You Clicker Training, or Training with a Clicker? 14
by Kathy Sdao

Beyond Clicking and Treating: The Power of Choice 19
by Irith Bloom

Is it Really All or Nothing? 26
by Ken Ramirez

Chapter 2: Getting Started 33
Fifteen Tips for Getting Started with the Clicker 34
by Karen Pryor

The Training Game 37
by Karen Pryor

Paying Attention—A Training Exercise for Puppies and Dogs 40
by Aidan Bindoff

Tucker's Top Training Tips 42
by Aaron Clayton

Chapter 3: Clicker in Action 47
The 10 Laws of Shaping Revisited 48
by Lori Chamberland

Shaping Success 56
by Sarah Dixon

How to Teach Your Pet to Target 60
by Laurie Luck

Targeting vs. Luring 63
by Gale Pryor

Ken's Top Tips for Reinforcement 66
by Ken Ramirez

How to Use Play as a Reward 69
by Laurie Luck

Controlled Tug Games: A Novel Reinforcer 73
by Aidan Bindoff

"Clicker Trainers Use No Punishment" and Other
Training Myths 77
by Melissa Alexander

Should You Use No Reward Markers? Examining the Debate 86
by Laura VanArendonk Baugh

When It All Goes Wrong: How to Respond to Failure 92
by Aaron Clayton

The Rules for Cues 97
by Karen Pryor

Adding the Cue 98
by Karen Pryor

Hurry Up and Wait 99
by Lori Chamberland

Reinforcing Doing Nothing 101
by Karen Pryor

My Dog Knows It, He Just Won't Do It! How to Achieve Fluency .. 103
by Laurie Luck

Chapter 4: Basics for Puppies 109
Clicker Litter 110
by Karen Pryor

All Ears! How to Train Your Puppy to Listen 113
by Aidan Bindoff

Where's the Potty? How to House Train Your Puppy 116
by Debbie Martin

How to Survive Puppy Teething and Nipping 122
by Casey Lomonaco

The Need to Gnaw: How to Prevent Puppy Chewing 131
by Rebecca Lynch

Chapter 5: Basics for All Dogs 137

How to Crate Train Your Dog 138
by Casey Lomonaco

Teaching "Off" with Positive Reinforcement 143
by Joan Orr

How to Teach Your Puppy Not to Jump 150
by Sarah Stoycos

How to Teach Loose-Leash Walking 154
by KPCT

What Squirrel? 10 Techniques for Training with Distractions 157
by Casey Lomonaco

Happy Together: How to Train Successfully in a Multi-Dog Household 163
by Irith Bloom

Five Training Tips for Old Dogs 171
by Lori Chamberland

Chapter 6: Socialization 175

What to Expect: Introducing a Puppy to Your Adult Dogs 176
by Laurie Luck

Overly Excited Greetings: The Good, the Bad, and the Ugly ... 182
by Nan Arthur

Help, We're Being Invaded! How to Train Polite Greetings 190
by Laura VanArendonk Baugh

Don't Socialize the Dog! 197
by Laura VanArendonk Baugh

Spa Day: How to Train Your Dog to Love a Bath, a Brushing, or Even a Mani/Pedi 204
by Colleen Koch

Chapter 7: Solving Problems 215

Ten Reasons Your Dog May Develop Behavior Problems 216
by Sarah Dixon

The ABCs of Barking 221
by Kiki Yablon

How to Put an End to Counter-Surfing 228
by Aidan Bindoff

How to Prevent Door-Dashing 231
by Casey Lomonaco

How to Keep Your Dog Calm When the Doorbell Rings 238
by Nan Arthur

How to Train a "Crazy" Dog! 247
by Laura VanArendonk Baugh

Desperately Seeking Snoozing—How to Help Your Dog Relax.... 252
by Nan Arthur

Separation Anxiety: When Alone Time Makes Your Puppy Panic .. 260
by Terrie Hayward

Chapter 8: Dealing with Anxious, Fearful, Reactive, or Aggressive Dogs 269

Aggressive Dogs: Nature or Nurture? 270
by Aidan Bindoff

The Four "Fs" of Fear.. 273
by Laura VanArendonk Baugh

Ben: An Aggressive Dog Case Study 277
by Emma Parsons

Muzzles—Not Just for Aggression Anymore! 282
by Nan Arthur

How to Help Your Fearful Dog: Become the Crazy Dog Lady.... 291
by Casey Lomonaco

Reducing Leash Reactivity: The Engage-Disengage Game 298
by Alice Tong

Erasing Fear: A Lesson (or Two) on Cues and Shaping 302
by Clint Matthews

How to Prevent Resource Guarding in a Multiple-dog
Household... 311
by Hannah Branigan

The Power of Ongoing Learning 315
by Ken Ramirez

Chapter 9: Creating the Thinking Dog 323
101 Things to Do with a Box 324
by Karen Pryor

When Animals Train Us... 328
by Lori Chamberland

Carnivorous Chairs and the Cone of Shame: Creativity in Action... 331
by Alena Van Arendonk

The Unexpected Benefits of Training............................... 336
by Ken Ramirez

Training Terms... 341

Author Biographies 351

Introduction

"I'll look for a trainer if my dog develops behavior problems."

"Training is mainly for those interested in competition or sport."

"Training is too time consuming and complicated."

These are just a few of the misconceptions and statements people have and make about training. However, training can be a simple and fun activity that helps build a better relationship with your dog. Positive reinforcement training teaches skills that makes life better for dogs and the people in their lives. The statement I wish all people *would* recognize and live by is that *"all dogs deserve and need training."*

Better together

There is no question that dogs add immeasurably to our lives, and with positive reinforcement training we can also add equally to theirs. Training creates a partnership that makes both you and your dog better together. There are so many training options open to pet parents that it can be hard to find clear information about how and why to choose certain approaches. This book takes you on a guided journey from starting the training process through problem solving and other advanced skills. We have selected various authors because each offers unique insights and revelations that will be helpful for beginner and advanced trainers alike. Each article brings a different perspective and voice to the topic, but they are all cohesive in the goal to guide trainers to teach as positively and humanely as possible.

Why train?

Dogs are naturally inquisitive and active creatures. Without guidance or direction, they will occupy themselves by digging up a garden, chewing a shoe, chasing rabbits, or barking at strangers. These are natural behaviors that our modern society has generally deemed inappropriate. If we want our pets to follow our rules, we have to teach them what we consider to be acceptable behavior.

Even more important than teaching dogs to live by our rules is recognizing the many benefits that training brings to a dog's life. Just as you would never consider having a dog without providing good veterinary care and appropriate food, you should think of training as being just as essential to your pets' lives. Training is a key to good animal care that enhances the welfare of your pets.

While we may choose to train dogs for many reasons, I have always felt that there are three primary reasons to focus on training. We should recognize the importance of activities that directly benefit the individual animal, such as physical exercise, mental stimulation, and cooperative behavior.

Physical exercise

Like most animals, dogs need to exercise. They have a natural desire to chase after things and sniff the world around them. If we don't provide them an outlet to get the exercise they need, they will find their own opportunities to release their energy. Training can be a way to keep dogs out of trouble and to get them a needed aerobic workout. Whether you focus on something basic like teaching a dog to walk on a leash without pulling or train high-energy retrieval games and tugging exercises, these are activities that allow you to control how and when your dog engages in exercise. Training allows you to set guidelines for your dog and teaches rules that allow your dog to get the exercise he needs and wants at a time and place that suits you.

Mental stimulation

When a dog is awake, his mind is active; it is just as important that dogs get regular mental exercise as it is that they get physical exercise. Toys, puzzles, and games give animals a focus for their hyper-alert brains. However, simply providing a toy or puzzle may not be enough. It is important to teach dogs the appropriate way to play with their toys. The timing of when you provide toys and games can be critical in determining what the dog learns and how he behaves in the future. A toy can be a great way to reinforce desired behavior or redirect an animal away from unwanted behavior. Successful use of toys and games requires an understanding of training and can help assure that your dog is mentally satisfied.

Cooperative behavior

In general, this is the first goal and main reason people think about training. Teaching a dog to walk on a leash, wait his turn to eat, or give his toys back when requested are helpful skills that make living with a dog easier. But I believe cooperative behavior should be much more than just getting a dog to comply with requests. One of the benefits of training is teaching the animal skills that will help in his care. Being able to trim a dog's nails, brush his teeth, or give medication when needed not only makes life easier for the trainer but also improves the quality of the animal's life. Training is so much more than a luxury; it is a necessary component of good animal care.

The power of the click

Another important benefit of training is the powerful relationship that can develop between you and your dog through the training process. Training provides a means of two-way communication between you and your dog. Positive reinforcement helps to create a stronger bond with your pet and can lead to a wonderful and lasting partnership. When training is a part of your everyday interactions, you will find that it is easy and fun. It establishes a framework that can keep behavior problems from developing, and it gives you a starting point for better communication with your pet.

You will notice that most of the articles in this book refer to the use of a clicker. The clicker is a tool that aids in making that communication happen. It is a way to indicate to your dog that he has just done something correctly. But, I'm getting ahead of myself! There are several articles in the first chapter of the book that will explain the clicker and how and why it is useful. Even if you don't want to use a clicker, you will find valuable information in every section of this anthology that will help you become a better trainer and build a better partnership with your dog.

Using the book

Good training should be an exciting and fun journey for you and your dog. You will run into roadblocks, have to make detours, and discover both challenges and joys throughout the process. This book ventures into those topics as well, and provides excellent advice on common problems—and a peek at advanced applications.

Better Together: The Collected Wisdom of Modern Dog Trainers is a collection of articles that were written for and appeared previously on the Karen Pryor Clicker Training website (www.clickertraining.com). Karen Pryor Clicker Training is a leader in positive reinforcement education. These articles were written by 28 different trainers, each a leader, innovator, or outstanding educator in the positive reinforcement community. If you come across ideas, rules, or concepts from different authors that seem to contradict each other, these differences often illustrate the artistic aspect of training and the fact that there are multiple correct ways to train. We included the differences on purpose, because each varied approach follows good training principles. We have chosen the articles carefully to provide a clear journey and a useful resource for trainers at any level. There is a logical flow to the articles; you can read the book from start to finish and build your training skills and knowledge sequentially. But, since each article was originally written as a stand-alone piece, it is easy to dive into any chapter or article and focus on a specific topic or problem.

Training is an essential component in providing the best care possible to our pets. Positive reinforcement makes the process fun and exciting for your dog and helps build a strong relationship between teacher and learner, a relationship that, ultimately, will make you better together.

Happy Training,

Ken Ramirez
Executive Vice President & Chief Training Officer
Karen Pryor Clicker Training

Clicker Principles

This book is devoted to the power of positive reinforcement training. The articles in this chapter focus on the philosophy and science behind clicker training, how it works, and why it is so effective. How does clicker training align with and fit into the science of operant conditioning? How can it help make you a better leader for your dog? How might it assist you in creating greater choices for your dog? Why doesn't just using a clicker make you a clicker trainer? This chapter provides an overview—whether you are just starting your journey into the world of clicker training or want to expand your view of positive reinforcement training.

Does Your Dog Require a Leader? If So, What Kind?..................... 8
by Aidan Bindoff

Operant Conditioning vs. Clicker Training 12
by Kellie Snider

Are You Clicker Training, or Training with a Clicker?.................... 14
by Kathy Sdao

Beyond Clicking and Treating: The Power of Choice.................... 19
by Irith Bloom

Is it Really All or Nothing? 26
by Ken Ramirez

Does Your Dog Require a Leader? If So, What Kind?
by Aidan Bindoff

The scientific study of behavior has led to some useful ideas and insights about how all animals learn. All organisms—dogs, cats, parrots, alligators, or humans—learn pretty much the same way. We each find different things reinforcing or punishing, and we experience sensory perceptions differently. Some species or individuals are more tenacious, others more sanguine, some sleep most of the day, some are capable of learning more complex skills. Our unique environments play a large part in shaping us. But whether we live under the sea or in the desert, spend most of our lives perched on a tree branch, eat grass, or hunt large prey, there are over-arching principles that govern how we learn.

Life's consequences
Operant conditioning has to do with how the environment acts on the organism. If you stand behind a horse, you might get kicked; if you eat your vegetables, you get ice cream. If you fail to put on a seatbelt, an alarm sounds repeatedly; if you remember your PIN, you can buy a new pair of shoes.

Not every consequence provided by the environment has to come directly from another conscious living creature. The seatbelt alarm comes from the car. The PIN attached to the bank account card is approved by a computer. If you don't look where you are going, you might trip and hurt your knee on a rock.

You don't always need a teacher to learn. Behavior is not always governed by decisions that either we or others make.

Adapting
Chances are, if a dog were left stranded on an island with access to food and water, he would survive just fine. He wouldn't become too lazy to get out of bed, he wouldn't go picking fights with animals he didn't plan to eat for survival, he wouldn't spend all day barking at nothing, he wouldn't dig

holes that served no purpose—and I'm pretty sure he wouldn't gamble all his money away or take to the bottle!

Continuing with this hypothetical scenario, if there were other dogs on the island, the evidence from stray and feral populations of domestic dogs suggests that they might form a group and work together, or they might not. Most of them would get along just fine either way. They would figure out what worked for them and how to survive.

Observations of stray dogs in Moscow suggest that dogs have even figured out how to ride the subway and when to cross the road according to traffic signals! Even in an almost completely human-made environment, the city, the dogs survive without human leadership—some even thrive.

Why does a "good home" introduce difficulty?
So what happens to create "dog behavior problems" when humans open the door and invite dogs into their homes? What is it about this particular environment that encourages dogs to become unruly, boisterous, noisy, destructive, dangerous, stubborn, or any of the other words that dog trainers routinely hear from their clients? Is it a lack of leadership—or something else?

Whether it's out on the savannah, on the streets of Moscow, or in the suburban family home, the environment is always providing consequences to behavior. Behaviors that bring favorable consequences are those that the dog will tend to repeat; behaviors that do not result in favorable consequences diminish over time.

The difference between life on the savannah and life in the family home is that the people in the home provide most of the environmental feedback. But, regardless of what the dog does, those people will still put the food in the bowl and keep him safe from predators. For the most part, it is a blessed life. Survival comes easily under human care.

The flip side of this environment is that dogs no longer need to hunt or forage. Those skills, as well as the ability to keep an ear out for danger, are not required as often as some dogs seem to think. This leaves dogs with a surplus of untapped potential; in some cases dogs are overflowing with potential.

There are two problems here: 1) a dog's primary survival requirements are being met regardless of his behavior, but 2) he still wants to use his energy and instinct to do something, even if that something is really annoying! Add to this the communication barriers between two vastly different species and decades of misinformation about how to bridge this communication gap (for example, the erroneously named "alpha roll") and you start to wonder how it is that dogs ever managed to find their place in front of our hearths. (Thankfully, dogs do love to sleep!)

Making it work

Leaders control the resources and make the rules. In the modern home, humans control the resources, or at least have the capacity to control them. They also make the rules, or at least have that capacity, too. The humans who care for them are a huge part of a dog's environment. This puts humans in the position where some degree of leadership is not just advantageous, but appropriate.

Attention, affection, play, shelter, safety, and food are some of the resources humans must provide dogs. Rules about how to greet others, how to enter or leave the house, how to walk on a leash, where to sleep, where to toilet, and how to play are all open to interpretation if the human doesn't lead the way effectively.

To take responsibility, as leaders should, not only for a dog's behavior, but also for his physical and emotional well-being, leaders should consider appropriate outlets for energy and the expressions of instinct or drive. At the very least, food should be earned in some capacity.

What a dog was bred to do should be taken into consideration, of course. All dogs have certain traits in common, though, and most are happy with any activity chosen for them as long as one is thoughtful about teaching how the behavior is associated with the activity.

Communication—the click can be the key

There are many ways to communicate with dogs. The clicker is one tool that makes communication easier by providing a means of communicating precisely which responses are being reinforced. Clicker training communicates clearly, at the same time giving dogs an outlet for their energy and

Chapter 1 – Clicker Principles

instincts that in turn leads to acquiring resources from the trainer. Clicker training takes advantage of a very natural and meaningful process in a way that tailors the outcome to suit modern life for pet dogs.

Leadership is about taking responsibility. Good leaders are clear and effective communicators who provide for the needs of those they lead. Leaders allocate resources effectively and appropriately. Take some time to understand your dog, see his role in your life, take stock of the resources available to you, and experience the benefits that come with being a good leader. Your dog will thank and reward you for this effort.

Operant Conditioning vs. Clicker Training
by Kellie Snider

While some use these terms interchangeably, others distinguish between "operant conditioning" (OC) and "clicker training." What is the difference, and how does understanding that difference make us better clicker trainers?

Operant conditioning is a natural behavioral phenomenon that occurs in the relationship between humans and animals and their environments. Clicker training is a technology developed in response to that phenomenon.

Operant conditioning was identified in the scientific laboratories of B.F. Skinner in the first half of the twentieth century. Skinner was always fooling around with inventions and experiments and accidentally figured out quite a lot about how the natural world of behavior operates. (Hang onto that word "operates." That's how the word "operant" in "operant conditioning" was derived.) Skinner's discoveries led to decades of controlled scientific experiments in laboratories as well as in real-world (applied) training and experimentation.

Operant conditioning is a concept that describes how behavior and the environment interact. Operant behavior exists because it has been followed repeatedly by a reinforcer in the environment. That reinforcer can be either positive, as in the case when something desirable is added to the learner's environment when he performs a behavior, or negative, as when something desirable is removed from the learner's environment when he performs a behavior.

When a reinforcer follows a behavior, the frequency of the behavior stays the same or increases. The term "operant" refers to behavior operating on the environment to produce reinforcers. The reinforcers may come from the fingertips of a clicker trainer or from the surrounding world. A baby's smile results in his mommy picking him up. Inserting coins in a soda machine produces a soft drink. A lover's kiss results in a hug.

Chapter 1 – Clicker Principles

OC occurs everywhere and anywhere there is an organism with the ability to act. Look at your spouse or roommate or child. OC operates in their interactions with their environments. Look out your window. See that squirrel, that grackle, that sparrow? There is OC at work in those organisms as well. Your dog, your cat, your parrot? There is OC there. See that cockroach, that worm, that ladybug? OC is also guiding their behavior. Even amoebas and germs learn by operant conditioning. Unattached muscle tissue learns by OC: muscles in human bodies can be taught to twitch through reinforcement without the muscle's owner being aware it is happening.

OC doesn't care whether we believe in it or not. OC just is, like evaporation or gravity or radioactivity. It's a phenomenon at work in the natural world. If I do not believe in gravity, I will still fall to Earth if I jump from the branches of a tree. If I do not believe in OC, I will still enter my house through the entrance that opened because I turned the key in the lock and pushed the door.

Some people have learned how to harness OC in effective teaching technologies. One of those technologies (but not the only one) is clicker training (and TAGteach, the parallel method for teaching humans). We can improve our clicker training skills by better understanding the principles of the phenomenon on which they are based. In other words, we reinforce improving our understanding of OC by getting better results in our clicker training!

Are You Clicker Training, or Training with a Clicker?
by Kathy Sdao

I began teaching people how to clicker train their dogs in 1996. At that time, most pet owners had never heard of clicker training and few class instructors took it seriously. Mine was the only advertisement in the local Yellow Pages that mentioned the word "clicker." I had to persuade students to even try this novel gadget.

Clickers are now common in dog training classes. But, I suggest, clicker training still is not common enough.

I believe "clicker training" is an unfortunate term for what we do. It's misleading in two ways:

1. **You can "clicker train" without ever touching a clicker.** I did this when I trained marine mammals. During those 11 years, I used various behavioral markers, including an adjustable-pitch Acme Silent Dog Whistle (with beluga whales), an underwater acoustic ping (with US Navy dolphins in the open ocean), the word "good" said with specific pitch and inflection (with a walrus named E.T.), and a single silent clap—a visual marker (with the dolphins at the University of Hawaii's Kewalo Basin Marine Mammal Laboratory).

2. **You can use a clicker for training, yet be doing something quite different than "clicker training."** I've met trainers who see nothing odd about holding a clicker in one hand and the transmitter of a remote shock-collar in the other. Their carrots are backed up by big sticks. Clearly, this is not clicker training.

So we're left trying to define genuine "clicker training" in order to distinguish it from "training with a clicker." Before I attempt this, let me acknowledge a few things:

- Clear definitions matter. They allow us to talk about abstract ideas with as little ambiguity in our conversations as possible.

Chapter 1 – Clicker Principles

- Definitions are social constructs. They aren't handed down from on high, etched into granite tablets. We—everyone who uses the language—create them, through discussion and consistent usage, though the opinion of experts does tend to carry more weight.
- Clicker training is a powerful behavior-modification process. It warrants delineation from other training approaches.
- It is needlessly divisive to define "clicker trainers" (versus "non-clicker trainers"). We are talking about a method and a philosophy, not a classificatory label. Though I passionately promote clicker training in seminars around the country, I sometimes use other training techniques, such as classical counter-conditioning. When working with animals, sometimes I'm clicker training and sometimes I'm not. Whether I (or anyone else, for that matter) should be labeled a "clicker trainer" seems beside the point.

And so, when you use a clicker to train your animal, are you clicker training (CT) or training with a clicker (TWC)? To answer this, consider the following questions:

Is the click an event marker?

- CT: The click pinpoints a behavioral instant, a moment of muscle movement. (With clicker-savvy animals, the click may sometimes be used to mark instants of non-behavior.)
- TWC: The click is used in a less precise way, as a general signal that the animal has earned a reward.

Is the click a release?

- CT: The click informs the animal that his movement met the trainer's current criterion; that is, his behavior was "enough" to earn reinforcement.
- TWC: After a click, the trainer may require further behavior from the animal before paying up (for example, after clicking, the trainer withholds reinforcement because the animal didn't stay in place, or didn't finish the weave poles).

Is the click meaningful?
- CT: It is essential that the animal recognize the click as an independently meaningful signal. Therefore, great care is taken to ensure that the sound of the click occurs in a sort of "stimulus void."
- TWC: Other stimuli salient to the animal that occur simultaneously with the click (for instance, a food lure on the dog's nose, the trainer's intentional movements toward food) often overshadow or block the click. As a result, the animal becomes desensitized to the sound of the click; he will not react to it in ways that indicate anticipation of food or play, such as flicking his ears, looking toward the source of the click, or wagging his tail.

Does the click predict a strong positive reinforcement?
- CT: The click is paired with the animal's deepest desires: food, toys, interactive games, social companionship, and so on.
- TWC: The click is often paired with weaker reinforcements such as praise and petting.

Is the treat delivered "in position"?
- CT: The emphasis is on delivering the treat as soon as possible after the click (though never simultaneous with the click). The trainer delivers the treat regardless of the animal's position subsequent to the click. The trainer knows that the animal's position at the instant of treat delivery is reinforced, and so, when planning a training session, considers various ways to provide reinforcement.
- TWC: The emphasis is on delivering the treat while the dog is still in the correct position. Treats may be withheld if the dog moves out of position when he hears the click (for instance, the dog forges ahead of heel position or gets up from a sit).

Who is doing more work—the trainer or the trainee?
- CT: The trainee is the more active participant, moving more than the trainer who remains relatively passive. The animal's job is to behave, that is, to move; the trainer's job is to observe the animal and to deliver timely, consistent, frequent reinforcements.

Chapter 1 – Clicker Principles

- TWC: The trainer is the more active participant, moving more than the animal that remains relatively passive. The trainer is focused on making behavior happen and uses food lures, body language, and physical prompts to "help" the animal.

Is speed of acquisition of a few key behaviors the most important goal of the training process?

- CT: Each training session is an investment in the animal's future ability to learn. Knowing this, the trainer sacrifices instant compliance to gain momentum toward the goal of accelerated learning, when the animal has "learned to learn" and training becomes virtually effortless. Trainers often accomplish this by allowing animals to get "unstuck" on their own, without lures and prompts.

- TWC: The priority is getting the animal to perform a particular behavior (for example, getting a dog to lie down quickly and completely). Lures, prompts, and physical molding—all behavioral antecedents—may be used to speed this process. The animal may learn this initial behavior quite quickly but also may be hindered in future learning situations by a tendency to remain passive, waiting for "hints" from the trainer.

Are all four quadrants of the operant conditioning grid used equally?

- CT: Clicker training is an intentionally "unbalanced" form of operant conditioning. It has a preferential option for positive reinforcement (the trainer adds stimuli the animal desires), and, to a lesser extent, negative punishment (the trainer removes stimuli the animal desires). In most cases, clicker training avoids using positive punishment (the trainer adds stimuli the animal dislikes) and negative reinforcement (the trainer removes stimuli the animal dislikes), knowing the fallout that can result. Clicker training gets rid of unwanted behaviors using extinction, the training of replacement behaviors, management, and negative punishment.

- TWC: The four possible consequences are used in proportions that are more equal. Positive punishments such as collar-pops, physical manipulation, and verbal reprimands are used to get rid of problem behaviors and to deal with the animal's non-compliance. These aversives are interspersed with clicks and treats.

Is the main emphasis control or communication?

- CT: Clicker training is an elegant and effective method for communicating with animals in a coherent way. It challenges humans to strip away the constraints of verbal language and to tap into a more universal way of conveying information. Control of the animal's behaviors then flows as a by-product of consistent, clear communication and effective motivation.
- TWC: Behavioral control is the principal goal of training. Communicating with the animal is the means to this end.

Is it important to realize the animal's full behavioral and cognitive potential?

- CT: At its best, clicker training maximizes each animal's potential. It strives to make the animal a fully active, thinking participant in the training process by constantly expanding the animal's behavioral repertoire and by providing ever-greater cognitive challenges.
- TWC: Training with a clicker may also aim high, attempting to tap into the animal's maximum potential. Often, though, the ultimate goal is a specific repertoire of discrete "obedience" behaviors, performed reliably on command.

Of course, when you come right down to it, a clicker has no inherent meaning. It can be used in all sorts of ways, both within animal training and outside that realm (for instance, US Airborne troops in World War II used clickers to identify friendly forces; Catholic nuns before Vatican II used them to cue the movements of students in church). My hope, though, is that the term "clicker training" will come to have a standardized meaning and that my colleagues who "train with clickers" will call their method something else.

Chapter 1 – Clicker Principles

Beyond Clicking and Treating: The Power of Choice

by Irith Bloom

If you're reading this article, you are probably interested in clicker training—and for good reason. The clicker is a wonderful tool. It lets us communicate more clearly with other species (as well as with our own, in some cases). It helps us focus on the behavior we want to see. It also enables us to train behaviors that would be extremely difficult, or even impossible, to train in any other way.

There's more to clicker training than just using a clicker, though. While clicking and treating are at the core of what most people think of as clicker training, to me clicker training is something that happens even when there is no clicker in the picture. You are probably thinking, "There are many markers other than clickers that trainers can use, such as whistles," and that is certainly true, but I'm trying to get at something more basic. Clicker training in its highest form goes way beyond formal training sessions. At its best, clicker training is the gateway to a world in which animals—and their choices—are better respected.

Training with a clicker

For the purposes of this article, I will refer to the use of a positive-reinforcement marker followed by something reinforcing to the animal as "training with a clicker," whether the trainer is using an actual clicker, a flash of light, a whistle, a tap on the water's surface, or any other short, sharp, salient stimulus as the marker. In other words, whatever the marker, if you are using one and then following it with positive reinforcement, that falls under "training with a clicker." I purposely call this "training with a clicker" as opposed to "clicker training," because I view "clicker training" as involving more than just technique. Back to that in a little bit!

It's fairly easy to train with a clicker. Watch a few videos, grab some yummy food, and, voilà, you're off and running. Unfortunately, there are many people out there who view clicker training as that simple—and that limited. The clicker is a tool they use only to train specific behaviors in formal training situations. Once the training session is over, though, these people go back to interacting with the animal in a very different way. For example, they may jerk the leash when their dog rushes ahead of them, throw a cat off the counter with an angry swipe of their arm, or use a crop to encourage greater speed in a horse.

Animals with handlers who behave like this live in a very confusing world. Part of the time they are asked to figure out how to earn a click and treat, which requires creativity and initiative, but the rest of the time the rules are different. In the formal training context, assuming the trainer is following the basic tenets of training with a clicker, if the animal happens to guess wrong, nothing particularly stressful happens. Outside of that context, though, if the animal misunderstands the signals the environment is sending ("misunderstands" as judged by the human, that is), the situation is completely different. In fact, creativity and initiative when the trainer isn't holding a clicker may very well result in painful or frightening consequences.

In my mind, the trainer of the confused animal is not a true clicker trainer. He or she is just a trainer who happens to use a clicker sometimes.

Clicker training as a lifestyle

At its best, clicker training is a way of life. It's something that happens between the animal and the handler all the time. As someone who lives with a non-human animal in my home, I spend a great deal of time looking for behavior I like, marking it in one way or another (our domesticated pets tend to be brilliant at reading the natural human behavior that precedes reinforcement), and then reinforcing it.

For example, if I am preparing food, I go out of my way to praise my dog and toss him an occasional treat when he is hanging out just outside the kitchen (as opposed to near the kitchen counters and underfoot). This behavior only took a short while to train back when we first adopted our dog, years ago. Within about a week, I went from tripping over my dog every time I was cooking to having a dog whose preferred spot is just beyond the confines of the kitchen—and I have an English shepherd, so being underfoot is more or less in his DNA.

Chapter 1 – Clicker Principles

In a formal clicker training session, the human's role is to look for correct behavior in the animal, mark it when it happens, and then reinforce it. The handler must have a clear picture of what "correct behavior" is so that s/he can see it and then mark and reinforce it. If the correct behavior doesn't appear, no click happens. If the correct behavior doesn't appear for extended periods (in the animal training world that often means anything longer than a few seconds), the handler needs to consider whether the criteria are appropriate and change them if necessary.

"I know, I know," you may be saying. "You don't need to explain to me how to shape behavior successfully." Those of you who have experience with the clicker are often fantastic shapers, and your use of the clicker in training sessions is a joy to watch. What I want you to think about, though, is what happens when you're not in the middle of a formal training session with a clicker in your hand. Do you react with anger when your cat jumps on the counter, or do you reinforce her for staying on the kitchen floor? Do you snap at your dog when he climbs on your bed, or do you offer him a cushy bed of his own in a nice sunny spot, and then praise and pet him every time he gets on it?

In a clicker training session, if the animal doesn't offer the correct behavior, the trainer doesn't yell at, hit, or otherwise punish the animal for failing to get it right. The trainer just waits and gives the animal a second chance (or the trainer adjusts the environment to help the animal get it right). Ideally, errors are not considered the animal's fault. True clicker trainers understand that it is the trainer's responsibility to set the animal up for success. After all, we are asking non-human animals to conform to human standards, while we speak a foreign language to them. The least we can do is help them out. And if this is true in formal training sessions, shouldn't it be true at other times as well?

Clicker training should be about more than just training interesting tricks. It should be about fair treatment and communication. It should also be about allowing the animal to make choices. We may use the click to encourage the choices that we want—a paw movement, for example, if we are training a "wave hello"—but, in the end, the animal gets to choose what to do. The animal also gets to decide whether or not making the choice we like is worth the reinforcer we are offering.

Clicker training and choice

Here's the bottom line: Done right, clicker training is much more than a formal training technique. It's a philosophy, a way of viewing the world. It means looking for and reinforcing behavior we like, and ignoring behavior we don't like unless it's truly problematic or dangerous (in that last case, it's a good idea to manage the environment until we can train a different behavior).

Clicker training at its best also means following this philosophy not just in training sessions, and not just when we have a clicker in our hands, but all the time. It's about reinforcing the animal for what we consider good behavior, whenever it happens. It's also about honoring the animal, respecting natural behavior, and guiding the animal to live more happily within our strange human rule structure.

Ultimately, clicker training, when done right, is about honoring animals' choices. While we may not always think of it in these terms, we click when we like the choice an animal has made. We often set up the environment to make the "right" choice more likely, but in the end we still have to wait for the animal to make a choice. We're not out there manipulating the animal using brute force; we're letting the animal choose what to do. That's extremely empowering for the animal. In fact, science tells us that choice (in other words, control) is one of the most powerful reinforcers out there.

The kind of aversive control I mentioned earlier—sweeping the cat off the counter and so on—reduces an animal's ability to choose how to behave. What's worse is that aversive control is likely to increase an animal's stress, as demonstrated in countless research studies. It's really not surprising when you think about it. Consider this: How would you feel if a giant hand came out of the sky, picked you up, and then put you down in a different place? To me, that sounds disconcerting, at best. Imagine how terrifying it must be to live in a world where that happens all the time!

Alas, what I just described is the world many small dogs experience. Is it any wonder that smaller dogs are often described as high-strung? People even complain that their dogs run away when they reach down to pick up the dog. To borrow a term from Dr. Susan Friedman, our "cultural fog" is so thick that often people don't notice the connection between being picked up willy-nilly and running away from reaching humans. It's so obvious to these people that they have the right to pick up their dog whenever they want, and to move the dog wherever is convenient, that the animal's opinion simply does not enter into the matter at all—and then they complain that the dog is high-strung, to boot!

Being able to choose what to do, freely and without compulsion, is an incredibly important aspect of life. Because we humans have the power to force behavior, we regularly fail to give animals the opportunity to make even the most basic of choices. For example, even though I try hard to give my dog many choices, he doesn't get to choose what he eats. Do I give him nutritious food that I believe is palatable? Yes, but it's still not his choice. This is just one situation where an animal living with humans doesn't get to make a choice. How many times a day do you make choices for the animals you interact with?

By being cognizant of when we allow animals to make their own choices, and by paying attention to what is reinforcing those choices, we can understand better why an animal behaves in a particular manner. When we take an animal's choices away, we lose that opportunity. That means that, strange as it may seem, letting animals make choices actually improves training and leads to better results.

Empowering animals

I believe it's important to empower animals to make choices. The road to empowerment starts with using choice-rich techniques such as clicker training in sessions where the animal has the choice to participate or not (as well as the choice to earn a click or not, of course).

When I visited Shedd Aquarium several years ago, I was delighted to discover that their animals can leave a training session at any time. If the trainer's rate of reinforcement isn't high enough to keep the animal interested, or if the animal is simply overwhelmed or tired, or whatever else, the animal can leave (in many cases, this involves swimming away). What a great gift this is to the trainer! The animal lets you know if a training session is reinforcing by remaining in your presence.

While we're on this topic, why would you ever want to force an animal to stick around, anyway? If training isn't a top priority for the animal, the animal isn't likely to learn much from the session. Consider how much more you learned in classes where you were truly engaged with the teacher or the topic as opposed to classes where you were forced to sit and listen but resented the whole experience.

I use the "free-to-leave" concept in all my clicker training sessions with domesticated animals. I may put up barriers (ex-pens for puppies, for example), but if the animal walks away from me, I honor the animal's choice and wait for the animal to reengage with me. If the animal keeps leaving the session, I know that something is wrong with the setup, and I adjust the environment accordingly (generally by changing my criteria and raising my rate of reinforcement).

Letting an animal choose to leave a session may seem like a very small change, but it's extremely significant. Willing participants are likely to learn more. Having the choice to leave also offers the animal a little more control over his life, and that is extremely beneficial in terms of stress.

Once you get comfortable with giving animals the choice to participate in formal training, start thinking about other ways you can offer more choice. For example, why not ask your cat if she wants to be petted, rather than just petting her "at will?" Another interesting (and often entertaining) exercise is a taste-test of different food treats with your pet. When my husband and I went through that process with our dog recently we were startled to discover, while comparing two specific food treats, that what we thought was our pet's favorite treat in fact comes in second to another treat, every time. What might you learn when you let an animal choose?

The great thing about empowering an animal to make choices is that his choices can help us understand what motivates his behavior. For example, if my kitten pounces happily on every leaf he sees blowing on the ground, I know that toys that behave like that leaf are likely to be good reinforcers for him. If, on the other hand, he spends more time stalking larger things that move in a more regular pattern, I would choose different toys for our training sessions. The choices he makes can help inform and improve my training in a million different ways.

Chapter 1 – Clicker Principles

Putting choice first

One of the difficulties with adding choice to our animals' lives is that it often requires us to give up the ability to make the choice we would like best in a certain situation. For example, if I decide I'm going to let a dog choose what pace to walk, that means I need to suit my pace to hers instead of the reverse. This entails a bit of adjustment—both physical and mental.

With some dogs, I'd probably need to walk faster a lot of the time, but I'd also need to be prepared to come to sudden stops when a particularly sniffy spot beckons. With other dogs, I might find the walk only goes a couple of hundred yards, and we dawdle the whole way. This may mean I don't get my heart rate up for an extended period, but it also means the dog gets to be much more proactively engaged in the environment than when we go on a forced march at my pace. It also means I need to give my dog attention, so that I can observe and promptly respond to changes in the dog's pace (no cell phones, please!).

These adjustments can make the first foray into giving animals more control a bit challenging, so be forgiving of yourself if you find it difficult at the start. Control and choice are just as reinforcing to us as they are to the animals we interact with. Giving up the ability to choose, even only some of the time, can be a bit daunting. For me, though, it's worth it to give the animals in my life more choices. It can take work, but the benefits are huge. In my experience, an empowered animal is calmer, more confident, more creative, and better able to navigate difficult situations. Doesn't that sound like a good thing to you?

Is it Really All or Nothing?
by Ken Ramirez

If I shared my travel schedule with people, most would be horrified at how much time I spend on the road! A good amount of the consulting I do is with professional trainers and programs looking for a way to transition to using positive reinforcement methods. I have been working with many of these organizations for more than 10 years now, and a great deal of that work I have carried with me into my role with Karen Pryor Clicker Training.

Coincidence…?

It has long been my mission to help more traditionally based trainers find useful solutions to the various training challenges they face by introducing them to positive reinforcement methodologies. Assisting people with a background in coercion-based training can be difficult, time-consuming, and filled with roadblocks. But, when we make breakthroughs and I see trainers use new tools and be successful with those new tools, it is rewarding and reinforcing for me! This is an area where I feel I can make a significant difference; my work over the past decade has convinced me it is worth the effort.

In a span of just a few weeks, I worked with five different groups that included several law enforcement agencies, a service dog organization, a guide dog organization, and a group of serious dog sports enthusiasts. As usual, each group had its own unique challenges and obstacles—and each stretched my training abilities in new ways. These varying needs and issues can be frustrating and exciting at the same time.

I wanted to share an obstacle that I faced on three separate occasions, an obstacle that came from an unexpected place. While each of the three conversations I had were different and sprung from completely different sources, they each presented me with an obstacle that was eerily similar. All of the encounters were private conversations that I had with individuals during the time I was working with their organization or group. I will detail one specific conversation for the purposes of this discussion.

Chapter 1 – Clicker Principles

Client: "I appreciate the knowledge you bring to us, Ken, but I can't drink the Kool-Aid! I can't really become a positive reinforcement trainer!"

Ken: "Why not? I am not trying to make you drink some artificial potion!" (I feel myself getting defensive, so I pull back my intensity and continue in a more calming voice.) "In fact, there is nothing hidden in what I am sharing with you. I am simply teaching various scientific principles and practical tools that will help you become a better trainer and improve your program. I want to give you new options for dealing with problem behavior so that you get better results!"

Client: "But some of the tools don't make sense for my needs (*he says in a rather snippy tone*)!"

Ken: "I know! That's why I am giving you lots of options, so that you can use the tools that are most appropriate for you and your style of training. Choose the tool or application that you understand and that makes sense for whatever particular challenge you face. I will help you apply the techniques effectively, over time."

Client: "But I was told that if I don't embrace the entire philosophy, then it is pointless to use just a few of the techniques. Mixing and matching coercion with positive reinforcement dilutes the effectiveness of both tools! And I am not ready to completely throw out my 25 years of training experience for a new fad!"

Ken: "Whoa, whoa, whoa! Hold on a minute! Let me figure out what you're trying to say. Where did you hear this? I think you have some misconceptions about positive reinforcement. What I am hoping to teach you is certainly not a fad nor is it new. Can you explain why you feel this way?"

Client: "I thought I would try to get a head start on understanding positive reinforcement by taking classes from a private trainer and using the techniques with my dogs at home. So, I signed up for a class and was told by the instructor that she would not work with me. If I wanted to learn about positive reinforcement, it was all or nothing. I could not use any corrections or it would negate all the work that we would accomplish using positive reinforcement. The instructor was pretty snooty about it and copped a serious attitude with me. So, I said 'forget that!' I have well-behaved dogs already; I don't really need her class."

Ken: "Do me a favor. Give me a chance this week and if you don't see a way that I can help you, we can say goodbye and you don't have to ever talk to me about positive reinforcement again! I think you may have misunderstood the instructor or caught her on a bad day, but let me clear up a few things for you…"

I won't go further with this particular dialogue but will simply say that this individual changed his point of view by the end of the week. He is looking forward to having me back to work with his organization again later in the year! If the conversation above had been my only conversation of that type, I probably would not be sharing this story. But I am sharing it because I had three similar conversations. Each conversation had slightly different specifics, but the people I spoke with all told me that they had reached out to or talked to another positive reinforcement trainer and were turned off to the use of positive reinforcement because of that interaction.

I had been on the road traveling for a few weeks in a row, but instead of being excited by the progress I had made at each organization and feeling happy to be headed home, I was troubled the entire flight home. All I could think about was that my biggest obstacle at each location had been conversations my clients had with other positive reinforcement trainers. Are we sabotaging our own cause without realizing it?

My must-solve issues

I am hopeful that these three incidents were just isolated and unique coincidences. I know many colleagues who share my philosophy and hope, so I find comfort in that fact. However, I also felt it was important to share this experience with readers, to share my initial thoughts on the topics that this experience raised for me. Here are the key issues for me:

1. Working with traditional trainers and determining how best to help them transition to the use of positive reinforcement
2. Talking with trainers whose approach differs from our own, using positive reinforcement ourselves

Positive options in a real world

These issues both apply to working with trainers who use coercive techniques regularly—the type of clients I worked with during my recent weeks of travel. I think the "all or nothing" philosophy comes from a well-intentioned

Chapter 1 – Clicker Principles

place, but it is unrealistic to maintain that philosophy dealing with trainers who already have a history of using aversive control and correction-based tools. There are options for handling the following obstacles these trainers present.

1. **Mixing reinforcers and punishers in the same learning environment.** The real world is filled with reinforcers and punishers; they are around us all the time. We, along with our animals, learn from these experiences every day. The existence of both reinforcers and punishers in our world does not by their very presence negate their effectiveness. We can recognize that a stovetop allows us to cook a delicious and reinforcing meal while also learning that touching the stovetop's hot surface with a bare hand is painful. Our long-term lessons about being around a stove will depend on the context and history of our collective experiences around that kitchen appliance. If every time we try to cook that delicious meal we always end up touching the stove and burning a hand, that experience (due to our clumsiness, ineptness, or inappropriate tool use) may teach us that the meal we crave simply is not worth it.

   But if taught to cook properly, with the right tools, we may avoid getting burned again, or at least rarely. Our comfort level using a stove and cooking our favorite meal will become more powerful than the rare times we are burned—thus, we'll still be eager to cook that meal. My point is that both punishers and reinforcers work in our environment side by side all the time. However, as positive reinforcement trainers, we recognize that the use of punishers, or any aversive, can break down the trust and relationship we have worked so hard to develop with our animals. This is one of the reasons we don't recommend mixing the two. Working with young or new trainers, we can teach them how to use positive reinforcement in a way that eliminates the need to introduce any corrections at all. But that is not the case if we are trying to help a traditionally trained trainer transition to the use of positive reinforcement.

2. **Using aversive control around animals that have never experienced it, or haven't experienced it in many years.** It is understandable that some trainers may want to prevent other learners in the

classroom (animals and people) from being exposed to corrections if those learners have not seen or experienced corrections before. That exposure can be a very upsetting and uncomfortable experience. This may be a valid reason for not wanting someone who uses corrections instinctively to be in a classroom setting. However, there are several options available besides simply denying the person access to classroom instruction. One option is to explain why you would like him or her to avoid using those tools in your classroom. Many trainers and owners are more than willing to try—as long as you set clear expectations and help them through the challenges they will face for the first class or two.

Another option is to offer a separate class (or a private class) to a handler who has a history of using correction techniques. This alternative prevents other students from being impacted by the use of aversive tools. You may find, as I have, that it only takes one or two classes for a handler to gain enough discipline to avoid using old standby tools in a classroom setting. After initial classes are handled privately, the handler can join a larger class. If we want to see coercion-based trainers make the transition, we need to find a way to work with them.

Step by step

My experiences over the years have helped me recognize that it takes time for someone who has used a skill or technique for many years to change to a new method or to use new tools. Just as we teach behavior to our animals in small steps, successive approximations, I have found that teaching trainers to move away from the use of corrections requires the appropriate steps and an adequate amount of time. We have to help these learners by setting them up for success. Give them steps and goals that are achievable and reachable, and move them toward our goal of using positive reinforcement in small increments.

If we are successful trainers, this is a process we have already used hundreds of times with our animals. Why not use it with our human learners as well? Successive approximation is the only method that I have used successfully as a consultant. There will be no change or progress if I come in and suggest that the client must stop doing everything that has worked for the past 30 years! I cannot, and do not, expect coercion-based trainers to leave all the tools they know behind and switch to a new set of tools all at once. Instead, I need to assess their needs and make the transition slowly one or two tools at a time.

This training process has to be executed thoughtfully so that the client can be successful in the transition. If we expect a client who wants to learn to use positive reinforcement to make the transition all at once, we are making the task far too difficult. Seeing success will be the most reinforcing event, and will lead the client to want to use more new tools. If I introduce the transition correctly, the client will often be eager to move even more quickly than I will allow. As much as I want eager clients to use the new tools, sometimes I am forced to slow down the pace to build a solid foundation before adding more layers.

Positive reinforcement: Offered to all!

A concern that has plagued me for years is that some positive reinforcement trainers fail to use the techniques they use so well with their animals when they are working with their human clients. I appreciate the passion with which we hold to our conviction that positive reinforcement is an effective and more humane approach to use when training animals. But sometimes that heartfelt emotion clouds our approach to talking about the science logically. More often than not, that approach makes our passion seem like harsh criticism of anyone who doesn't train the same way we do. I fear that some who profess to embrace positive reinforcement forget that unless they are grounded in the science and use positive reinforcement with the people around them, they will fail to make an effective case and fail to convert anyone.

In each training environment that I worked in, the people with whom I worked reported that they were turned away from positive reinforcement not because of the science or practical elements of its application but because of the attitude of the trainer who tried to convert them initially. This is not the first report of this news, but it alarmed me to face that obstacle three times in the span of just a few weeks. I know many positive reinforcement trainers who are equally good at the application of reinforcement with the animals they train and the people they teach. Until we can all move in that direction, we will fail to convince those considering new tools to make the switch!

2

Getting Started

When you are new to a skill, like clicker training, you may be unsure about where to start. When should you click and when should you treat? What does it feel like for your dog? The articles in this chapter give suggestions that can help you begin training successfully from managing the clicker to understanding what it's like to be your dog. You and your learner will acquire key skills that will set you both up for success.

Fifteen Tips for Getting Started with the Clicker 34
by Karen Pryor

The Training Game 37
by Karen Pryor

Paying Attention—A Training Exercise for Puppies and Dogs........... 40
by Aidan Bindoff

Tucker's Top Training Tips 42
by Aaron Clayton

Fifteen Tips for Getting Started with the Clicker

by Karen Pryor

Clicker training is a terrific, science-based way to communicate with your pet. It's easier to learn than standard command-based training. You can clicker train any kind of animal, of any age. Puppies love it. Old dogs learn new tricks. Here are some simple tips to get you started.

1. Push and release the springy end of the clicker, making a two-toned click. Then treat. Keep the treats small. Use a delicious treat at first: for a dog or cat, little cubes of roast chicken, not a lump of kibble.

2. Click *during* the desired behavior, not after it is completed. The timing of the click is crucial. Don't be dismayed if your pet stops the behavior when it hears the click. The click ends the behavior. Give the treat after that; the timing of the treat is not important.

3. Click when your dog or other pet does something you like. Begin with something easy that the pet is likely to do on its own. (Ideas: sit, come toward you, touch your hand with its nose, lift a foot, touch and follow a target object such as a pencil or a spoon)

4. Click once (in-out.) If you want to express special enthusiasm, increase the number of treats, not the number of clicks.

5. Keep practice sessions short. Much more is learned in three sessions of five minutes each than in an hour of boring repetition. You can get dramatic results and teach your pet many new things by fitting a few clicks a day here and there in your normal routine.

6. Fix bad behavior by clicking good behavior. Click the puppy for relieving itself in the proper spot. Click for paws on the ground, not on the visitors. Instead of scolding for making noise, click for silence. Cure leash-pulling by clicking and treating those moments when the leash happens to go slack.

Chapter 2 – Getting Started

7. Click for voluntary (or accidental) movements toward your goal. You may coax or lure the animal into a movement or position, but don't push, pull, or hold it. Let the animal discover how to do the behavior on its own. If you need a leash for safety's sake, loop it over your shoulder or tie it to your belt.

8. Don't wait for the "whole picture" or the perfect behavior. Click and treat for small movements in the right direction. You want the dog to sit, and it starts to crouch in back: click. You want it to come when called, and it takes a few steps your way: click.

9. Keep raising your goal. As soon as you have a good response—when a dog, for example, is voluntarily lying down, coming toward you, or sitting repeatedly—start asking for more. Wait a few seconds, until the dog stays down a little longer, comes a little farther, sits a little faster. Then click. This is called "shaping" a behavior.

10. When your animal has learned to do something for clicks, it will begin showing you the behavior spontaneously, trying to get you to click. Now is the time to begin offering a cue, such as a word or a hand signal. Start clicking for that behavior if it happens during or after the cue. Start ignoring that behavior when the cue wasn't given.

11. Don't order the animal around; clicker training is not command-based. If your pet does not respond to a cue, it is not disobeying; it just hasn't learned the cue completely. Find more ways to cue it and click it for the desired behavior. Try working in a quieter, less distracting place for a while. If you have more than one pet, separate them for training, and let them take turns.

12. Carry a clicker and "catch" cute behaviors like cocking the head, chasing the tail, or holding up one foot. You can click for many different behaviors, whenever you happen to notice them, without confusing your pet.

13. If you get mad, put the clicker away. Don't mix scoldings, leash-jerking, and correction training with clicker training; you will lose the animal's confidence in the clicker and perhaps in you.

14. If you are not making progress with a particular behavior, you are probably clicking too late. Accurate timing is important. Get someone else to watch you, and perhaps to click for you, a few times.

15. Above all, have fun. Clicker training is a wonderful way to enrich your relationship with any learner.

Chapter 2 – Getting Started

The Training Game
by Karen Pryor

The Training Game is a great way to sharpen your shaping skills and have fun at the same time. It allows you to see and experience other trainers' decision points and to be aware of what you might have done instead. It also allows trainers to make mistakes and learn from them without confusing some poor animal or unsuspecting person! Maybe most valuable of all, it allows you to see the training process from the viewpoint of the trainee, which is often a highly illuminating experience. The training game also helps us get rid of the superstitious behavior of putting the blame for problems on the person or animal we are working with instead of on the training contingencies, where it belongs.

The rules

While two people can play this game, larger groups are more fun. In a classroom or larger group, divide up into groups of six to eight. In each group, one person is selected as the Animal and goes out of hearing range. The others choose a Trainer and a behavior for the Trainer to shape.

The behavior must be something easy to do physically, which everyone can see. Some favorites are turning in a circle, pouring or drinking water, turning on a light switch, picking up an object, opening or closing a door or window, or marking on a blackboard. Avoid two- or three-step behaviors unless you are deliberately working on behavior chains.

The behavior must be something socially acceptable—no disrobing, no behavior (like lying on the floor or standing on a table) that is not polite in public. Don't pick a behavior involving touching other people! The behavior may involve a prop.

The Trainer will use a clicker, handclap, or other noise as a conditioned reinforcer. Each time the Animal hears the sound, he or she must return to the trainer and get an imaginary treat. (This prevents the Animal from just standing in one spot and trying to think, which gives you nothing to reinforce.)

There should be no talking during the shaping; the point of the game is that shaping is a non-verbal process. However, cheers, groans, laughter, and applause are not only permitted but encouraged. When the Animal accomplishes the behavior, most groups tend to burst into applause. The Animal then becomes the Trainer, and the group chooses another Animal. The new Animal leaves the room; the group chooses a new behavior, and the session starts again. When everyone has been both Trainer and Animal, the game is complete. This usually takes 60–90 minutes. An open discussion after the game can be useful and entertaining.

Helpful hints

If you get totally "stuck," and the Animal has either stopped working altogether or is uselessly repeating the same action over and over, here are some things you can try:

- Change the environment by taking the group to another part of the room.

- Try a new behavior. Once your Animal is working again, you can go back to the target behavior.

- Be generous with reinforcements; it's better to reinforce some behavior, even the wrong behavior, than to reinforce nothing at all.

- Try using a prompt. For example, to get someone to bend over, you might drop an object on the floor—a key ring, say—and reinforce the person for leaning down to pick it up.

- Check to see if you are trying to train two behaviors at once, or if what you want is really a chain; if so, remember that you will have to train the end behavior first.

Variations

The built-in delay (by Marian Breland Bailey and Robert Bailey): Have three people hold hands. The one at the right-hand end of the group is the Trainer. When she wants to reinforce the Animal, she squeezes the middle person's hand; that person squeezes the hand of the third person, who then clicks or says "Good." Watch what goes wrong with the shaping.

Chapter 2 – Getting Started

The group cheer (by Janet Lewis): Instead of picking one Trainer, let the whole group cheer and clap when the Animal does something deserving of reinforcement, and fall silent when the behavior is not improving. The group can travel around in a building or outdoors, teaching the Animal to fetch something from a distance, go over an obstacle, and so on. Fun for kids, especially!

Adding a cue: Divide the group in half. Separate the two groups. Inform one group that they are the Trainers. They will pick a word to use as a reinforcer, and an action (patting the hair, coughing, pulling the ear) as a conditioned stimulus. Tell the other group that they are the Animals. Pair up each Trainer with an Animal. Each Animal will offer one or more simple behaviors, such as turning, clapping, or waving. The Trainer must select a behavior, reinforce it, and then bring it under control of a conditioned stimulus. To do this, the Trainer establishes the behavior on a variable ratio schedule (that is, the subject is able to repeat the behavior two or three times for each click and reinforcer). When this has been accomplished, the Trainer presents the action that is going to be the cue, and reinforces the behavior in the presence of the cue. The Trainer does not reinforce any behavior that occurs in the absence of the cue. By alternating between short periods of cue-present and cue-absent, the Trainer can shape the behavior of responding with the correct behavior when the cue has been given, and waiting, without offering other behavior, when the cue is absent.

The task is completed when the Trainer can demonstrate to others in the group that his Animal waits for the cue (a cough, say) and then, when the cue is given, immediately performs the behavior correctly until clicked. At this point it is always worthwhile to ask the human subject these two questions: 1) What is the behavior? (They will usually answer correctly) and 2) What is the cue? (They may not have the faintest idea). One can often demonstrate good stimulus control of an operant behavior, in a human subject, without the subject being consciously aware of the nature of the cue. Apparently the part of the brain that learns environmental cues of this sort is not the verbal, "aware" part of the brain. This exercise often serves as a nifty demonstration of that fact. It can be surprising and illuminating to the spectators.

Paying Attention—A Training Exercise for Puppies and Dogs
by Aidan Bindoff

Does your dog know how to pay attention to you? Here is a simple training exercise you can use to teach your dog how to pay attention to you in all situations. By the end of a week, your puppy or dog will be paying more attention to you—guaranteed!

We're going to use the principle of positive reinforcement to teach this behavior, through a simplified process known by animal trainers and behaviorists as "shaping." Shaping occurs when you "shape" a behavior like a piece of clay. You start off with something simple and mold it into something you can use. It's not difficult to do using positive reinforcement, but you need to be able to relax a little and trust the process.

What you're going to start off reinforcing is any effort your dog makes to pay any sort of attention to you. That means any glance in your general direction, or even a step toward you. You're going to be quiet and still and wait for your dog to do this: do not try to get your dog's attention during this exercise.

You'll use food as a reinforcer. You're going to work in 10-minute sessions using a rate of reinforcement of 1 food treat every 10 seconds, so you'll need 60 treats. Count out 70 just in case you need more. The reason you count out your treats is so that you know that you are reinforcing simple-enough behaviors. Many trainers wait for too much behavior to begin with, and the dog doesn't learn as much as he could if he were reinforced more frequently. If you have any more than 10 treats left over at the end of a 10-minute session, then you're asking for too much and need to relax your criteria a little.

You need to find safe areas to let your dog off lead where you don't have to worry about cars or losing your untrained dog. The more of these safe areas you can think of within driving distance the better, because the more times and places you do this exercise over the next week or so, the more effective it

Chapter 2 – Getting Started

will be. Dog parks at quiet times, dog-friendly beaches, friends' houses, and playing fields are some of the places you can use. If you can't think of a safe area to let your dog off lead, then use a long leash, but don't use the leash to get your dog's attention.

Once you get to a safe area, you can let your dog off leash (first checking that it is safe to do so). If your dog glances at you, makes eye contact, or walks toward you (even just a step), then praise "Good dog!" or click your clicker and toss a food treat (just one). When your 10 minutes is up or you're out of treats, you can collect your dog and go home. The more you can repeat this exercise in as many different locations as possible, the better.

Troubleshooting

"My dog won't eat the treats." Make sure you're using something he really likes, even if it is something you wouldn't normally give him. Cheese, chicken, and ham are favorites. Make sure your dog is hungry. Don't try this exercise after a meal; you could even withhold a meal to build hunger. Some dogs won't take treats because they are stressed. Find a quieter location. It could be that other dogs, people, or noises are upsetting your dog. You can try this location again later.

"I can't possibly give all 60–70 treats." Chances are, you can, but you're just not trained yet to see the little things that are worth reinforcing at this early stage of training. Watch carefully and relax your criteria. The briefest glance in your direction, or an accidental step toward you, is worth a treat.

"I run out of treats before the 10 minutes is up." Congratulations! This is a good sign. Now you can start raising your criteria. Wait for your dog to take more steps toward you, or to "check in" with you, giving eye contact rather than a vague glance in your direction. Or find a busier location.

A dog that has learned to "check in" and keep an eye on you is a dog that is ready for more advanced training, so this exercise is a worthwhile foundation, and I hope you and your dog enjoy it!

Tucker's Top Training Tips
by Aaron Clayton

Tucker is my Labrador puppy. He's stop-dead-in-your-tracks handsome. Really. Cars have pulled over to tell me how handsome he is. Spend some time with him and you find out just how sweet and calm he is, too. He's so calm, people can't believe it. ("That's the calmest Lab I've ever seen. Golly Jed, come over here. Do you see this sweet puppy? He's real different from my daughter's Lab. Is it the same breed?")

Now, not much of this is my doing. I just haven't messed it up. We got Tucker from Kate Fulkerson of Highgarth Labradors. Kate is a wise lady and an innovative breeder. She clicker trains her pups right after whelping. She keeps the pups with their littermates for 14 weeks. She does lots of other innovative things, which gave me a great pup to begin with.

Now, can you imagine the pressure I am under to have an extraordinary dog? I work with Karen Pryor; I'm president of the company. People might even assume I have a lot of experience training dogs. Wrong. Whoa. Hang on. Although I've been studying the principles of clicker training, and I have been practicing with people since I joined Karen at Karen Pryor Clicker Training (KPCT), it wasn't until my youngest child turned six that I wanted to bring a puppy into the house. So, let's face it, though I have a pedigree by association, I am a beginner clicker trainer with many wise teachers in the offices next door!

As a beginner I have had some real "Oh, so that's what I should be doing" moments when I went from theory to implementation. Along the way, I kept jotting down thoughts that I wanted other people to know—especially stuff that I simply missed or didn't realize until I really started training.

Here are the first few....

Maintain a huge rate of reinforcement

You are going to reinforce a lot! I mean a *lot*... more than you think you would when you read about clicker training. When you are training, clicking and reinforcing is the mode of communication, so just plan on doing it a lot and don't worry about overdoing it. When I started loose-leash walking Tucker at four months, I clicked and treated him 100 times in our 10-minute walk. Really. 10 times in a minute, or once every six seconds (on average). What about weight gain? I just subtracted what I used for treats from my pup's regular diet.

Raising criteria: The "must-have" skill

You aren't going to be stuck at that rate of reinforcement for life because you'll learn to raise and shift criteria so the dog has to do more, and longer, for each click and treat. What a core skill! At ClickerExpo, Steve White once said that this was *the* skill that tripped people up. I agree. This is so important. When I wanted Tucker to learn to sit quietly on the floor at home, I clicked and treated him every 5 seconds at first. Now we're up to 15 minutes. He'll just lie there for an hour in the same spot, waiting, as long as I give him a reinforcer every 15 minutes or so. You have to learn how and when to raise your criteria (or lower them). It takes some practice. Jump in there and start practicing.

Basic theory: Don't leave home without it

Learn the basic theory. Don't assume you know it. There are several times when, uncertain about what the outcome would be, I fell back on some part of operant conditioning theory to help make my decision. (I used the books or I just turned to my in-house experts.) In either case, a basic grasp of the theory helps you think through what is happening or why it is not happening and helps you solves problems.

Live in the learning moment

This isn't some New Age mantra. Consider that just about every interaction with your puppy is a learning opportunity. Sometimes I learn, sometimes he learns, sometimes we both learn. For example, if I give a cue to come and he doesn't respond, I've learned that he doesn't know that cue. So what do I do? Well, for one thing, I have to make a decision not to use that moment to teach "come or else." Instead, I might decide to go get him and to save the real learning for later. What has he learned from this episode? Maybe nothing. But it's what he didn't learn that also matters. He didn't learn that he earns a reward for *not* coming. He also didn't learn that the consequence of getting something wrong will result in something unpleasant.

You must recognize that good behavior is an important learning moment. Always reward good behavior! It is so unnatural for us to reward everyday good behavior in our dogs or in anyone else. Work to drop that point of view. Tucker, did you sit by my feet even if I didn't ask for you to? Click, treat. Did you lie down in the kitchen quietly without a cue? Click, treat. Did you look at my sock but not actually put it in your mouth and run around the room? Good decision! Click, treat. If you miss these moments, you are not really clicker training as powerfully as you could, so you are slowing your pup's and your own learning.

Chapter 2 – Getting Started

3
Clicker in Action

Here you will find many of the key techniques and tools needed to be a good trainer. This chapter focuses on several diverse but equally important components to training. They include how to get behavior through shaping and targeting, the importance of reinforcement, what to do when mistakes happen, and how to put behaviors on cue. These articles contain essential information that every trainer should know.

The 10 Laws of Shaping Revisited 48
by Lori Chamberland

Shaping Success 56
by Sarah Dixon

How to Teach Your Pet to Target 60
by Laurie Luck

Targeting vs. Luring 63
by Gale Pryor

Ken's Top Tips for Reinforcement 66
by Ken Ramirez

How to Use Play as a Reward 69
by Laurie Luck

Controlled Tug Games: A Novel Reinforcer 73
by Aidan Bindoff

"Clicker Trainers Use No Punishment" and Other Training Myths 77
by Melissa Alexander

Should You Use No Reward Markers? Examining the Debate 86
by Laura VanArendonk Baugh

When It All Goes Wrong: How to Respond to Failure 92
by Aaron Clay

The Rules for Cues 97
by Karen Pryor

Adding the Cue 98
by Karen Pryor

Hurry Up and Wait 99
by Lori Chamberland

Reinforcing Doing Nothing 101
by Karen Pryor

My Dog Knows It, He Just Won't Do It! How to Achieve Fluency 103
by Laurie Luck

The 10 Laws of Shaping Revisited
by Lori Chamberland

One characteristic of a good shaper is flexibility—a willingness to change course based on new information. Good science shares that characteristic. As Susan Friedman once said, "A fact is only a fact until it's replaced by a better one." I love this pithy reminder that although something may seem obvious or indisputable, rather than becoming complacent, we continue searching for something even better.

This is as true in the training community as it is in the scientific community. Every year we grow and evolve. We discover faster, better, more creative ways of training. For example, at ClickerExpo, the epicenter of groundbreaking positive reinforcement training, faculty members themselves never fail to learn something new from each other every single year.

As good shapers, we must be willing to revisit the principles by which we train—no matter how comfortable and familiar they have become. In that spirit, "The 10 Laws of Shaping" (see p. 50) have evolved since Karen Pryor first published *Don't Shoot the Dog!* We have learned more and more about the science that powers the clicker training engine.

Variable schedule or natural variety?

A few years back, Karen Pryor and I were working together on updating some of the information in Karen Pryor Academy's (KPA) Dog Trainer Professional program. During that update process, it was hard to overlook the fact that the third original "law" of the 10 Laws of Shaping was no longer consistent with what we actually teach in KPA.

The original 10 Laws of Shaping were published in 1984 and, as Karen said, "We've learned a lot since 1984! We've gotten much better at shaping over the years." The original third law states:

During shaping, put the current level of response on a variable schedule of reinforcement before adding or raising the criteria.

Chapter 3 – Clicker in Action

That suggestion conflicts with what we now firmly believe and advise people to do in KPA: when training a new behavior, use a continuous schedule of reinforcement (CRF). In shaping, we advise using a CRF schedule for the approximation we are strengthening. So, a dilemma. We certainly didn't want to remove the still-very-valuable 10 Laws of Shaping from the course, but we didn't want to confuse people with conflicting information either. So we decided it was time to update the beloved 10 Laws of Shaping (now "The Modern Principles of Shaping," p. 51), beginning with law Number Three.

"As soon as the animal learns that if it doesn't hear a click, try again, it's already entering the world of natural variety," said Karen. That natural variety Karen refers to is built into the shaping process inherently. Animals are not robots. They don't exhibit the exact same behavior every time. They can't. Their speed, position, and muscle movements are inherently variable. We humans are not robots either. We don't perceive the animal's movements the same way every time. We click a fraction of a second (or more!) sooner or later than we did last time. We withhold a click for a brief moment and see if the animal will give us something a little different, a little closer to our goal. If it does, we click that instead.

Consider the following example of a shaping session:
- Animal dips its head and gets clicked for it.
- Animal dips its head in a slightly different way and gets clicked for it.
- Animal dips its head, but his trainer is slightly too slow, so animal dips it again. Click!
- Animal tries something different—a sit—and hears no click.
- Animal dips its head again. Click!

The natural variety is built in, and a variable schedule isn't necessary. "If you actually put each criterion on a variable schedule before moving on, it would slow you down and interrupt the flow of the shaping process," says Karen.

Original intent and early uses of variable schedules

The original thought behind advising trainers to sometimes withhold a reinforcer until an animal performs two iterations of a given behavior (which

The Ten Laws of Shaping
By Karen Pryor

1. Raise criteria in increments small enough so that the subject always has a realistic chance of reinforcement.
2. Train one aspect of any particular behavior at a time. Don't try to shape for two criteria simultaneously.
3. During shaping, put the current level of response on a variable ratio schedule of reinforcement before adding or raising the criteria.
4. When introducing a new criterion, or aspect of the behavioral skill, temporarily relax the old ones.
5. Stay ahead of your subject: Plan your shaping program completely so that if the subject makes sudden progress, you are aware of what to reinforce next.
6. Don't change trainers in midstream. You can have several trainers per trainee, but stick to one shaper per behavior.
7. If one shaping procedure is not eliciting progress, find another. There are as many ways to get behavior as there are trainers to think them up.
8. Don't interrupt a training session gratuitously; that constitutes a punishment.
9. If behavior deteriorates, "Go back to kindergarten." Quickly review the whole shaping process with a series of easily earned reinforcers.
10. End each session on a high note, if possible, but in any case quit while you're ahead.

From Chapter 2 of *Don't Shoot the Dog!* by Karen Pryor

Chapter 3 – Clicker in Action

The Modern Principles of Shaping
by Karen Pryor

1. **Be prepared before you start.** Be ready to click/treat immediately when the training session begins. When shaping a new behavior, be ready to capture the very first tiny inclination the animal gives you toward your goal behavior. This is especially true when working with a prop such as a target stick or a mat on the ground.

2. **Ensure success at each step.** Break behavior down into small enough pieces that the learner always has a realistic chance to earn a reinforcer.

3. **Train one criterion at a time.** Shaping for two criteria or aspects of a behavior simultaneously can be very confusing. One click should not mean two different criteria.

4. **Relax criteria when something changes.** When introducing a new criterion or aspect of the skill, temporarily relax the old criteria for previously mastered skills.

5. **If one door closes, find another.** If a particular shaping procedure is not progressing, try another way.

6. **Keep training sessions continuous.** The animal should be continuously engaged in the learning process throughout the session. He should be working the entire time, except for the moment he's consuming/enjoying his reinforcer. This also means keeping a high rate of reinforcement.

7. **Go back to kindergarten, if necessary.** If a behavior deteriorates, quickly revisit the last successful approximation or two so that the animal can easily earn reinforcers.

8. **Keep your attention on your learner.** Interrupting a training session gratuitously by taking a phone call, chatting, or doing something else that can wait often causes learners to lose momentum and get frustrated by the lack of information. If you need to take a break, give the animal a "goodbye present," such as a small handful of treats.

9. **Stay ahead of your learner.** Be prepared to "skip ahead" in your shaping plan if your learner makes a sudden leap.

10. **Quit while you're ahead.** End each session with something the learner finds reinforcing. If possible, end a session on a strong behavioral response, but, at any rate, try to end with your learner still eager to go on.

Karen called "asking for two-fers") was to get a naive animal used to the idea that it doesn't always get reinforced. The idea would prevent the animal from potentially suffering the frustration of an extinction burst when it suddenly fails to earn a reinforcer for a previously reinforced behavior.

Decades ago, some trainers would use these frustration-filled attempts at gaining reinforcement to select for more intense behavior. While "surfing the extinction bursts," the trainer would purposely withhold reinforcement, inducing brief frustration in the animal. That frustration often resulted in a bigger/higher/faster/harder behavioral response that s/he could then click and treat.

But, based on what we know about extinction (it is very frustrating for the animal, slows learning, and can lead to aggression or quitting altogether), using extinction bursts deliberately to produce behavior directly conflicts with our desire as clicker trainers to keep animals confident, stress-free, and happy throughout the shaping process. The focus on the animal's comfort with the training process results in stronger, more reliable behaviors and a much better overall training relationship.

The whole shaping process is a dance between trainer and learner. The more skilled the trainer, the more fluid the dance. If the trainer has poor observational or mechanical skills, it probably leaves the animal feeling as if his partner has two left feet. But even a bad dancer who is trying hard and is fun to be with is better than a dancer who suddenly leaves the floor without warning.

Additions to the 10 Laws

While the deletion of the third law was the most significant update to the 10 Laws of Shaping, we made some other important changes as well, including adding two new principles.

1. **Be prepared before you start.** So many times, the trainer misses that very first "clickable moment" in a shaping session. When that happens, it sets the whole session off to a bad start. This result is especially common with trainers using a prop or a target of some kind. It's so important to be ready to catch that very first inclination the animal shows toward your goal behavior. "Grab whatever goes by that's in your general direction," says Karen.

Chapter 3 – Clicker in Action

When we click and treat an animal for looking, sniffing, or pawing at the mat or the platform on the ground, we are not only saying that the goal behavior has something to do with that object, we are also reinforcing his curiosity and his braveness. The more times we reinforce curiosity and braveness, the more confidence the animal gains. We end up with an animal that is creative, is excited about interacting with novel things, and readily offers new behavior. That kind of animal is much easier to train.

When we miss that very first clickable moment like the sniff, the glance, or the paw touch, we are telling the animal: "It's not that object. Try something else." Often the animal will do just that. The animal asks the trainer a question with the sniff, look, or touch: "Is it this?" The lack of a click tells him: "No, it's not." We owe it to our learners to be good dance partners and not miss a beat.

2. **Keep training sessions continuous.** This principle was added to help reduce the amount of "dead air time" in shaping sessions. Just like those times when the TV displays snow or the radio emits static, if only for a moment or two, dead air time can be the kiss of death in shaping. If the animal is left hanging, it might be because the trainer waited too long to click, set up the environment poorly, or is holding out for too much too soon.

If your animal, for whatever reason, is left hanging, you're doing something wrong. He will find a way to fill that dead air time—often with behaviors that have nothing to do with what you were looking for, or with displacement behaviors brought about by the stress of lack of information. As Karen puts it, "He should be working or thinking the entire time, except for the moment he's consuming/enjoying his reinforcer."

On changing trainers midstream

To make room for the two new laws, the other law we decided to remove was "Don't change trainers midstream." While this is still sound advice, it can be difficult to adhere to in some cases. In addition, we felt that the principles relating to the process of training and how a training session takes place are more important than who is doing the training.

For maximum shaping efficiency, it is indeed ideal for one trainer to work on shaping a behavior throughout the acquisition phase. Once the behavior is on stimulus control, the cue can then be transferred to other trainers. This is fairly simple to adhere to in a household setting, but sometimes more difficult in a zoo, aquarium, shelter, or other environment. While the efficiency of shaping that behavior would suffer a bit, as long as the second trainer is a proficient shaper, progress toward the goal behavior should resume fairly quickly with either trainer.

Switching trainers has less to do with the principles of shaping and more to do with best practices in training. We removed that law to make room for the others and keep it to an even 10.

Breaking the "Laws"

The 10 Laws of Shaping aren't actually laws at all. "Principles," said Karen. "We should call them principles instead." They don't fit the definition of a scientific law, such as the law of gravity, which is a statement of fact based on repeated observations that describes some aspect of the universe. Nor are they laws in the criminal sense. There are no shaping police to come and lock up shaping scofflaws. "Principles" better describes Karen's training guidelines, as the word does not have the same connotation as the word "law."

Also included in the new "10" title is the word "modern." This is by design as well. Just as clicker training is the modern way of training, these principles, at Karen's suggestion, are described that way as well. "We need modern in the title," she said emphatically and with a smile.

TAGteach-friendly phrasing

Finally, we wanted the new Modern Principles of Shaping to fit with TAGteach-friendly phrasing. In TAGteach, instructions are phrased in the positive. So, rather than "Don't interrupt a training session gratuitously" (old law), it's "Keep your attention on your learner" (modern principle).

Each principle is succinct (usually five words or fewer) and phrased to tell the learner what to do, instead of what not to do. This, of course, is exactly what we do in clicker training.

Chapter 3 – Clicker in Action

The characteristics of a great trainer

Looking at the changes made to the original 10 Laws of Shaping, it is quite remarkable how much we didn't need to change! Used by trainers all over the globe, Karen's guidelines on how to conduct a good shaping session are still so applicable more than three decades later. Given that, it would have been easy for Karen to respond with "Not a chance" when I swallowed hard, approached her one day, and said, "I think we should rewrite The 10 Laws of Shaping." Instead, she said unhesitatingly, "Great idea. Let's do it."

That's Karen. Humble. Flexible. Always willing to learn and improve. Always displaying the characteristics of a great scientist and a great trainer.

Shaping Success
by Sarah Dixon

Free shaping is a powerful training tool that teaches behaviors in gradual steps using a marker, like a clicker, and rewards. Shaping can be a great way to teach some difficult behaviors, expand your animal's capabilities, exercise your animal's brain, and build your chops as a trainer. A recent trend is toward employing free shaping as much as possible, but it can be frustrating for the learner if the shaping is done poorly. Free shaping is sometimes not the most effective training option.

Timing

If you want to be successful building behaviors with shaping, you will need to have good timing. There are lots of games you can play to practice timing with a clicker. Try bouncing a ball and clicking every time it hits the ground. Or, while watching TV, take a few minutes and click every time the camera angle changes. If you don't have good timing, you're not going to be able to click your animal's behavior, and you might end up shaping some pretty bizarre actions.

Plan ahead

Before beginning shaping sessions you should plan what the probable steps of the behavior should look like. Start with something the dog can and likely will do easily and build up in logical steps to the finished behavior. For example, if I wanted to train my dog to bow, my steps might look something like the following:

1. Dip the head in a standing position
2. Dip the head halfway to the floor
3. Dip the head so that nose is close to touching the floor
4. Bend elbows
5. Touch elbows to floor, rear in the air—a bow!
6. Establish criteria and reinforcement rate

Chapter 3 – Clicker in Action

A common misconception about free shaping is that it provides little information to the learner. The truth is that if you are free shaping well, you will provide plenty of feedback to the animal. Your goal should be about 15 clicks a minute—that is feedback an average of every 4 seconds. With that rate of feedback and reinforcement, your dog should be having lots of success, understanding what you are looking for, and working eagerly for you. If you notice your dog getting frustrated, then you are probably asking for too much and need to adjust your criteria.

When you are getting the 15 clicks a minute consistently after a few training sessions, then it is time to wait the dog out before offering the next step of your shaping plan, to see if he offers a bit more of the target behavior. Keep your training sessions short, only a minute or two in length, and track how many treats you go through so you know what your rate of reinforcement is. Count out a certain number of treats before the session, and count what was left afterward to know how many clicks per minute you logged.

Cues to communicate

Another objection to free shaping is that it causes dogs to be frantic and to offer behaviors continually. While this definitely can happen, I don't feel it is the fault of free shaping itself. I believe that dogs get this way because their trainers do not add cues early enough. It's commonly accepted in the clicker training world that you do not add a cue until the behavior is perfect, but delaying adding a cue gives the animal plenty of rehearsals of the behavior without a cue attached. The more times the dog does the behavior without being cued and gets reinforced for it, the more likely it will be that the dog will offer that behavior when it hasn't been asked (cued) to do so.

So, when do you add a cue? As soon as possible! When you can predict with relative certainty that the dog will do some form of the behavior, start attaching a cue. Once you add a cue, do not reinforce un-cued responses afterwards. You can always change your cue once you get the behavior exactly the way you want it so your final cue is not attached to the imperfections associated with training.

Provided that your dog has a good understanding of the concept of cues and you are diligent about getting behaviors on stimulus control, this practice will help avoid frantic offering of behavior. Your dog will know the difference between when it is time to experiment (shaping) and when it is time to perform a specific behavior when asked. Another trick that seems to help dogs develop a "shaping off-switch" is to use "game on" and "game off" signals to indicate when you are going to start shaping and when you are done. I use "Are you ready?" to mean we are going to start training and "All done" to tell the dog our session is over.

Reward placement

One of the single most effective actions that can speed up your shaping sessions (and training in general) is using the placement of rewards to aid learning. For example, you can deliver your reinforcement in a physical location that will jump-start your dog to offer the next repetition. Reward placement comes down to planning, but also to thinking on your feet. Where do you want the dog to be positioned to set up for the next rep? If you want the dog to stay in position, deliver the food directly to the dog. If, for example, you are trying to train a dog to go around an object, click for just moving beside it and toss the food so that the dog has to move even farther around it. Instead of having the dog return to you to get the food, jump-start the behavior of moving around the object by using your food reward placement to get the dog there. If you want to set the dog up to repeat an action, go to a platform, for example, toss the food away from the platform after you click so that the dog moves off and has the opportunity to return to the platform.

Many people think that they have to be extremely sterile during clicker training, and during shaping in particular. Not true! Put some heart into it! If you are engaging, your dog is going to enjoy the process so much more. Training should be a game that both of you enjoy. While you should remain quiet before you click, there is no reason why you cannot praise the heck out of your dog after a click for a big breakthrough or at the end of a session. Relax and have fun!

Shaping—just one tool

While shaping can be a really cool way to teach some behaviors, it is not always the most efficient or effective way to train a skill. This is why shaping is not something I use to train all the time; I use shaping if I cannot get the behavior easily in another manner, or if I want to challenge myself and my dog. To avoid frustration and make training go smoother, I suggest that you pick a method that will get the behavior started as quickly as possible. Often, this choice will not be shaping. Using prompts such as targets, setting up the environment, or even just capturing may be much faster means of training. You can even mix a combination of targeting, shaping, and so on— whatever works best to explain to the animal what you are looking for.

One wonderful benefit of shaping is that there are no prompts to fade, since the training process is based completely on the dog offering behaviors. If you are going to use a prompt, it is important that you do not use it more than is necessary. For example, if the animal will do the behavior naturally, you don't need to set up the environment. If you can set up the training area to get the behavior easily, try not to use targets. If you can get the job done with targets, avoid using a lure. The less you prompt or lure, the less you have to fade. Remember, if you are using a prompt or lure, you want to fade it as quickly as possible to avoid the animal's reliance on it. Get the prompt or lure out of the picture as quickly as you can.

Some dogs prefer shaping more than others. If one of you, you or your dog, does not really like shaping, that's just fine. There are plenty of other training tools to teach your dog to perform wonderful tricks and behaviors. My 5-year-old Belgian shepherd, Dexter, loves to shape and is really fun to work with, so I do shaping with him often, just because he is so enjoyable to train this way. In contrast, my young Australian shepherd, Brew, finds shaping a frustrating process, so I limit the amount of shaping I do with him. I do shaping with Brew occasionally since it is good practice for him to think and use his brain in that way.

A useful technique

Shaping is often misunderstood and can be difficult to do well. But if you have well-developed timing and planning skills, with some practice it can be a helpful addition to your toolkit—especially since there are some behaviors you can shape that are difficult to train in another manner. Overall, shaping is an excellent way to enhance your skills as a trainer and exercise your dog mentally.

How to Teach Your Pet to Target
by Laurie Luck

Imagine teaching your dog to put his hind feet—just his hind feet—on a mat. Or, imagine teaching your dog to give a high-five. What if you could teach your dog to use his nose to ring a bell to go outside?

These fun and useful behaviors are all examples of targeting a body part to a specific object. Training your pet to touch a target is not only a fun game to play, but it is easy to teach and can extend to more complicated behaviors or to tools in administering veterinary care.

Targets can be almost anything. Use a kitchen rug as a settle mat for your dog; the dog targets his whole body onto the kitchen rug so he won't be underfoot while you prepare dinner. Your cat can sit on a drink coaster while you fix dinner; as long as her feet are on the coaster, she can't jump on the counter and pester you. Teach your dog to ring a bell, and you have a doggie doorbell for him to use when he has to go outside. Targeting the dog's nose to the bell is the easiest way to avoid damage to the bell. Teach your horse to target a hoof to a bucket, and you have made soaking the hoof a lot easier (for you and the horse!).

Nose-first
It's easiest to begin by teaching an animal to touch its nose to a target held close to the nose. Use just about anything as a target: a sticky note, a pencil, or even your hand. These targets all work well for smaller animals like dogs and cats. For larger animals, a larger target may be easier. You can use a tennis ball on a dowel rod as an inexpensive target stick for horse training.

Step-by-step
Here's how to get started using a target with your pet:

1. Choose an appropriate target. For a dog, your hand or a sticky note is a good choice.
2. Present the target swiftly and about ¼" in front of the animal's nose.

3. Click and treat the instant your animal looks at the target. (If your dog touches it right away, click that!)
4. Again, present the target ¼" away from your animal's nose.
5. When the dog touches the target, click and treat.
6. Next, progress to presenting the target a little to the left, a little to the right, a little higher, a little lower—clicking and treating every time your animal touches the target. For now, make it easy for your animal by continuing to present the target close to your animal's nose.
7. If your pet is overexcited and tends to bite at the target, click just as he moves toward the target instead of waiting for him get the target in his mouth.
8. Work in short sessions, no more than 3–5 minutes at a time.

Following the target—for business and tricks!

After you have taught your animal to touch a target, move to a more advanced targeting skill: following a target. Think of how easy it would be to move your pet from one location to another (loading your dog into a car, for example) if all you have to do is place a target in front of your pet's face and then move the target to where you'd like the animal to go!

Other uses for targeting include getting an animal onto the scale at the veterinary hospital, moving your pet off the sofa so you can have a seat, and moving your dog away from another dog walking down the path. You can also use a target to teach your dog to move away from you. Stick the target on the wall and the dog will learn to move away from you in order to earn a click and treat.

Here's how to teach your pet to follow a target:
1. Present the target stick.
2. As your pet moves to touch the target stick, pull the target about an inch away so the animal has to stretch its neck to reach the target. Click and treat.
3. Continue at the same distance for a few repetitions so that the animal has a fun and easy time with the task.

4. Begin to move the target a little further away as the animal stretches.
5. Over the course of a few training sessions, your animal should be happy to follow the target around for a few feet.

Using the target stick makes teaching tricks easier, too! Imagine how easy it would be to teach your dog to turn the lights off or to close the refrigerator door for you. You can accomplish this, and realize other dreams, all by using a target stick!

Targeting behavior comes in handy if you would like your dog to walk on a loose lead. Simply present the target next to your leg; click and treat the dog for walking at your side (in other words, for following the target). Targeting is a great tool for horse owners, as well. Using a tennis ball on a dowel makes loading your horse into a trailer a breeze. There are so many practical and entertaining applications of targeting!

Whatever needs targeting can fill for you and your animal, remember to work toward your goals slowly and positively. Steady success makes training so much more enjoyable for all!

Chapter 3 – Clicker in Action

Targeting vs. Luring
by Gale Pryor

How does the use of targeting to "get the behavior" differ from luring a behavior?

Soon after learning that a click marks the exact behavior and tells the animal what earned its reward, newcomers to clicker training wonder how to go about getting that clickable behavior. On this point, the answer they hear depends on whom they ask.

"Get the behavior" is one of the adages of clicker training. The saying reinforces the creativity enabled by the method: however you get there is fine; just get there. Or, as Karen Pryor points out, "There are as many ways of training a behavior as there are trainers." In general, however, trainers tend to turn to one of four methods to get the behavior: shaping, capturing, targeting, or luring.

When working with newcomers to clicker training, some teachers suggest they begin with luring their animal into the desired position, then click and reward. Others ask their students first to teach their animal to touch a target with its nose (or paw or hoof or beak) and then to move that target to put the animal into the clickable position or motion. Using a lure or a target can jump-start a behavior, getting a trainer from point A to point M, T, or X in a few short steps. (Shaping is rich with its own benefits, but relies on clicking and rewarding incremental steps, and can be derailed by jumping over those steps. Capturing, a one-step training method, relies on a behavior being frequent and observable.) Both a food lure and a touched target lead an animal into position. Both "get the behavior." Is there any real difference between the two methods? Why do some trainers rely on luring while others opt for targeting?

We asked trainers and teachers with experience with a range of animals and training goals these questions. Their consensus is that the methods have some similarities and important differences.

Both methods require an eventual fade of the lure or the target so that they don't become the final cue for the behavior. Both carry a risk of the trainer becoming as dependent on a physical prompt as is the animal to complete the behavior. Pet class teachers often hear the lament, "I can't get him to lie down without food in my hand. If I don't have it, he won't do it." These beginning trainers fear losing the progress they have made toward a desired behavior without the method that got them there. (Experienced trainers are not immune to this worry and may also hesitate in fading a lure or a target.) The speed with which luring got the trainer to see the desired behavior is reinforcing to the trainer, and reinforced behaviors endure in trainers as well as learners.

Despite the apparent similarities, however, there is an essential difference between luring and targeting. As Ken Ramirez, Chief Training Officer of Karen Pryor Clicker Training, explains: "In luring, the animal is focused on the food. The trainer uses the food to guide the animal toward a desired behavior, just as a trainer would use a target to guide the animal. What goes on in the animal's head, however, may be significantly different. Luring keeps the animal thinking about the reinforcement or the treat, while targeting gets the animal thinking about the task."

While both methods may succeed in getting the behavior, a lured animal may be so focused on the treat that he is not aware of what behavior he has just accomplished to earn the reinforcement, so he has learned less. An animal that follows a target, on the other hand, may still be working to receive a treat, but because the treat is not right in front of him, he must think about the actual behavior. The result is an animal that is more engaged in the process, has accomplished more learning, and is more able to apply that learning to any number of other behaviors.

Kay Laurence of Learning about Dogs prefers targeting to luring because of the flexibility it offers. She asks her Border collies and Gordon setters to touch targets with their noses, their paws, their tails, and their hips. The result is an ability to combine a series of cues to direct the dogs into desired positions: left back paw on step, nose on right front paw, and so on in infinite variety. Kay's fine tuning of the use of a target underscores an important principle for newcomers and experienced trainers alike: Many behaviors we

Chapter 3 – Clicker in Action

humans think of as a single behavior are, in fact, combinations of multiple behaviors. A down is a down, but there are many ways in which a dog can lie down (front feet first, back legs first, on its side, or legs tucked under its belly). Creative use of a target can help a trainer to guide the components that make up a completed behavior rather than a broad approximation of the behavior.

At its essence, targeting engages the animal's mind, rather than its appetite. It allows the use of food to be maintained as a reinforcer of behavior rather than as a stimulant of behavior. And it enables trainers to be as creative as they wish and to extend the applications of clicker training as far as they can imagine.

Ken's Top Tips for Reinforcement
by Ken Ramirez

I have many different guidelines and rules for using reinforcement effectively. But when I teach people about non-food reinforcers, more questions come up than usual.

Developing the Karen Pryor Academy (KPA) course Smart Reinforcement, I included the following tips to help trainers as they consider the possible explanations for the challenges they face. These are not all-inclusive rules. They are simply thoughts to keep in mind when training, points designed to guide you as you make your reinforcement strategies stronger.

1. **Don't take any reinforcer for granted.** There is no single reinforcer that will *always* be reinforcing. Remember that reinforcers are context-specific and may lose their effectiveness under certain conditions. As an example, kibble may be a great reinforcer for a dog in the confines of his home, but in the park it may not measure up to the reinforcement of the squirrels, other dogs, and new people in that environment. When you take reinforcers for granted, you are likely to be disappointed eventually.

2. **Understand the motivating factor behind each reinforcer and make sure to maintain its strength.** Each reinforcer has some aspect to it that makes it valuable to your animal. For the doggie treat it may be the smell or taste of bacon, for the tennis ball it may be the chance to chew it, and for the tug toy it might be the relationship and the play with you. If you fail to pay attention to the factors that make certain reinforcers motivating, you will see the reinforcement value of that item decrease—or in some case disappear altogether. When you change treats, you may see the dog refuse the new treat immediately, or the enthusiasm diminish. But sometimes it is not so obvious. What if the motivating factor of a tennis ball is the opportunity to chew it, but you throw it for the dog, asking that it be brought back immediately and assuming the

reinforcer is chasing the ball? If you take the ball away too quickly, the dog never receives the value of the reinforcer: actually getting to chew the ball. If you are unaware of this subtle but important difference, the value of the tennis ball can decrease gradually over time. Always be aware of the factors that make each reinforcer effective, and work hard to maintain them.

3. **Evaluate the effectiveness of reinforcers constantly.** I ask myself regularly, "Is this reinforcer working?" If I am not able to determine the answer easily, I begin to set up a formal evaluation process to look at factors like "focus." I have always found that the level of an animal's focus is directly related to the power of the consequences being used in that training session. While there are many factors that impact whether or not a reinforcer is effective, I have discovered that by observing the animal's level and intensity of focus I can quickly determine if the reinforcers being offered have value. High-value reinforcers create razor-sharp focus, while low-value reinforcers create wandering eyes, and sometimes even wandering feet.

4. **Be aware of the expectations your animal has developed regarding reinforcement.** Depending on how and when you use certain reinforcers, animals will develop expectations about those reinforcers. If you always use a high-value treat for certain behaviors, or are in the habit of giving a set number of treats in certain circumstances, your animals will come to anticipate and expect that level or value of reinforcement. You may find that if you change or lower the value of the reinforcer, the animal is disappointed. The animal may actually find the offered treat aversive, because it did not match the expectations. If you want an animal to accept variety in the types of reinforcement you offer, that acceptance must be taught. I encourage the use of reinforcement variety early in every animal's training.

5. **Understand the value of access to reinforcement.** Always remember that if an animal has regular access to a reinforcer, its effectiveness may diminish. This goes hand-in-hand with understanding the motivating factors behind reinforcement, discussed above. I leave certain toys around for my dogs to play with when I am not home.

Since some of the reinforcing value comes from the social interaction of playing with me, the toys are still effective reinforcers even though the dogs have access to them all day. However, if the primary value of the toys is chewing them, the toys may not have as much value if the dogs have had the chance to chew them all day long. Being aware of these possibilities can help you make sure that reinforcers have value when you are ready to use them.

6. **Look at behavior—the key to successful training.** Ultimately, it is most important to look at your animal's behavior to determine whether your use of reinforcement is successful. If you are seeing behavior that you like and want, your use of reinforcement is working. If you are not seeing desirable behavior, then something in your reinforcement plan needs to change.

Chapter 3 – Clicker in Action

How to Use Play as a Reward
by Laurie Luck

Have you ever wanted to reward your dog for a job well done but didn't have food treats with you? Consider playing with your dog to reinforce good behavior! Not everyone wants to spend life storing food in pockets. (Have you ever found a pocket full of food after it has gone through the laundry? It's not pretty!)

Instead of being a slave to food treats in my pocket, I introduce my dogs to "real-life rewards." Occasionally, play takes the place of food as payment for a job well done. My dogs find the opportunity to chase a ball, to chase me, or to have me chase them even more fun—and unexpected—than food.

Dogs, like humans, play long after they have "grown up." I think that's one of the many reasons we get along so well with our canine friends. Play is just as much fun for us as it is for our dogs. The one-on-one attention your dog gets from you during a play session can be as reinforcing as the play itself—and can contribute to a strong relationship between you and your dog.

Benefits of play

Aside from sheer enjoyment, there are other benefits from using play as a reinforcer. Start with convenience: when you have a few games you can play with your dog, you always have a way to reinforce your dog's behavior. Some games require a toy (fetch, tug), but other games don't require anything but you and your dog. You can play a game of fetch with just about anything that's around—a stick, your glove, your car keys. Anything your dog can pick up safely is a possibility!

Another benefit of using play is the increase in the variety of your reinforcers. With more options, you can mix it up for your dog. Sometimes the reinforcer is a yummy treat; another time the reinforcer is a quick game of chase. Keep your dog guessing—sometimes the surprise is the reinforcer! If you're teaching your dog a behavior that needs to be quick and snappy (heeling, for instance), play is the perfect reinforcer because it can rev up your dog and speed up the behavior.

One of the most important benefits of using play as a reinforcer is that it helps strengthen the relationship between you and your dog. Play is fun, and involves both you and the dog. It makes you a team. Finding a game that you and your dog enjoy and then using that game as a reinforcer increases your value to your dog and helps your dog enjoy you more. With a deepening relationship, every interaction between you and your dog is more fun and more rewarding. With play, you can create a dynamic that will enrich not only your training, but your lives together!

Types of play

In addition to the games mentioned already, tug and fetch, there are other games you can play with your dog. I categorize play into two types—interactive play and passive play. Interactive play requires that you and the dog are equally engaged in the play. Examples of interactive play include tug, chase, being chased, and other running or moving games. In interactive play, you are part of the game.

I think of passive play as something that I start, but I'm not really an integral part of the play. Fetch is an example of passive play. I'm needed to throw the toy, but then the dog takes over and is the primary player of the game. I just make the toy come alive. My dog, Nemo, enjoys a passive version of the chase game. I "sneak off" (so that he can see me) and hide behind an evergreen in our backyard. My sneaking off is Nemo's cue to "stalk" me. Once I jump out from behind the evergreen and "scare" him, he runs around the yard, feinting left and right, as if he's being chased by imaginary dogs. Occasionally, I'll need to jump out and "scare" him again if he slows, but for the most part Nemo's out there running in the yard.

In this game, I'm merely the catalyst to get the behavior going. But from Nemo's point of view, I'm pretty darn valuable to him and the game. That viewpoint will help take our training further than if I simply dispense treats as reinforcers.

Finding and fostering play preferences

Some dogs are natural retrievers—fetch is their game of choice. Other dogs like to chase or be chased. Still other dogs like physical play—roughhousing is fun for them. To determine which type of play your dog enjoys naturally, watch your dog when he's with other dogs. Does he like to body

Chapter 3 – Clicker in Action

slam and wrestle with his doggie friends? Chances are he might like to do the same with you. Does he chase other dogs? Does he like it when other dogs chase him? See if you can engage your dog in these same kinds of games.

Maybe your dog loves the water? Find a water-worthy toy and get him involved in play in his element. Does your dog go crazy for squeaky toys? Buy several toys with different squeakers and see which type of squeak your dog likes the most.

If your dog doesn't seem to like any particular game or toy, there are toys with little pockets you can fill with food. Lure your dog into interacting with a toy to jumpstart play.

We have Labrador retrievers, but not all of them find retrieving fun. Retrieving is pretty low on Lily's list of fun things. She would much rather chase something than retrieve it. For Lily, I put a toy on a string and whip it around—left and right, up in the air, over her head, under her belly. She loves it! You may need to go beyond what's normal and typical for your dog's breed to find out exactly what your dog likes.

Once you determine your dog's play preferences, make a concerted effort to work play into your daily interactions with your dog. Spend a few minutes initiating play with your dog. Grab the tug toy, swish it around on the floor a few times, and encourage your dog to pick it up and begin tugging. When your dog does this, praise him, tug gently, and watch his reactions. Ideally, you'll see excitement and enjoyment of the game.

Keep your initial play sessions short and fun. Keep the game at an appropriate level, too. If the dog escalates out of control (in the tug example, if the dog starts to re-grip the toy and his teeth touch your hands, or if he shakes the toy so hard that it's difficult to maintain your grip), simply drop the toy and walk away from the game.

For dogs developing their play skills, keep your play at a level where the dog's efforts are rewarded, not punished. For instance, if your dog is just beginning to enjoy fetch, throw the toy a short distance, not 40 yards away, or you could destroy that preference for fetch by asking for too much effort too soon in the learning phase. Just like training, you want to keep your rate of reinforcement high. Keep the dog engaged in the game and having fun.

Choosing the right toys

When you know your dog's play preferences, next comes the fun part: shopping for toys! There are so many toys on the market, you are sure to find one that fits your dog's preferences. If your dog likes to chase things, take a look at toys as in Kong Tails. There are lots of little fabric flaps to whisk around on the floor for your dog to chase. Or, try the Chase 'N Pull—a stick-like pole with a sturdy rope to which you can attach just about any toy. Whip the Chase 'N Pull back and forth or up and down, and your dog will be hooked!

If your dog loves the water, look for bright, floating toys that you can toss into the surf. Kong makes several types of water toys, including floating versions of the Kong. For example, Aqua Kong has a rope at the end (for easy tossing) and is filled with a buoyant material to make it float.

Most bumper toys are water-worthy and fun for your dog to retrieve. If you have tennis balls around the house, they float well, too! If your dog is just learning to fetch, attach those toys to a River Rope, in case your dog decides not to fetch the toy. With a River Rope you can pull the toy back in easily, without having to go into the water yourself. The rope also keeps the toy from going downstream or out with the tide!

If squeaking is what your dog is after, your options are almost limitless. Check out the Kong toys that have squeakers built in (my dogs' favorites!), like the Air Kong Squeaker or the Wubba.

Top choice = you!

Don't forget that the opportunity to play with you can be the most rewarding activity of all! Run away from your dog, and see if he follows you. Give chase after your dog; my dogs seem to enjoy this game most of all. That one is a win-win choice—we're having fun together and we're both getting exercise!

Working play into your daily interactions with your dog is valuable for a myriad of reasons. First of all, it's impossible to measure the fun! Fun is an effective reinforcer in training, too, whether you are training basic manners or more advanced skills and tricks. Don't forget that amazing side effect of playing with your dog—your relationship with your dog gets better and better.

Now get out there and play with your dog!

Chapter 3 – Clicker in Action

Controlled Tug Games: A Novel Reinforcer
by Aidan Bindoff

Many dogs just love playing tug-of-war games. Of those who don't, most can be taught to play and end up loving it. If a dog loves doing something, what should a clicker trainer do with it? That's right, use it as a powerful reinforcer for other behaviors!

There are plenty of myths and old wives' tales surrounding tug games with dogs. Some people maintain that tug games encourage aggression, biting, and "dominance." While it is true that playing *uncontrolled* tug games can lead to behavior problems, the opposite is likely when you play *controlled* tug games.

Apart from being a powerful reinforcer, controlled tug games also exercise your dog's body and mind, teach some important foundation behaviors (self-control, holding, and letting go of objects in the mouth), and provide a fantastic outlet for the innate drives within your dog. When you learn how to teach and play tug games, you learn how to combine aspects of canine ethology and behaviorism in a practical and fun way!

Getting started

Choose a suitable tug toy. To start with we'll use a clean rag. Actually, we'll use two rags; you'll find out why in just a moment.

With an uninitiated tugger, we need to incite a bit of prey drive. How do we do this? We make our rag act as prey would act. Would prey move toward a predator? No way! Prey always moves away from a predator. Your puppy is the predator, so make that rag move away from puppy and never toward him. If prey started moving toward the predator, the predator might get a little intimidated and defensive, and we want to avoid that because it will end the game faster than anything.

Prey also likes to keep the predator guessing so that the predator is unsure of when to go in for the kill. To do this, prey changes direction often—but always away from the predator.

Some dogs will play this game with just the slightest wiggle of the rag; others demand you put a bit of energy and enthusiasm into it—so be prepared to work up a sweat. We can't do all our clicker training from the recliner during ad breaks on television.

Of course, your domestic predator needs to actually win this game and catch the prey to play tug, so make your prey act a little wounded and slow down just enough for puppy to pounce and take the rag in his mouth.

At this point you can click to mark the biting behavior, then pull the rag gently to encourage holding on. You don't want to yank the rag out of pup's mouth, you just want enough pressure to make pup fight to keep hold of the rag for a few moments.

Then drop the rag and pull the second rag out of your pocket. The first rag goes dead—all the fun evaporates out of the first rag. The second rag now starts to come alive. All the fun that was in the first rag has found its way into the second rag and is calling the pup to come and party.

At the instant that your dog drops the first rag, click and let him bite the second rag and play the tug game for a few moments.

Then drop the second rag, and pick up the first rag. Again, make the rag in your hand come alive and wait for pup to drop the other rag. As soon as pup drops the other rag, click and let him bite the rag in your hand.

Play the game in this fashion until your dog is reliably dropping the rag in his mouth when you wiggle the rag in your hand. This can happen in one session, or it could take several sessions. What do we mean by "reliably dropping the rag"? In five trials, pup drops the rag immediately at least four times when you wiggle the other rag.

This is a good time to add a cue, such as "give" (Note: if you are training for a sport, don't use the cue you will be using for that sport just yet). Just before you wiggle the rag in your hand, say "give." Pretty soon pup will learn that when you say "give," he lets go of the rag in his mouth.

"Give" is a useful behavior for a puppy or dog to know. If pup steals your underwear out of the laundry—or your kid's homework—it's very useful to be able to cue "give" and have the item freely surrendered. Pup needs to learn that it's always worth dropping the object in his mouth quickly, and that there isn't always a rag in your hand being wiggled when you ask.

Your dog has very likely got the idea that he is to drop the rag in his mouth when two things happen together: 1. You say "give," and 2. You have another rag in your hand. Now you want your dog to drop the rag whenever you say "give" on its own.

Cue "give" without another rag in your hand. If you're very lucky, pup will immediately drop the rag in his mouth, in which case you can click, pick that rag up, and play tug with it. If you're not quite that lucky, it's worth waiting for a count of five (silently). Chances are, pup will get bored and/or confused and drop the rag, in which case you can click and play tug with the dropped rag. If not, then cue "give" again with another rag in your hand. Try again without the rag in your hand later.

Generalization: Anything, anywhere, anytime

So far, your dog has learned how to tug a rag and drop it on cue. Now is the time to start introducing other objects—short lengths of hose, tennis balls, soft toys, squeaky toys, and so on. You can also start playing this game in different places—different rooms of the house, front and back yards, at the park, on-leash in a car-park, outside your vet clinic, and so on.

Every so often, instead of clicking and picking up the toy for a game of tug, click and treat with food, pick up the toy, wait a few seconds, then invite pup to play tug again.

A quick word on "latency"—performing the behavior quickly when asked

Some dogs won't respond immediately when you give the cue. For these dogs, it's worth investing some time early on to remedy this problem. Figure out how long your dog takes to respond to the cue; let's say it's four seconds. Give your dog five seconds to respond to your cue, and if he responds within that time, click and continue play. If he fails to respond within that time frame, end the game and try again later.

When your dog is reliably responding within five seconds in four out of five trials, reduce the time allowed to four seconds. Keep whittling down the allowed response time, second by second, until you have reduced it to less than one second. Maintain that standard from then on.

Now that you have this fun game in your toolbox, think about how you might use it. Most dogs learn to really love playing tug, which makes it a great reinforcer for things like coming when called, or at the end of an agility run. If you compete in Schutzhund, ring, retrieving, or flyball, think about how you can shape the "give" into a reliable "out" or retrieve to hand.

Some dog owners have even discovered that playing tug can be an effective stress release for their dog during difficult training sessions, or at other times of stress.

Play by the rules, but above all, keep it fun.

Chapter 3 – Clicker in Action

"Clicker Trainers Use No Punishment" and Other Training Myths
by Melissa Alexander

Before starting this article, I polled the ClickerSolutions mailing list about the training myths—about both clicker and more traditional training—the members had heard. The responses poured in. It became obvious that misunderstandings, miscommunications, and half-truths abound, creating unnecessary walls between trainers. Let's debunk some of these myths.

"Traditional training doesn't work" and "Clicker training doesn't work"

Of course they work. Thousands of pet, competition, and working dogs out there prove the efficacy of both types of training. As long as a specific method follows the principles of learning for an individual dog, that method will work.

"No one method works for all dogs."

True—at least as written. A method is a recipe, step-by-step instructions for training or modifying a behavior. No one recipe works for all dogs, and this is why so many alternative methods—many of them just slight alterations of their predecessors—have been developed. The history of training can, in fact, be traced trainer to trainer through methods.

Unfortunately, methods are limiting unless the trainer also understands the underlying principles. In the past, trainers taught methods rather than principles, and as a result, individual dogs (and sometimes entire breeds) that didn't respond to the methods taught were incorrectly labeled too "stupid," "stubborn," "dominant," "soft," "driven," "aggressive," or "easily bored" to train.

Clicker training, though it contains recipes, is not a method. It is a technology for changing behavior that emphasizes principles of learning heavily. For the first time, the ability to evaluate a method for an individual dog, to modify it, or even to create an entirely new recipe is taken out of the indefinable realms of "instinct," "experience," and "talent" and taught and explained to everyone—from beginning pet owners to professional trainers.

Clicker training, applied skillfully, will work for every dog mentally and physically capable of learning, because no dog is immune to the principles of learning.

"Traditional training is cruel and inhumane," and "Traditionally trained dogs are fearful/aggressive/miserable," and "Dogs that behave fearfully must have been traditionally trained and abused."

These myths are frequently spouted—and they are both unfair and incorrect. Are there people who use aversives inhumanely in the name of training? Of course. Are there traditionally trained dogs that fail in traditional programs and become fearful, aggressive, or miserable? Unfortunately, yes. However, many remain happy workers, and a seemingly miserable dog is not necessarily a sign of abusive training.

"Because all training can be explained using operant conditioning terms, all trainers are operant trainers."

Children can make some darn cool chemical reactions with a chemistry set, but that doesn't make them chemists. My husband built a functional table—that didn't make him a carpenter. I can follow a recipe in a cookbook and can occasionally even throw together ingredients for my own unique dish—that doesn't make me a chef. Being a chef, a carpenter, or a chemist requires an understanding that goes far beyond the level of following step-by-step instructions or doing simple experimentation. The same is true of operant training.

Just because a training method can be explained using operant conditioning terms, that doesn't mean the trainer applying the method is an operant trainer. To be an operant trainer, the trainer must understand those principles inside and out and be able to apply them and modify them in any situation to any individual. "Operant trainers" are not limited to clicker training methods (nor is every clicker trainer an operant trainer), but because clicker training so heavily emphasizes the principles of learning from the earliest stages of learning, more operant trainers are clicker trainers.

"Clicker training isn't effective because no clicker trained dogs have achieved (fill in your favorite elite title)."

Clicker training is not a new technology, but it is relatively new in the dog world. Because of grassroots efforts, it has slowly increased in popularity over

Chapter 3 – Clicker in Action

the past 15 or 20 years, so that now clicker training classes have begun to appear with any regularity. Prior to that, trainers were largely on their own, teaching themselves with the help of mailing lists, websites, and a limited selection of books and videos. Even now most classes are geared toward the pet owner.

A potential competitor who wants to traditionally train his dog has lots of resources at his disposal because many, many people have been down the road before him. There are many existing methods, many experienced competitors to help, many instructors to teach, and many books and videos to supplement.

People who want to clicker train for competition aren't that lucky. Some sports—like agility and canine freestyle—are dominated by clicker trainers and have accumulated a wealth of resources, but other sports—like field training—have little to help the new competitor. The old traditional recipes usually don't translate; the trainer—often a beginner himself—must start from scratch.

In order to get a title (in any sport!), you need

- a trainer who thoroughly understands the training style he is using
- a trainer who thoroughly understands the sport he is participating in and the individual behaviors he needs to train
- a dog that has the talent and physical ability to do the required behaviors at a precise-enough level to win consistently
- the desire to train and compete enough to obtain the title
- the money to train and compete enough to obtain the title
- the time to train and compete enough to obtain the title
- the skill to train to obtain the title

You have to have every single one of those elements. Every one. The reality is it takes years to become good enough to train to the upper levels of any sport, even if you have the resources to help you get there. For those trainers who are pursuing sports where no one has yet forged a path and invented recipes, the road is infinitely tougher and harder.

It will happen. Every year another boundary comes crashing down. All we need is the time to have all of the elements fall into place. *[Editor's note: Since this article was first published, clicker trained dogs have won all sorts of titles, and continue to do so.]*

"Clicker trainers use no punishment."

Incorrect. Clicker trainers use negative punishment, which is the removal of something the dog wants. For example, "penalty yards" is a common method used in teaching loose-leash walking. The dog sees something it wants. As long as the dog walks nicely, the trainer lets it walk toward what it wants. However, if the dog pulls, the trainer walks the dog backward. Walk nicely; get what you want—positive reinforcement. Pull; lose what you want—negative punishment. This method is extremely clear to the dog, because getting or losing what it wants is controlled by the dog's actions.

"Adding an aversive (positive punishment) is more severe, but more effective, than removing a reinforcer (negative punishment)."

Is positive punishment more severe than negative punishment? Is it more effective? What about positive reinforcement? Is it more or less powerful than negative reinforcement? Is it more or less effective?

Every application of reinforcement and punishment, positive and negative, falls on a continuum from mild to extreme. Exactly where the particular application falls on the continuum depends on the individual dog and the specific situation.

Similarly, punishment and reinforcement are defined by their results so, by definition, they work and are effective. Even if used correctly, aversives may have side-effects. Both punishment and reinforcement take skill to apply correctly, but the potential for negative impact to a training program and the dog is higher if the trainer misapplies an aversive.

"Corrections are vital to ensure a dog knows it must obey."

False. Reliability is a number. Data. Cold data with no relation to "choice" or "control"—or to the method used to get the result. Reliability is obtained through reinforced repetition. True reliability is achieved at fluency, long after the animal is past the point of performing solely because of consequence, positive or negative.

I've been driving cars with manual transmissions for more than 10 years. In that time, I've had an incredible number of reinforced repetitions (meaning the car did what I wanted it to do) for using the clutch.

Chapter 3 – Clicker in Action

I remember learning to use the clutch. It was horrible because I'm not terribly coordinated. Shifting once the car was moving wasn't too hard, but getting started from a stop was murder. So we did lots of reps. We started in a parking lot—no distractions, few restrictions. When my reliability improved, we raised the criteria and went to a neighborhood street. I was back at square one in that environment. But through practice, I improved. Then we went to more populated streets. Whoa—drop in performance again! But again, I quickly improved. Gradually the streets got busier and harder. We added hills. We added the pressure of cars behind me at a stop light. Man, I had thousands of repetitions before I got relatively smooth at getting that car started.

For a very long time, using the clutch to start the car was a deliberate, conscious behavior. I had to think about it every time. Over time that changed, and I don't think about it anymore. I don't have to. I'm fluent in the behavior. Latency is immediate. Reliability is near 100%.

Near 100%. Once in a blue moon, I stall the car. It happens. I ain't perfect, even after more than 10 years of repetitions. And still the behavior is under my control. I can choose not to use the clutch any time I want to. I can pop the clutch intentionally. Never, never, never will that behavior be out of my control.

To get a truly reliable behavior, there's only one way to do it. Practice with intent. Generalize the behavior. Practice in the conditions in which you need the behavior reliable. Work on latency. Keep records and train until you've achieved the level of reliability you need, whether it's 9 of 10 or 999 of 1000.

You determine which cues are the most reliable and have immediate responses by training them that way. But never fool yourself into thinking training, no matter how severe the aversive used, overcomes free will.

"The click must be followed by a food treat."

False. The click must be followed by a reinforcer—something the dog is willing to work to obtain. You have a variety of reinforcers available. Some of the most commonly used include:

- Food
- Toys
- Praise, attention

- Opportunity to do something the dog wants to do
- Opportunity to perform a well-known behavior

In a formal training session you want to get as many repetitions as possible. Food is an excellent reinforcer because it can be cut into tiny pieces and eaten quickly. Toys are also a good reinforcer, but playing with the toy takes time, meaning you get fewer repetitions in a session. Praise and attention are wonderful additions to food or toys, but are often not desired enough by the dog to use alone, particularly in distracting situations. The opportunity to do something else is sometimes the most powerful reinforcer you have.

The most important thing to remember is that the dog determines what is and isn't a reinforcer in a certain situation. If the dog doesn't want what you're offering, it's not a reinforcer.

"Clicker training won't always work because food isn't a strong-enough reinforcer," and "Instinctive drives and self-rewarding behaviors are so powerful that you must use corrections to ensure reliability."

As mentioned in the last section, food isn't the only reinforcer available. No matter which reinforcer you choose, consider its relative value. One food might be worth more than another food. Your dog's tug toy might be worth more to your dog than food in certain situations. The opportunity to greet another dog may be the best reinforcer of all! It all depends on your dog and the particular situation.

One commonly cited concern is that there are things the dog wants in the environment that he can't have. Or that the dog has a powerful, instinctive drive to perform a certain behavior, and the trainer can't find a positive reinforcer more powerful than that drive. Guess what—you may not! So that's when clicker trainers move beyond operant conditioning and employ techniques based in classical conditioning, such as desensitization and redirection. Desensitization lowers the strength of the animal's response to particular stimuli. Redirection can be used to transfer the focus of the drive from an undesired outlet to a different—even unrelated—desired outlet.

Imagine a Border collie staying on task next to a soccer field filled with screaming, running children. A sporting breed remaining focused in the

Chapter 3 – Clicker in Action

presence of joggers, squirrels, birds, people throwing balls, and other dogs cavorting. A high-drive Malinois breaking off an attack on a single command without getting that oh-so-desired bite. That's how powerful desensitization and redirection are.

"Clicker-trained dogs will work only when food or the clicker is present," and "You have to use the clicker and food treats forever and carry them everywhere you go."

People are terrified of being tied to the clicker and food treats. Fortunately, they need not fear. The clicker is an event marker, used to identify correct performance during the early learning stage of training a behavior. Once the behavior is fully shaped, on cue, and strong, you don't need its precision anymore. You can simply replace it with a verbal marker/release word. If you don't have a clicker with you, you can always mark verbally—or even just deliver the reinforcer directly.

Food, as explained in earlier sections, is not the only reinforcer you have available. Yes, you do need to continue reinforcing behavior—at least occasionally—but that reinforcement doesn't have to be with a food treat or even with anything you "give" the dog. Instead the reinforcement might be the opportunity to do something he really likes or, if you're lucky, the behavior itself might become self-reinforcing!

Food can be misused, of course. Some people complain that their dog will do anything as long as food is present. That is an example of how wonderful dogs are at discriminating. If food is visible every time you train—whether used as a lure or in a treat bag around your waist—the dog will quickly come to believe that food is part of the equation. This problem isn't limited to problems fading food. Dogs are frequently trained to perform behaviors only when they are directly in front of their trainer, when their trainer is standing, or in a specific location. All of these problems can be avoided by making sure that you vary during training everything that isn't tied directly to the behavior.

"Clicker training is a snap to learn," and "Clicker training is too difficult for beginners."

Unfortunately and fortunately, neither of these is true. Clicker technique is simple, but it isn't easy. Even if you have a good recipe to follow, it takes a certain amount of skill to clicker train correctly. Fortunately, however, the dog is an extremely forgiving species that works very hard to figure out what his trainer wants. Although "timing" is often touted as the be-all, end-all for clicker training, the reality is that all pet behaviors (and a great number of competition behaviors) can be taught by someone with utterly abysmal timing.

Other people are overwhelmed by the amount of theory in clicker training. They just want to follow a recipe and train their dog. That's okay too! Many people are finding and following recipes with little or no understanding of how they work. They aren't operant trainers, but they're still achieving their goals.

"The clicker is a magic, necessary tool for training."
I'm amazed at the number of people who point the clicker at their dog, click it, and, when nothing happens, complain that clicker training doesn't work. The clicker is not a remote control.

The clicker is a tin noisemaker. When you first use it, it's completely neutral. However, by associating it with food or other reinforcers, it takes on reinforcing qualities. Its power, however, is not as a reinforcer but as an event marker. As an event marker, it is (in skilled hands) a scalpel, capable of shaping incredibly precise behaviors. A verbal marker is, by comparison, a butter knife. What do you need? If the butter knife is adequate, sure, you can train without a clicker. But if you need a scalpel, the clicker—or other similar, species-appropriate marker—is a superior way of getting precise behavior without the risks associated with aversives.

"The clicker cues behavior," and "Clicker trainers go around with a million uncued behaviors," and "Clicker-trained dogs constantly throw behaviors."
A cue "names" and elicits a behavior. The clicker marks that behavior when it occurs. For two reasons, clicker trainers don't add a cue until the dog is offering exactly what we want.

- When the pup is learning the behavior, we want him to concentrate on the behavior. At that point, the cue is meaningless to him anyway—just another bit of "noise" to sort through. In

Chapter 3 – Clicker in Action

the beginning, make learning easier on your dog by minimizing distractions, including meaningless cue words.

- We want the cue to be associated with the final, perfect form of the behavior. If you add the cue in the beginning, you run the risk of having the unfinished version of the behavior crop up when you least want it to—like during the stress of competition—even though you continued to shape a more precise behavior.

First get the behavior you want in the form you want it. Then add the cue as soon as the dog is actively offering the behavior you want. For a simple behavior that could happen the first day!

More complex behaviors may take more time to shape. If the behavior is extremely complex—a behavior chain, for example—you can add cues to the individual parts of the chain, and then add a cue for the entire chain when it's complete. Or, if the behavior is a single but very elaborate behavior, you can use temporary cues as you shape the behavior, replacing them with a permanent cue when you've shaped the final behavior.

"You can't praise your dog when you clicker train."

Of course you can praise! After you click, praise all you want. I do encourage trainers to be quiet before the click so the dog can think about what will earn him that click. Once he has earned it, however, celebrate all you want. Let training improve the relationship—love your dog!

I love clicker training, and I'd love to teach you about it, but not by using half-truths or attacks on a perfectly valid way of training. All trainers, no matter what kind of training they practice, have the same goal: to make life better for dogs and their humans. Learning new techniques is about solutions, not about condemning old techniques. Facts. Education. Understanding.

Editor's note: This article was originally written for The Commentator, *the newsletter of the Curly Coated Retriever Club of America.*

Should You Use No Reward Markers? Examining the Debate

by Laura VanArendonk Baugh

What is a No Reward Marker (NRM), and is it a useful tool or an awful mistake?

Should a good clicker trainer use an NRM, and, if so, when?

It's out there, lurking. At times you feel it stalking just behind you. At last, it springs as someone asks, "Why don't you tell your dog it was wrong?"

The NRM debate has been reopened once more.

The debate arises in cycles, but next time you'll be prepared for it, no matter how stealthily it creeps.

What is an NRM, anyway?

On the surface, an NRM is rather straightforward. At times, though, there is considerable debate regarding its true nature. The No Reward Marker is usually described as "conditioned extinction," since its intention is to inform the learner that no reinforcement awaits down the path he is considering. One of the most well-known examples of NRM is the children's game Hot & Cold, where feedback of "getting warmer" guides the participant to a goal object, while "colder" indicates that the participant should try another route.

At first glance, this looks like a good use of continuous feedback. However, a closer examination reveals that the "cold" feedback is really unnecessary. Savvy players start by spinning until they hear "hot." They do not waste their time passing through the room experimenting with how many "cold" responses they can get. In fact, the lack of a "hot" response is equivalent to a "cold" response, as anyone who has played a shaping game can attest. In the clicker trainer's version of Hot & Cold, the feedback is click and no-click respectively. In both the children's version and the clicker version, the cold answer—"cold" or no click—adds no further information.

Chapter 3 – Clicker in Action

Conditioned extinction or aversive?

There is far more to the NRM debate than this, however. Stand back, since this is where I'll step on some toes…

By the time an NRM has real meaning for the learner, it has become positive punishment.

An NRM may cue extinction, but in doing so it also signals a loss of opportunity. The chance of earning reinforcement has closed. If the subject changes his behavior to avoid the NRM—and that is the whole point of its use—then the NRM is by definition an aversive. It may be a mild aversive or it may be severe, depending on the learner's mindset, but it is a stimulus the learner is actively working to avoid. Because the trainer introduces the NRM upon the learner's mistake (adds an aversive stimulus that modifies behavior), the NRM is positive punishment.

Is the NRM necessarily evil? Probably not, but it's not the completely neutral stimulus that many claim. The punishment continuum runs from fairly mild to extremely harsh, and it is the learner who interprets the severity of any given punisher. If a trainer wishes to avoid the use of positive punishment, he should be aware of all its forms, including the form of an NRM.

Observe a contestant on a game show. When he answers a question and then hears the buzzer marking a wrong answer, does his body language indicate that the buzzer is a neutral stimulus, serving only as useful data? Certainly not! The disappointed contestant may exhibit slumping posture, frustrated displacement gestures, perhaps profanity—even if he does not lose points or money, only the opportunity to earn more of the same. For someone who really wants to be right, being wrong feels quite aversive. (A learner who doesn't care about being right is facing a motivation problem, not a data problem. An NRM won't help and may even hinder the development of motivation.)

Broken contracts

Some trainers use NRMs not only to shape a new behavior but to indicate any mistake a learner makes, including a failure to respond properly to a cue (no response or an incorrect response). For example, if a trainer sends a dog to select a scented object from a collection and the dog retrieves the wrong one, the trainer might say "oops" as the dog picks up the incorrect object.

While, superficially, this seems to be relevant data, it can break down careful training. Positively trained cues are themselves tertiary reinforcers. An NRM after a failed cue breaks the contract of reinforcement, offering P+ after a tertiary reinforcer—and creates serious risk of poisoning the cue (and rendering it useless for future use in chains).

(Note: If you find yourself using an NRM after a cue, review the cue. Why isn't it working? The issue is probably not the NRM at all!)

> **Testing NRMs in humans**
>
> At a Shedd Aquarium training workshop, Ken Ramirez led us through a variety of training games to develop skills in timing, cueing, chaining, and more. After several days, he gave us a new challenge: train a human subject to perform three simple cued behaviors using both a conditioned reinforcer and an NRM. Our task would not be complete unless the three behaviors could be performed successfully—and the subject could recognize and define our NRM stimulus.
>
> The results were amazing. Even though we had been discussing NRMs so recently and the concept was fresh in our minds (unlike the minds of our usual animal subjects), only one learner out of fifteen guessed that the extra stimulus was supposed to be useful data as an NRM.
>
> Meanwhile, every learner exhibited frustration, and even occasional aggression (sometimes veiled as jokes and sometimes not). About half of the learners never completed the tasks in the allotted time, while they had been highly successful in the other games. In my own learner, I saw cue inversion (frustration and confusion with the NRM caused confusion in other areas) and a general loss of enthusiasm. Even though I was making everything as plain and simple as possible—marking errors with the same precision as I would click correct responses, and trying to follow errors with a chance for success—I could see her attitude souring. Yet as a group we'd done well. Ours was the first session in the years of Ken's teaching where someone had not stormed out angrily during the NRM challenge.
>
> This experience cemented my current opinion on the NRM. With this confusion and frustration in humans who already knew the NRM concept, why risk those feelings with those who cannot discuss it with us?

Chapter 3 – Clicker in Action

Many animals (and humans) exhibiting stress in challenging conditions are stressed not only by the tasks they face, but by the changing schedules of reinforcement and the increased chance of punishment. Is the dog really finding scent discrimination so difficult—or is the dog frustrated by the learning conditions?

Is this data necessary?

Proponents argue that NRMs are simply data to inform the learner. They say that it's not fair to leave a dog guessing; it's kinder to tell him what's not working.

Why tell the dog that he wasn't successful? This question is usually asked in a more philosophical way, but I mean it very practically—if the dog needs an NRM to realize that he isn't being reinforced, the trainer has screwed up badly. Why doesn't the dog know already? Clicker training is pretty much yes/no. If training has been set up so that the dog can't tell if he's been successful, and he needs supplemental information, then something is wrong! (See "Fixing behaviors without an NRM," p. 91, for more on this.)

Can it ever be useful?

So is it always wrong to mark a behavior as non-reinforcing? Keep in mind that blanket generalizations are always wrong (irony intended!). Some informational cues could be called NRMs, because they signal the lack of potential for reinforcement—a red light rather than the more common and cueing green light. My dogs have learned if I say "shoo" while I'm at the computer, I'm not available to play, while at other times a nose poke might elicit attention. In this situation, "shoo" is a signal that future offered behaviors will not be reinforced. (Most pet owners will recognize that our pets know a host of these types of cues, mostly non-verbal.)

Most of the time, however, I see NRMs used as a crutch where the initial training was not clean and precise. This puts the burden of the trainer's mistake on the learner, who didn't receive adequate data in the first place and must now sort through additional cues, stimuli, and frustration. The vast majority of the time, the "need" for an NRM can be avoided through proper attention to training basics—good timing, appropriate criteria, and a high rate of reinforcement.

I think there is an application for NRMs in a situation where click/non-click is not clear to the subject, but these situations are rare and most trainers will not encounter them. This makes training an NRM "in case of need" a waste of effort. Spend your time training more cleanly in the first place and you'll never need the NRM.

Alternatives to a punishing NRM

So what's a trainer to do when a learner errs? There are several alternatives to the NRM as unintentional punisher. A time-out (usually the removal of the trainer's attention and/or opportunity) is negative punishment, rather than positive punishment. A least-reinforcing stimulus (LRS, a complete lack of response from the trainer or environment) is true extinction—and generally the best response to an error. A trainer working at a good pace (15–20 reps per minute for a simple behavior) may pause only a second for an LRS and then move on with the next repetition, but that is enough to note the error and its (lack of) consequence.

Training without aversives

Even potentially useful tools can be harmful, especially if they are a crutch for the sloppy use of preferred tools. In *Animal Training: Successful Animal Management Through Positive Reinforcement*, Ken Ramirez wrote, "I frequently discourage [novice] trainers from ever conditioning a 'no' signal, because if there is not a signal for 'no' it cannot be overused."

In the process of writing this article, even though I am arguing against the use of NRMs, I have found myself using more NRMs in my own training—having them on my mind made me more likely to use them even though I knew better!

While it is true that many learners can work through NRMs, it is equally true that many cannot (and many who can, do better without). It is a difficult habit for a trainer to break. Having the option can create the opportunity or even the need. As songwriter Jonathan Coulton noted, "We do what we must because we can." To avoid aversives in training, be aware of them in all forms, and plan accordingly.

Chapter 3 – Clicker in Action

> **Fixing behaviors without an NRM**
>
> Training my dog Shakespeare the (admittedly silly) behavior of putting his head into a bucket for a shaping demo was going smoothly, until I inadvertently reinforced my paw-oriented dog for moving his paw as he dipped his head. Within seconds I had a dog convinced that I wanted his right paw in the bucket! While many trainers might have resorted to an NRM to discourage the paw behavior, I chose to repair the behavior using only good timing and careful placement of reinforcement.
>
> At first Shakespeare was frustrated by his low rate of success. Would his attitude have been improved if I'd told him that his behavior was incorrect? Would an NRM have helped him know exactly how to modify the behavior the way I wanted, or would the NRM have been associated with bucket interaction itself? To fix the behavior, I tightened up my timing and temporarily reduced criteria. With the resulting jump in rate of reinforcement, the learner was able to quickly grasp what I wanted and retain it. The superstitious paw movement persisted and then faded under the weight of reinforcement for the desired behavior.
>
> Note that it was far more tempting for Shakespeare to place his paw in the bucket as he approached it from a distance; the test for this behavior was his ability to approach from across the room and place his head in the bucket cleanly.

When It All Goes Wrong: How to Respond to Failure

by Aaron Clayton

What's the right response in the first minute after a performance failure? For many clicker trainers, the immediate answer is to try to create a neutral response—one that doesn't reward or punish. But that goal, while admirable, isn't realistic and may lead the trainer to miss the bigger picture.

Canine sports and human sports

Trainers often ask, "What do I do with my dog right after a mistake? How do I act? What do I do to get back on track?" Human team-sport competition provides an excellent analogy to canine competition of any kind and can help illustrate the answers to these questions. Why human sports? The dynamics are compellingly similar.

A sports team is a product that is asked to perform when it doesn't know if it's ready. Trainer Steve White points out that a working or sport dog is exactly this—a "product" that is almost always in public before it's "finished!" We hope the product (the team or the dog) is ready, but every week at "game time" one team finds out it's not!

Looking at the sport of soccer—a sport I have coached at the youth level—there are other similarities. Soccer is a particularly challenging sport for a coach because he/she exercises little control once the game begins. There are no timeouts during play, so there is no opportunity to communicate changes. Plus, the size of the field makes it virtually impossible to dictate strategy or tactics to players while the game is on. For these reasons, a soccer coach in France is called the "selector" and not the "coach." He trains the players, selects the players who will play, and then hopes they go out and perform what they've been trained to do best. Any dog handler will recognize the soccer coach's challenges as his or her own!

Dog handlers train rigorously and compete regularly in complex environments. Course layouts change, and squirrels appear from nowhere. Courses

Chapter 3 – Clicker in Action

are dry when you practice and muddy when you run them. Similarly, my youth soccer team works hard—we have training sessions twice a week in both the spring and the fall, and we play games on Saturdays. We compete on surfaces that are very different, on fields whose sizes vary, and with additional variables like weather, referee skill, and more. Whether you compete in canine sports or coach sports, one of your chief challenges is a complex web of environmental variables.

Finally, in both arenas competition against other teams means the same thing: The competitive venue is where you see how well the skills you've been teaching and training are internalized.

The Case of the Goalie Error

In the soccer environment, I've learned some lessons about how to handle the mistakes my players (in my case, always kids) make on the field. Are these lessons that can help the canine handler?

Consider the following scenario: In a tight match, my goalie makes a mistake that costs us a goal and, quite possibly, the game.

Now what?

The nature of the mistake (not coming off her line to cut off a ball) tells me clearly that she hasn't yet internalized what we have worked on at practice. Yes, I am frustrated—by the goal, by the failure, and by the prospect of more goals given up if the right behavior doesn't take root!

What are my possible responses immediately following the goal?

- Keep her in goal and say nothing.

- Keep her in goal and ask her an interrogatory question of some kind (open-ended: Why didn't you come off your line?) or (yes/no: Should you have come off your line?).

- Keep her in goal and instruct her to do something different that could help in the future (Come off your line earlier next time!).

- Keep her in goal and say something encouraging (Keep your head up!).

- Take her out of goal, talk with her about what could be done differently, then put her back in goal.

- Take her out of goal, but put her back in the field.
- Take her out of goal, have her sit on the sideline, and say nothing.
- Take her out of goal and express some level of incredulity at her mistake.

The fallacy of the neutral response

What should I do? It's appealing to try to find a neutral response, one that neither encourages nor punishes. But none of the choices listed above are neutral responses. They all will have consequences—some more predictable (and aversive) than others. Hurt feelings, tears, loss of focus, loss of confidence, or a complete shutdown are all possible. But, it's also possible to see the following consequences: a bounce back with more energy, a determination to do better, or anger channeled into focused energy.

So how should I, as a clicker trainer and a coach, respond? First of all, if I've really internalized my lessons, my response should not be a conscious choice but a reaction. You can recognize masterful clicker trainers—their first reactions under stress are all in the right direction. But many of us (me included) are not yet masters and are working to overcome some unproductive patterns, especially in stressful situations. In those circumstances, I use a series of questions/reminders that can help me make the right decision.

Four questions

Here are the four questions I ask myself, as well as my answers as they apply to the case of the goalie error:

1. **Is this a real moment of training?** No. This is a game situation. I am not in a training situation where I can improve player skills. I can't fix the skill right now.

2. **What is the objective?** Since the objective is not "fix this problem skill right now," what is it?

    If I want this player in goal again, my objective is to be sure that at our next practice the player will be receptive to learning and will continue with confidence. Alternatively, if I have lost confidence in this player at this position, then I want her out of the net in this game. But, I also want her to feel prepared to learn again at our next training session. If I have to pull her out of goal, I want to try to redirect her energy into a task where she can feel successful and supported—perhaps in the game in a field position.

While it is true that every moment is a teaching moment, not all all teaching moments serve the same purpose. Some teaching moments only serve to set up larger teaching opportunities later. That's how I see this situation. My response should be focused on setting up the player to learn later, and not on fixing something now!

3. **Am I feeling neutral?** (Ha!) Be real about the stakes and emotions. No matter how neutral I want to feel, I have to acknowledge that I'm frustrated. I probably can't ask anything of, or tell anything to, the player that won't be taken as critical because I do feel critical. My goalie is feeling frustrated herself. The reality of these feelings makes me even less eager to pull her out and talk with her about how to improve. Neither of us would be very good at it at the moment.

4. **What don't I know about the issue?** A lot. I don't know what was going on in the moments before the error. Did this player make the error because she was thinking about her new puppy dog? Did she make an error in judgment but recognized the situation? Maybe she didn't recognize the situation, or maybe she did not know what to do in that situation. Maybe my player can explain the moments before the error, but it's more likely that she can't.

At this point, not knowing exactly what caused the error or where the error began isn't important. I know that I have to go back to a more basic level where my goalie is comfortable and build the skill back up from there. Knowing that I don't know is important—I won't be inclined to dictate a wrongheaded solution right now!

Decision time

In this situation, I choose to keep the goalie in. I cheer the whole group (including her) but don't say anything individually to the goalie. It's true that my silence (lack of explicit support for her) might be taken as an expression of my disappointment, or even a reproach. I don't really know. On the other hand, if I shout out encouragement to the goalie only, she might take that public effort as insincere and insulting—even as an attempt by me to place the blame on her in a public way. Again, I can't be sure.

Either of those responses would probably be fine. Both provide the opportunity for me to keep the player in the game and set up my player for successful training sessions later.

The "Big Picture": What trainers miss

The "Big Picture" is what I feel dog trainers and many coaches sometimes miss. In asking, "What do I do right after a mistake? How do I act? What can I do to get back on track?" they are quick-fix oriented. In the moment of failure, the "fix-it" orientation is often counterproductive. Instead, my answer to any of the "what to do" questions above is simple—go back and train some more. The error demonstrates that the skill is not sufficiently internalized.

In other words, how we respond in the first minutes after failure is important. Use those moments to prepare the player to internalize the right skill later; it's not the time to attempt to dictate the right skill then and there.

My team plays and competes every Saturday whether we're ready or not. We play in situations where I expect some failure all the time. Some failures have small consequences (mishandling a ball, missing a shot); some have larger consequences (mistakes that lead to goals by the other team). When you are in the performance arena, there's very little that can be done to fix mistakes. At halftime, I can inspire players to put into use the skills they have but are not using, or to deploy the skills that they have in a better way, but that's about it. If a mistake is an anomaly, then it's not likely to happen again so there is no need to get all upset about it. If it's a skill that is not yet fluent, the only way to fix it is in training sessions!

Preserve the opportunity to learn

In youth soccer, as well as in dog training, the neutral response is not attainable. Keep in mind the teaching objective, remember that you don't know much that's important about the circumstances of the error, and remember that there is little that can be fixed during the competition. Act instead to create and preserve the opportunity to fix errors in future training sessions. Make changes in training that set everyone up with the best chance for success. After that, hope for the best when you get to the unpredictable field or competition ring. No one wins gold without some luck on their side! Good luck with your own responses!

… Chapter 3 – Clicker in Action

The Rules for Cues
by Karen Pryor

The technical name for a cue is a discriminative stimulus.

Here is how you can tell if you have built a truly powerful cue that will always work for you and your dog.

Test one:
The dog always does the behavior you asked for, when you ask it. (That is, when you say "sit," or "bark," or "high five," the dog does what you asked, and immediately. For most people, this constitutes obedience, but it is only a start of creating real reliability.)

Test Two:
The dog never offers that behavior (sit, bark, high five) when you didn't ask for it. The dog never gives you that behavior just because it's bewildered, or hopeful, or wants a cookie.

Test Three:
The behavior never occurs in response to some other cue. For example, if you say "roll over," and your dog sits, barks, or lifts a paw for the high five, you have just learned that a) your dog doesn't yet understand what you mean by roll over, and b) your dog doesn't yet understand the cue for the behavior it did give you, either.

Test Four:
No other behavior occurs when you give a cue for one specific behavior. When you say "high five," the dog does not respond by licking you, rolling over, sitting, and so on.

To have a really reliable dog (in the show ring, obedience ring, hunting field, search-and-rescue, wherever) train at least two or three behaviors to meet all four tests. When a behavior meets all four tests, the cue for that behavior becomes an immensely powerful tool. When a dog has learned to refine its attention to cues to this level, it becomes a tremendously astute partner in learning new cues. You can develop the skill, or fluency, of understanding and recognizing cues, using any behavior, including tricks.

Adding the Cue
by Karen Pryor

When we first start out clicker training, we tend to get very excited about the fact that we can teach the dog a new behavior in just a few clicks. Suddenly we have a dog that sits, does a belly flop down, a spin, a paw wave, and six other things—but all at once. You're hoping for a sit/stay, and the dog is running through his entire repertoire trying to find something you'll click.

All this means is that you haven't named the behaviors yet. You haven't added the cue, as we say. Here's a quick and painless way to do that: work two opposite behaviors at once. For example: in your living room, after the dog has learned that sitting makes you click, and coming towards you makes you click, teach this lesson: You say "sit," the dog sits, you click and treat. Step backwards, bend over, call the dog with the word "come," the dog comes forward a step or two, click, treat. Step toward the dog, say "sit," the dog sits, click, treat; step away from the dog, say "come." After three or four rounds stop moving forward and back and just use the words. (Toss the treat after the sit, to get the dog far enough away from you to be able to "come.") In three minutes, with twenty clicks or more and a steady stream of successes, you have two behaviors and two new cues for the price of one.

As for that frantic whirlwind of tricks, the dog is telling you that he has no cues for those behaviors yet. Add those cues at the rate of one or two per five-minute session. With each cue, it gets easier. Once a dog has acquired three cues for three behaviors, and can respond to them confidently in new rooms and at different times, the dog will have the picture and you'll be able to "explain" subsequent new cues in just a few clicks.

Chapter 3 – Clicker in Action

Hurry Up and Wait!
by Lori Chamberland

Those of you with exuberant, fast-thinking dogs, imagine that your dog is offering solid repetitions of a new behavior and that you're ready to attach a cue. But, before you get a chance to give your cue, your warp-speed dog forges ahead and offers the behavior in anticipation of a click/treat—again and again. He won't let you get a word in edgewise! Now what?

In the early stages of attaching a cue, it's common for a dog to anticipate and offer a behavior before you ask for it—especially if you have not trained a specific default behavior for the dog. The dog has been reinforced at a rapid rate many, many times for doing a certain behavior. And now, all of a sudden, you ask him to break his familiar rhythm, notice the brand-new cue that you are introducing, and wait to perform the heavily reinforced behavior until after he perceives the brand-new cue!

When you are teaching dogs to wait for a cue, it's easy to forget that waiting itself is a behavior, and a pretty tough one at that! You are asking the dog to stand/sit motionless, with full attention on you until you give further instruction. That's a lot to ask of an eager dog! When you first attach a cue to a new behavior, you are interrupting the previously established rhythm of the training session by adding another few steps into the sequence. Rather than "Behavior, click, treat" then "Behavior, click, treat," the new sequence looks like this: "Dog waits for cue, trainer gives cue, behavior, click, treat."

There are many ways to help a dog learn the concept "wait until I give you the cue before you do that behavior." Here's a quick method:

If you have a previously established "wait" behavior, use it to your advantage! A great way to isolate the cue for a new behavior is to insert your "wait" cue just before you ask the dog to perform the new behavior. So, it's "wait, (dog waits), new cue, (dog does new behavior), click/treat!" The opportunity to do the behavior is the reinforcer for "wait," and the click/treat is the reinforcer for the behavior. Be sure to click/treat the dog for the "waits" sometimes as well, so that behavior on its own continues to pay off for the dog.

Now, here's the cool part: You'll probably find that after you've reinforced the dog for the wait behavior three or four times, he will start to anticipate. Dog: "She's just going to ask me to wait, so I might as well go ahead and wait first." Perfect! He has just offered the behavior of "wait for the cue" all on his own, which is exactly what you wanted in the first place. Soon you can probably fade out having to say the word "wait" every time you issue the cue for the new behavior. The wait will come on its own.

This is one instance where a dog's tendency to anticipate what you want can work to your advantage, because you now have the sequence of events you're looking for: "wait for the cue, new cue, behavior, click/treat." You are also continuing to strengthen the dog's reinforcement history for waiting. Every time the dog waits successfully, he is given the opportunity to perform a behavior for a click/treat.

Using a properly trained "wait" cue also gives the dog something to do, rather than throwing in other well-known behaviors, trying to guess what's going to make you click.

Once your dog has experienced some success using the cue "wait," you can try rotating among the new behavior and other known behaviors as well. So, it might be "sit" (dog sits), click/treat, new behavior cue (dog does this), click/treat, "down" (dog downs), click/treat.

All of this training will help strengthen the dog's understanding that he should wait to hear a cue first in order to earn reinforcement for a given behavior. Give it a try next time you're attaching a cue to a new behavior. Offering your dog something to do in that brief moment before you issue the new cue can cut down on confusion and frustration—for him and for you.

Chapter 3 – Clicker in Action

Reinforcing Doing Nothing
by Karen Pryor

Some dogs do a number of behaviors reliably on cue but go crazy and start offering many behaviors the second the clicker comes out. Other dogs only seem to listen when the clicker is visible.

What's going on?

Part of learning a cue is doing the behavior when you get the cue for that behavior. An *equally important* part is *not* doing the behavior when you don't get the cue. We teach this by picking an easy behavior, cueing it and reinforcing it several times, and then methodically giving the cue *only* when the animal is standing or sitting still. You reinforce "doing nothing" by giving the cue to do "something." You thus use the clicker to teach the animal to wait for and attend to a cue. When you have done this with three behaviors, that random throwing of behavior will die down. You also will improve your own timing and observation skills with this process.

When dogs don't respond until they see the clicker, they do not yet understand the real meaning of the click. They know food is available when they see the clicker, and they assume it's only available then. They have not yet learned that their own actions make you click, and that it's *their* own behavior that produces value. Probably the trainer is a) clicking much too late, after the behavior is over, b) luring the behavior so the animal has no idea it could do the behavior on its own, and/or c) pointing the clicker at the animal as if it were a TV remote so the animal assumes the sight of the clicker is important.

It's a beginner's problem, and easily overcome. A good clicker trainer keeps the clicker out of sight (in your hand, behind your back, or in your pocket) so the dog doesn't pick it up as a false cue. A good clicker trainer *never* moves the treat hand before or while clicking, or the dog will watch the treat hand instead of listening to the click.

A good clicker trainer reinforces lots of routine behavior outside of the clicker sessions, with a mouth click, a special word, and a pat, a smile, or sometimes a treat. Coming when called around the house, waiting at the door, standing still to have the leash put on, all are worth a verbal marker and some minor reward, thus teaching the animal that there are many ways to earn reinforcement through its own actions.

Chapter 3 – Clicker in Action

My Dog Knows It, He Just Won't Do It! How to Achieve Fluency
by Laurie Luck

The dog was huge. An adolescent Great Dane (about 150 pounds) walked calmly into the bustling restaurant by my side. He was the largest service-dog-in-training I'd ever worked with, and even I wondered if I could keep him out of the way of the wait staff and patrons. After we were led to our table, I laid the dog's mat next to my chair, cued "mat," and spent the next hour or so enjoying a lovely meal while the dog relaxed quietly on his mat and remained out of the way.

That's fluency at work. The dog's successful mat experience was due to his ability to perform the behavior with distractions, for a substantial length of time, and with a great deal of precision (if he wasn't squarely on that mat, he would have been a tripping hazard).

What is fluency?

So what exactly is fluency? Why should you care about it? And how can you improve your dog's fluency? First, look at fluency from a perspective that's already familiar: language. You are fluent in your native language. For me, that's English. I can read, write, speak, understand jokes, come up with synonyms and antonyms, understand syntax, and more in English. I *know* English. I don't have to think about it—it's a part of me.

I study German, but just because I know some German doesn't mean I'm fluent in the language. I have a small vocabulary; my comprehension is much better if I'm reading the language. I have to stop and think about a translation if I'm speaking with a native. I don't understand any jokes, and if I'm nervous or scared, I forget everything. My German is passable if I am just trying to ask where the bathroom is, but it needs a lot of work.

The same goes for dogs and behavior. Just because dogs know how to sit doesn't mean they can do it anytime, anywhere, under any circumstances.

That is just like me with my German; I can't hold a conversation about the latest political landscape simply because I know a few German words.

Training the highest level of fluency is how you get the behavior you want the dog to do, when you want him to do it. When people say "My dog knows it, he just won't do it," they mean that the dog is not fluent in the behavior in all circumstances. Fluency is the difference between a dog being able to sit in a quiet room and a dog being able to sit while visitors enter your house. It can also be the difference between a dog that sits almost before you finish saying "sit" and a dog that sniffs around, looks at you, then sits. Really, it's about how well you have taught the behavior.

Fluency: the sum of all parts

There are six pieces of fluency related to your dog's ability to "do" a behavior.

1. Precision: Does the behavior look perfect (you define what "perfect" looks like)?
2. Latency: Does the dog start doing the behavior as soon as you ask?
3. Speed: Once the dog starts the behavior, does it happen quickly enough for your needs?
4. Distraction: Can the dog do the behavior no matter what's going on around him?
5. Duration: Does the behavior last as long as you need it to?
6. Distance: Can the dog do the behavior away from you?

Using the "mat" behavior (dog goes to his mat and lies quietly) as an example, the components of fluency are easy to see.

1. Precision: The dog needs to be placed on the mat squarely (not just partly on, but centered on the mat).
2. Latency: The dog should start the behavior within one second of being asked.
3. Speed: The behavior should be completed within 3-ish seconds.
4. Distraction: The dog can do this behavior anywhere (ballpark, airplane, dentist's office, restaurant, and so on)

5. Duration: To expect a duration of 60 minutes is reasonable for the mat behavior (the length of a typical dinner out, doctor visit, and so on).
6. Distance: For this behavior, distance is not a big issue, as you will be with the dog. You do need the dog to be able to stay while you walk away, however.

Your criteria for each aspect of fluency might be different than what is listed above. The criteria are totally customizable to meet your need. For example, if you're working on the mat behavior and you define precision as "dog lies centered on mat," then shape the behavior until it meets your criteria.

Train the cue first

Before you start to work on fluency, make sure the behavior is "on cue." That means you have both taught the dog to do what you want and developed a signal to let the dog know when to perform the behavior. For my example, the cue is the word "mat" (of course, the mat needs to be there for the dog).

Train and enhance fluency

Where do you start with fluency when the behavior is on cue? Work on one aspect of fluency at a time. Why train one aspect of fluency at a time? It is really hard on the learner when requirements are stacked. Using the German language example, if my German teacher wants to improve my pronunciation (the precision with which I speak the word), the focus is on just that. For that time, no one cares that my rate of speech (speed) is quite low. The teacher and I won't worry about how long I need to think about how to answer a question (latency); we're working on pronunciation (precision) only. Imagine how hard it would be for me to stack those requirements on top of each another. What if after I get pronunciation down, my teacher adds on rate of speech (speed) while still holding me to the original high level of pronunciation? What if s/he then stacks another requirement—latency: the length of time I pause before answering a question? How soon do you think I will be quitting my German lessons?

The smart and efficient way to teach is to work on only one component at a time. Work on each aspect of fluency until your dog has achieved success at each level. Master each component individually, then come back and start pairing them together. Follow the same path with your dog as you would for yourself.

I find it easier to work on fluency in the order I've listed above. Start with precision, because you want the behavior to look right from the start. After that, you can work on other pieces of fluency, such as speed (does the behavior happen quickly enough?). If you're working on precision, it does not matter how long it takes the dog to do the behavior, if he can do it with distractions, or if any other part of fluency is demonstrated. What matters is if the behavior looks as it should. If it does, click and treat the dog whether or not other aspects of fluency were met.

After you've reached your goal for precision, set that aspect of fluency aside (just temporarily, don't worry) and work only on latency. The precision you worked so hard to get will likely deteriorate a bit while you're working on latency—that's OK. Let precision fall apart. You'll get it back, I promise.

Must-know: The average

In order to improve any behavior, any aspect of fluency, you need to know where you and your dog are currently. The way to do this is to find the average level of behavior, and then click only the behaviors that are at least at the average.

What you need: 10 treats, paper, pencil.

To find the average, put 10 treats on the table. Ask your dog to offer the behavior you want to improve. Click and treat every attempt. After every attempt, write down a number. For instance, if you're working on latency in the sit (how long it takes the dog to start doing the behavior), silently count the number of seconds it takes for your dog to start to sit after you ask him—that's your first number for the latency average. After 10 trials, add up those numbers and divide by 10. That number is the average amount of time it takes your dog to start the behavior.

With the average for whichever component of fluency you are working on, you have everything you need to improve your dog's behavior. Using the mat example again, if the average amount of time it took your dog to start moving toward the mat was three seconds, click and treat your dog whenever he starts to go to his mat in three seconds or less. If it takes him more than three seconds, abort that attempt. Shuffle your feet and move so your dog is reset for the next attempt. Very quickly, your dog will understand that only the faster responses get clicked. Soon you should have fewer below-average responses. Calculate the new average and then click and treat only those faster responses. Continue to improve the average until you've met your latency goal.

Start with success

Working with the last three aspects of fluency—distraction, duration, and distance—it's easier to start from a point where you know the dog can be successful. Raise criteria systematically from that point. For the mat behavior, if you were working on distractions start in a quiet room, and simply wave your hand while you ask your dog to move to the mat. Remember, when you are working on distraction, don't worry about any of the other aspects of fluency. So with the focus on distraction, it doesn't matter if it takes your dog five seconds to start toward the mat. As long as he gets there, he earns a click and a treat. Once distractions are at an appropriate level, only then work back up to the previously achieved level of latency.

Troubleshooting

If your dog isn't successful at a particular point, you may have overestimated your dog's abilities. If your dog can't get it right within three attempts, reduce the level of difficulty so the dog has a good chance of getting a click and treat.

Remember to work on only one aspect of fluency at a time. It's easy to think "he's mastered the distractions, now I'll add distance." That's a sure way to set your dog up to fail. Instead of adding on distance, drop out distractions and work only on distance. As always, keep training sessions short (5–10 minutes, shorter if your dog becomes less interested sooner).

Masterful performance

Working carefully through the six components of fluency will improve your dog's confidence and ability in a behavior. The result will be that reliable, crisp, and impressive behavior—and a dog that responds quickly, enthusiastically, and correctly whenever you ask.

Basics for Puppies

Most of the articles in this book apply to animals of all ages. However, training a new puppy presents unique challenges at a time when your young dog is most impressionable. If you practice good training from the start, it can set up your puppy for success. In this chapter you will find articles about how to get started with puppy training, how to teach your puppy to listen, how to house train your puppy, and how to deal with the common problems of teething, nipping, and chewing. These are the basics for puppies.

Clicker Litter 110
by Karen Pryor

All Ears! How to Train Your Puppy to Listen 113
by Aidan Bindoff

Where's the Potty? How to House Train Your Puppy 116
by Debbie Martin

How to Survive Puppy Teething and Nipping 122
by Casey Lomonaco

The Need to Gnaw: How to Prevent Puppy Chewing 131
by Rebecca Lynch---

Better Together

Clicker Litter
by Karen Pryor

How soon can you begin training puppies? As soon as their eyes and ears are open, according to some breeders who are using the clicker on whole litters of pups, even before they are weaned. Why would you want to do that? Well, the clicker means good things are coming. The puppy that makes that connection can then learn that its own actions sometimes cause those clicks that lead to treats. And the puppy that makes that discovery has a big start on a happy future.

Here's how it works. As soon as supplemental feeding begins, the litter owner clicks as the pan of food is set down among the puppies. Some people click just once, and some click as each puppy's nose actually reaches the food. Dog trainer Steve White, who breeds German shepherds, begins clicking even earlier, every time the dam goes into the litter box to nurse her babies—surely a very important event for the pups.

After some exposure to the clicker, start taking each puppy away from the litter for a short session on its own. Click, and treat. A dab of pureed baby food meat on the tip of your finger makes a great treat, even for the tiniest breed. Then pick something the puppy happens to do, such as lifting a front paw, and click as the paw goes up. It may take 10 or more clicks before the puppy begins lifting the paw on purpose, but then you'll be amazed at how enthusiastic the puppy becomes. "Hey, look! I can make that huge person give me food, just by doing *this!*"

Choose any simple behavior at first: it doesn't need to be something useful. A sit, spin, wave, play bow, back up, or lie down are all possibilities. You can teach all the puppies the same behavior, or, if you have them identified individually, teach them each something different. Don't try to coax or lure your students into a particular behavior; you want each puppy to discover that its own actions make you click. This teaches the puppy a major life lesson: "I like to find out what people want me to do." That discovery won't happen if the puppy just learns to wait to be shown what to do.

Chapter 4 – Basics for Puppies

How much time does this take in your busy life? Two or three clicker lessons of no more than two to five minutes each are enough to develop some cute little behaviors. No need for a lot of drilling; once a puppy learns what to do for a click, it won't forget.

More importantly, these brief lessons can convert a puppy of five weeks or so from an oblivious blob into an eager, observant learner.

You can capitalize on this awakened state in many ways. For example, when people come up to the litter box, do the puppies rush over and leap on the walls, begging for attention? Probably. So use clicker sense and make a new rule—a rule for puppies and for family and visitors, too: only puppies that are sitting get petted, or lifted out of the pen. It doesn't take long to get the whole litter sitting; you can click them all at once for doing that. Now, when supper comes, the puppies will have to sit and be clicked before the dish goes down. Instead of repeatedly and unintentionally reinforcing jumping up, a behavior most pet owners really hate, you are building a bunch of pups with better manners than that, even before they leave home.

"Come when called" is another skill the whole litter can learn with clicks and treats, and it is a fun one for children to teach. Two or three children can take turns calling a puppy back and forth between them, clicking and treating when the puppy goes to the child that called. You're going to give your buyers a puppy that already has a head start on this important behavior.

How far can you go? Training with absolutely no corrections, just informative clicks and enjoyable treats, you can go a long way, even with a baby. When my last border terrier puppy arrived on the airplane, a long-distance purchase bought sight-unseen, she was just nine weeks old. I brought her home, set her down, and gave her a little toy. She picked it up, carried it to me, and dropped it at my feet. "Surely this is an accident?" I thought. I tossed it. She went and got it, brought it back, and dropped it again. Using clicks and treats, the breeder, as a treat for me, had taught this tiny puppy a nice retrieve!

Breeders with clicker trained litters usually give their buyers a demonstration of what the puppy has learned, a simple list of instructions or suggestions for using the clicker (several lists are available free online—search for clicker training sites), and of course a clicker or two. People love taking home a puppy that already knows a trick; what a smart dog! Your early work starts them off with an attentive and cooperative pup that is ready to learn more—a puppy that has a far better chance of fitting in to its new world than a puppy starting from zero.

Melinda Johnson, a long-time breeder of soft-coated wheaten terriers, began clicker training litters several years ago. Like many breeders, Melinda will always take a dog back if it doesn't work out in its new home. Melinda reports that since she started clicking litters, her return rate has dropped to zero, and her file of letters from thrilled and happy owners has grown enormously. "Smartest, most attentive dog I've ever had." "A laugh a minute, how did we get along without her?" These puppies still have a lot to learn, of course. But they start their new lives knowing how to learn, and ready and eager to learn more. Click!

Chapter 4 – Basics for Puppies

All Ears! How to Train Your Puppy to Listen
by Aidan Bindoff

Do you find yourself repeating instructions to your dog or puppy? You can learn how to train a puppy or dog to listen to you the first time, and every time.

Many dog or puppy owners blame the dog for not listening. When you have invested time and effort in training, it can be disappointing when your dog suddenly decides to stop listening to you—or when he decides that something else in his world is more exciting or interesting than you. The truth is that dogs do what works for them. It is up to you, as a puppy or dog owner, to teach your pet to listen—by making listening to you work for the dog. Believe it or not, many dog owners inadvertently teach their dogs to ignore them!

So how do you teach a dog to listen?

More is not always better
Dog owners frequently repeat commands over and over. If your dog didn't respond the first time, repetition isn't going to help. Repeating commands teaches a dog that the command is meaningless, or that it's OK to respond in his own sweet time!

What are the odds?
Never ask for a behavior that you aren't at least 80% sure you will get the first time. If there are too many distractions, if it is a new situation, or if the behavior just hasn't been learned well, then you probably won't get the behavior you want.

Keep it quiet—and succinct
Train quietly. Bellowing commands at a dog is left over from the old military-style dog training. Dogs have a powerful sense of hearing and can hear our tiniest whispers. That's not to say that a command shouldn't be clear and

audible, but if you only roar commands during training, don't expect your dog to pay attention to you unless you are roaring. A dog that has learned to listen carefully will tend to pay more attention.

A bit of meaningless chatter is fine every so often, but dogs don't speak our language and you don't want cues to become lost in the noise. When training, try not to talk too much. Effective communication comes through quality and clarity, not quantity.

Basics build success

If you find yourself in a situation where your dog won't respond to a cue, and you're sure he knows it in other situations, think about what is different about the situation. It could be that there are too many distractions for your dog to focus, or it could be that the situation is vastly different from training situations in the past.

Go back to basics when this happens. Remove distractions if you can, and re-introduce them slowly. Start at the beginning in a new situation, even if it means using a food lure briefly in order to get the behavior. If there's too much going on, move away from the action a bit.

Remember to set your dog up for success. If your dog can't succeed, you can't reinforce. If you can't reinforce, nothing useful has been learned.

Timing is everything

Make sure your rewards are meaningful. Reinforcement is only reinforcement if it increases or maintains behavior. A satiated dog offered lousy treats, or a dog-tired dog offered a chance to chase a ball, is probably not going to be too interested in training.

And remember to quit while you're ahead. If you train for too long, you'll get sub-standard behavior. Reinforcing sub-standard behavior will only produce more sub-standard behavior in the future.

Some final advice

- **Don't feel as if you have to reinforce every behavior.** Once the behavior is well learned, stop reinforcing the worst offerings. If your dog is trained to come when called, don't reinforce if he takes too long to respond. Set him up for success; reinforce the faster responses only.

Chapter 4 – Basics for Puppies

- **Train often.** Dogs need to "learn to learn." By training often and training consistently, your dog will learn how to play the training game with you—and it should be a game. If training isn't like playing a game, it stops being fun for both of you.

- **Be worth listening to—someone your dog trusts and respects.** Be predictable, confident, calm, and decisive. When you make a decision, stick with it. If you decide that your dog can't sit on the couch, lead him onto his mat every time he sits on the couch. Don't give in just because he's giving you "those eyes." (It's another matter altogether if you decide to invite your dog onto the couch as a reward for some other behavior you asked for.)

Where's the Potty? How to House Train Your Puppy

by Debbie Martin

House training might be the most important behavior to teach a new puppy that will live indoors. Few dog owners will tolerate a healthy adolescent or adult canine that lives indoors and urinates or defecates indiscriminately in the home.

Not being house trained is a common behavioral reason that dogs are relinquished to shelters. Other behavioral reasons for inappropriate elimination include separation anxiety, urine marking, submissive urination, or excitement urination. These reasons are not related directly to learning, but to anxiety, fear, or emotional arousal. This article will focus on house training related to lack of training. As the most prevalent location where house training occurs is outside, the focus will be on this location specifically. However, the same methods can be used for any designated elimination location (pee pads, dog litter box, and so on).

Encourage instincts and a preferred location

Once they are mobile, puppies naturally leave the "nest" to eliminate away from their resting area. A puppy will seek a location that is porous (absorbent) and away from his eating or sleeping locations. To a puppy, a rug or bath mat may meet the criteria for an appropriate elimination location. Puppy parents need to teach the puppy the preferred place to eliminate.

Though not inherently difficult, house training a healthy puppy successfully requires consistency, predictability, and patience from the caretaker. Patience is key! Like a parent potty training a young child (going from diapers to using the toilet), teaching a dog an appropriate location for elimination does not occur overnight. Accidents are bound to happen, even with diligent supervision. Progress should be seen in house training by 4-6 months of age, yet some dogs may take 9-12 months to be completely house trained.

Chapter 4 – Basics for Puppies

Positive steps to house training

It is important that the learning process be carried out positively. Punishment and reprimands have no place in house training, as they will only teach the puppy that it is not safe to eliminate in front of people. In fact, punishment might teach a puppy to sneak off to eliminate, making teaching the puppy a human-approved location to eliminate extremely difficult.

There are 5 key steps to successful house training (adapted from *Puppy Start Right: Foundation Training for the Companion Dog*)

1. Prevent accidents from occurring.
2. Reward elimination in appropriate areas.
3. Anticipate when a puppy needs to eliminate.
4. Know what to do when accidents happen.
5. Clean soiled areas.

Prevent accidents from occurring

Close supervision and management are crucial. Set up the puppy for success by controlling the puppy's learning history so that urination and defecation are more likely to occur in a preferred location. Most puppies have an inherent desire for cleanliness and do not eliminate in locations where they sleep or eat. This instinct can be used as an advantage for management and prevention of accidents.

Three management techniques can be helpful: using a crate, using an exercise pen, and the umbilical method. Ideally, all three methods should be incorporated into house training a young puppy.

A crate can make elimination training much easier by providing a safe location for the puppy to be while the owner is otherwise occupied. Rest time and feeding can occur in the crate, and, when properly acclimated to a crate, most puppies find it a comforting place. For house training purposes, the crate should be large enough for the puppy to stand up, turn around, lie down, and stretch out comfortably. If the crate is too large, the puppy might sleep in one area and use another corner for elimination. Once the puppy is house trained, the larger the crate the better.

Another option is to use an exercise pen and enclose a small area for the puppy. The exercise pen will likely be larger than the crate area and can be used for short periods. Just remember that if the area is too large, the puppy is likely to find an elimination spot.

The umbilical cord method is a great way to both enjoy having the puppy with you and keep an eye on him. This method involves keeping the puppy on a leash attached to you as you move about the house. Having the puppy close means that you are more likely to notice when the puppy starts to show subtle signs of impending elimination (sniffing the ground, circling, pulling to move away).

Reward elimination in appropriate areas

Maintain a routine for taking the puppy outside. Use a keyword or phrase, such as "Outside" or "Do you have to go outside?" Always use the same exit and take the puppy outside on leash even if you have a fenced-in yard. Go to a designated elimination area in the yard (one that is full of odors from previous eliminations) and "be boring" (ignore the puppy).

Wait for up to 5 minutes. If the puppy eliminates, immediately after he completes the void reward with a small food treat. Even better, just as the puppy finishes, mark it with a click and then give a treat. Keep your body and hands still while the puppy is eliminating. If you begin to reach for the treat or start talking, the puppy is likely to stop before emptying completely.

The primary goal is for puppies to be rewarded with a food treat just after eliminating in a desirable location. Timing of the reward is important. Too early, and the puppy is likely to not begin or to stop eliminating in order to get the treat. Too late (when you have returned inside, for example), and the puppy does not form the association between eliminating in a desired location and getting a treat. The importance of using a food reward is to impress on the puppy that the best place to eliminate is outside. The puppy would be content using the area rug in the house. Either location would meet the puppy's criteria for an appropriate elimination location, but the treat comes after eliminating outside.

After receiving the treat for elimination, the puppy can be given some off-leash play time with you if you are in a securely fenced area. Play and attention follow elimination. This additional lesson helps teach a puppy to go outside and "do his or her business" so the fun can begin.

If after 5 minutes of waiting the puppy has not eliminated, return inside and supervise (umbilical cord method) or manage (crate or exercise pen). Try again in 10–15 minutes.

Anticipate when your puppy needs to eliminate

Physically, urinary and bowel sphincter control, or the ability to hold it, takes several months to develop, even up to 16 weeks of age. This means that once the bladder or colon is full, the puppy cannot wait to go if the muscles are not developed enough physically to prevent elimination. A general rule for how long a puppy can go between elimination opportunities (in hours) is 1 + the puppy's age in months. For example, a three-month-old puppy might be able to hold it for four hours. When active, puppies might have to eliminate more often.

Puppies often have to eliminate after stopping one behavior and starting another. After waking up, playing, and eating are all good times to provide an opportunity to eliminate. Set up the puppy to succeed by anticipating when he will need to eliminate. Be proactive rather than reactive. Initially, you might take the puppy outside 10–15 times in a day and he eliminates only 5 or 6 times. By providing frequent opportunities, you will be more likely to have him in the desired elimination location when he needs to eliminate, thus providing opportunity for reinforcement.

Watch for subtle signs of impeding elimination: suddenly stopping what he is doing, sniffing the ground, circling, or wandering toward the door.

Keep a written log of activity and eliminations. With a set routine for meals, training, play, walks, and elimination opportunities, a pattern of elimination frequency will develop. Keeping a log documents improvement and also identifies problem areas in the house training (the puppy continues to have accidents between 3:00-4:30 p.m. when the kids arrive home from school, for example).

Feeding a highly digestible diet consistently and at set times two to three times a day will help determine a defecation pattern. Provide a 20-minute window of opportunity for the puppy to eat; remove any leftover food once the puppy has walked away from the bowl.

Water should be freely available. Restricting water intake could result in a puppy that ingests a large volume at one time. The consequence of that might be excessive and frequent urination.

Know what to do when accidents happen

If your puppy starts to have an accident in front of you, cue "outside." This might delay the elimination for the few moments you need to get him outside. Reward elimination in the appropriate location.

Verbally reprimanding or physically punishing a puppy for eliminating in front of you will only teach him it is unsafe to eliminate in front of people. The puppy will sneak off to go, where it is "safe." If a puppy is reluctant to eliminate in front of people, then it is difficult to reward him for eliminating in the desired location.

If you find an accident after the fact, just clean it up and review your supervision and management strategies.

Clean soiled areas

Because dogs are drawn to spots where previous elimination has occurred, thorough cleaning of the area is imperative. Avoid any products containing ammonia, vinegar, or bleach because these smells can act as an attractant.

Soak up or pick up as much of the accident as possible. Apply an enzymatic cleaner and allow it to dry on the area for 24 hours.

Once the area is dry, apply a scent to deter future elimination in that area. Citrus and pine scents are good options, but the slight scent of mothballs has been found to be the most effective. To lay down the scent, either wipe the mothball directly on the area to leave a residual scent or powderize the mothball (place in two sealed bags and crush outside) and apply 1/8 of a teaspoon deep into the pile of the carpet or fabric. Remove any residual powder. You should not be able to smell the mothball when you enter the room, but only if you smell the exact location where it was applied (and there it should just be the hint of the odor).

Chapter 4 – Basics for Puppies

Caution: Mothball crystals are toxic if consumed by dogs or people. Do not use mothballs on bedding, in areas where a puppy is confined, or on objects that may be chewed or ingested.

Success!

With these guidelines and consistent, positive training most puppies can be house trained successfully. Lack of success with house training or regression in house training may indicate a medical problem that should be evaluated by a veterinarian. Vaginitis and urinary tract infections are common in young and adolescent dogs.

With a healthy dog, one that is set up for success and positive reinforcement, house training will be among the earliest behaviors where you and your dog find success together. With an elimination routine in place, everyone in the family can enjoy home sweet home.

How to Survive Puppy Teething and Nipping
by Casey Lomonaco

I am firmly convinced that the evolutionary process made puppies adorable so that we would overlook the fact that their mouths are full of razor blades—blades they do not hesitate to put to frequent use. Nipping and chewing rank high on the puppy-parenting complaint list and are symptoms of teething, a developmental stage associated with both human and canine infants.

Why puppies bite

There are a number of reasons puppies nip, bite, and chew. This behavior starts before puppies even leave the litter—as soon as they begin to develop teeth, they begin receiving feedback on their bite strength from their mothers and littermates. With their litters, puppies learn that biting hard leads to loneliness or, worse, hunger! Bite a littermate too hard in play? She'll likely yelp and stop playing with you until you've reclaimed your wits. Bite Mom too hard while eating? You may wind up missing the snack bar as she walks away. Poor, lonely, biting puppies. That is, until they calm down. Then the play party is back on!

Puppies also bite and nip to learn the social mores of dog culture. Dogs don't play with Legos, video games, and Barbie dolls; they chase, race, tackle, play face-bite games, pounce, tug, and wrestle. This play actually serves a more serious purpose, teaching the lessons that need to be learned so that a dog can survive in canine society. Dogs don't communicate with verbal language; they communicate physically, through body language and contact. Because dogs don't have "wars of words," when the going gets tough, there is often a physical scuffle.

When well-socialized dogs find themselves in conflict, the interaction often looks very scary—teeth flashing, growling. More often than not, these interactions are brief, however, and both dogs walk away without injury. It's a lot of bluster, but it is a highly ritualized display. If one or more of the dogs

Chapter 4 – Basics for Puppies

is under-socialized, though, the interaction pattern changes, and a player is likely to get hurt.

While bite-inhibition training begins while a pup is with its litter, training must continue throughout the dog's life, with special emphasis during puppyhood. My dog, Mokie, will be six this July, and we still practice bite-inhibition exercises occasionally.

Here comes trouble (one more reason!)

Puppies bite because they are teething and learning to control their bite strength, and because nipping is a way to explore and join the social life of dogs. Another reason puppies bite is because it makes exciting things happen; biting earns attention.

Biting for the reaction usually happens after the puppy enters its "forever home." The typical scene is where the family is quiet, relaxing after a long day. Mom is checking her Facebook account, dad has his feet up watching the game, Suzy is studying, while Johnny plays Xbox. Everyone is ignoring the puppy. Ho-hum.

The bored puppy muses, "How can I get this party started?" Biting often works to get attention, so the puppy zooms around the room leaving a wake of torn pant legs in its path. Ignored no longer, now the entire family is looking at and touching the puppy, and "barking" with excitement (yelling at the puppy). Every family member has put aside what was previously interesting in order to focus on the puppy. Mission accomplished—the party has started! Puppies are very good at training humans to pay attention to them.

Mouth manners for the long-term

Puppy training should emphasize behavior problem prevention in the adult dog. While most puppy classes teach basic manners and cues like "sit," "down," and "settle on a mat," it is far more important to offer exercises and lessons that prevent behavior problems from occurring in the adult dog. Most of my puppy classes have a heavy emphasis on socialization, prevention of resource guarding, and development of bite inhibition.

Dogs that are confident and comfortable in their surroundings are less likely to bite. Appropriate and extensive socialization helps dogs learn to be confident and comfortable in many different environments. Teaching bite inhibition, controlling the pressure exerted behind a bite, helps stop a dog from causing significant damage in a situation where the dog feels the need to defend itself with teeth. There is a difference between gentle mouthing (a "nip") and a bite that sends someone to the hospital. Bite-inhibition training helps puppies learn polite, gentle mouthing—and that human skin is very delicate!

Before discussing techniques and strategies for addressing puppy nipping, I should clarify that nipping and chewing are symptoms of a developmental stage that may last 6 to 9 (or more) months from birth. This is not an issue that will be fixed in a single training session. Consistency is required throughout this puppy period, and regular attention to your dog's bite strength is a good idea even well into adulthood.

"Do" the right thing

There are things you can do to ensure that your dog develops appropriate "mouth manners."

DO wait until your puppy is at least eight weeks old before separating him from his littermates. Puppies learn a lot of lessons about appropriate social interaction, including bite strength, from their dam and littermates. Taking puppies away from their litters too early can prevent them from learning these valuable lessons. Be wary of adopting "singletons," dogs born without littermates. These puppies miss out on a lot during critical stages of development, including essential feedback about the force they are putting behind their bite!

DO consider letting your puppy stay even longer with the breeder/litter if the breeder is doing a great job with socialization.

DO reserve your spot in a well-taught puppy class before you even bring your puppy home! While many veterinary professionals once recommended starting classes with your dog when the puppy reached six months of age (and completed a full round of initial puppy vaccinations), behavior-savvy veterinarians are now changing their positions. Many are now recommending that puppies start in a group class at an early age, as young as eight weeks old! Refer to the *American Veterinary Society of Animal Behavior (AVSAB) Position Statement on Puppy Socialization* for more details. While most puppy-biting is simply nipping, there are cases of aggression developing early in puppyhood; an experienced instructor will realize the difference and help you address the issue promptly.

Chapter 4 – Basics for Puppies

DO make sure that you have plenty of chew toys on hand—bully sticks, Nylabones, frozen stuffed Kong products, or even old washcloths soaked in low-sodium chicken broth and frozen are all great treats. Supervise your puppy when he is enjoying his toys.

DO hand-feed your dog. Hand-feeding is a great way to improve your bond with your dog, and it offers you lots of opportunities to practice rewarding him for using his mouth politely! Hand-feeding also teaches the dog that you are a very exciting and rewarding person to spend time with—a bonus! Other family members should practice hand-feeding; encourage guests to hand-feed the dog as well. Of course, small children should not feed nippy puppies by hand. If there are elderly individuals in the home, they should practice this exercise last or wear light gardening gloves when practicing the initial stages of training. Since skin tends to thin as people age, there is a greater likelihood of puncturing.

DO manage and redirect. Crates and tethers are valuable management tools. You do not want to associate crate time with punishment, so when your puppy needs to go in the crate to relax for a bit, offer one of the chew toys you have prepared. Doing so allows you to redirect your puppy's teething instincts to an appropriate outlet. If you are using a tether, make sure that your puppy is securely attached in an area that has been puppy-proofed. Neither the crate nor the tether area should make the dog feel socially isolated (keep both in a living area and not in a damp, musty corner of the basement).

DO set up play dates with appropriate puppies and tolerant, well-socialized adult dogs. Your puppy-class trainer will instruct you about how to select appropriate playmates, read canine body language and stress signals, and how and when to intervene if play gets out of hand.

DO make sure your puppy is receiving adequate physical and mental stimulation. Sometimes, puppies bite because they are bored and it's something to do. If it makes people scream, run, and otherwise "freak out" as well, it's a real party starter for a brassy young pup just looking for a good time. Physical exercise and mental stimulation alone will not eliminate the nipping (maturity and training, however, will), but both can often reduce the frequency and intensity of mouthing behavior.

DO learn to "be a tree." You hardly ever see dogs chasing, nipping, or biting at trees. Why? Because they're boring—they don't move, squeal, run away, scream, give eye contact, or push the dog away. Trees are just there. "Be a tree" is a technique that all family members should learn, but it is especially wonderful to teach small children. Contact Doggone Safe (www.doggonesafe.com) to learn more about the "Be a tree" program and to access some wonderful dog-bite prevention resources.

DO give a dog binary feedback on bite strength. Acceptable use of teeth is rewarded with treats, attention, affection, or whatever the dog likes. Unacceptable use of teeth results in redirection (chew on this in your crate for a while) or negative punishment/removal of opportunity (biting makes people walk away from you). For puppies that continue to chase and bite at you when you move away from them, the tether can be especially helpful. Simply walk out of the tether area, cross the room, sing a verse of your favorite song in your head while ignoring your puppy, and then return to begin a new training session. It is essential that this removal of opportunity is unemotional and that it happens instantly and consistently as a response to using unacceptable bite force.

DO teach your puppy to use his mouth politely. There are many great resources on the Internet and several different techniques you can use. As with all puppy training, work in short sessions (average 10 treats per session). Here are some of my favorite training exercises:

- Teach hand-targeting (see "How to Teach Your Pet to Target" by Laurie Luck, p. 60) and/or put "kisses" on cue. These are great new behaviors for your dog to learn but they also teach an appropriate way to interact with hands that can earn reinforcement opportunities!

- Play "I'm OK with that," (see next page). My favorite way to train bite inhibition comes from a Karen Pryor article that details how to train your puppy not to nip at things (hands, skirt hems, ankles, and so on) near his face.

If your puppy bites your hand hard during any of the exercises, stand up, turn your back on the dog, and walk away or "be a tree." Consider practicing when your dog is tethered so he cannot chase and nip you.

Play "I'm OK with that!"
by Karen Pryor

Teaching the puppy to use his mouth gently is an important part of training. Doing it the clicker way creates clear communication without punishment. This technique is very simple, and very powerful. You are simply rewarding the puppy for choosing not to nip. When the puppy makes the right choice, he earns his click and reward! You are helping him learn to make good decisions. Please do it carefully to avoid small injuries to yourself. Follow these easy step-by-step instructions for using the clicker to help eliminate puppy nipping.

- Take your closed fist and put it in front of the puppy's face. Click and treat if he doesn't nip—even for a second! Repeat this. If your puppy bumps his soft nose against your fist, that's great. Click this!
- Next, take your closed fist and wave it slowly around in front of the puppy. If your puppy does not try and nip you right away, click and treat. Repeat this several times.
- Raise the criteria for a click by both lengthening the amount of time the puppy can have your fist in front of his nose without nipping, and by altering the distance from his face and the speed of your hand flying around his face.
- Repeat this exercise with a toy or chew bone. Click and treat for calmness and for waiting rather than grabbing at the object. If at any time the puppy tries to nip, stop, put your fist or other object out of sight and start again a little further away. When you have clicked and treated him several times for staying calm, click and give him the object and let him enjoy it. He is learning that you will give him nice things but only if he waits for permission.
- Repeat this step at several distances around the puppy's nose and mouth. Be sure to do this exercise several times during the day.
- Do the same with your open hand. Do the same with your index finger. Try it with your shoes and your clothing.

Your puppy can definitely learn not to nip things that are near his face, and since this is when most nipping occurs, reinforcing his correct choices is crucial. You should see immediate improvement with this technique, but because he's a puppy, you'll need to repeat it over and over, especially when you have tempting smells on your clothes and hands!

Soft-mouth shaping

Ian Dunbar has a categorization system for ranking the severity of dog bites. The scale may look a little different for a young puppy without severe aggression but with a normal nipping problem. Here's a sample 5-category scale for that situation, with 1 being the least amount of pressure exerted, 5 the maximum pressure.

1. The puppy sniffs or licks the hand.
2. The puppy gently mouths the skin. You can feel teeth without pressure.
3. Moderate mouthing. Slight pressure is applied to skin, but not enough to cause any puncture or tear.
4. The puppy bites hard enough to cause pain, but does not break the skin.
5. The puppy bites hard enough to break the skin.

There could be additional levels of biting beyond five (the puppy tears the skin, the puppy repeatedly bites the skin, puncturing it, the puppy bites and shakes the hand, and so on). If your puppy is biting at level 5 or higher frequently, consulting with a qualified behavior professional immediately is not optional but necessary!

Soft-mouth shaping is another technique for teaching a puppy to use its mouth politely. To start shaping a soft mouth, place a low-value treat in your hand and present it to your dog. Any reaction at level 3 or lower earns the puppy a click and the opening of the hand; feed the puppy from a flat palm. A level 4 reaction results in a 5-second removal of the hand (place it behind your back and ignore the dog). Level 5 reactions result in a temporarily lonely puppy—walk away from the dog for 7 to 10 seconds before reengaging him in training. As the puppy develops better control over his mouth, increase criteria so that only level 2 or level 1 responses earn reinforcement.

Mouthing manners: Helpful hints

- Introduce movement. It is one thing for a puppy to ignore a stationary hand, but it is much harder to avoid chasing and biting at moving objects. Introduce movement of hands and other body parts slowly while practicing these exercises. If at any point your dog becomes overly aroused by the current level of motion (a six-inch wave of the hand in either direction, for instance), reduce the level of movement (a wiggle of the fingers or a three-inch wave of the hand, perhaps). Reduce movement until your dog is more settled and composed, and then raise your criteria slightly again.

- Some dogs are more inclined to bite ankles than hands. If this is true for your puppy, teach your dog to play with a tug at your side. Redirecting the dog's natural tendency to chase and bite at things keeps your pant legs safe and builds great toy drive, a valuable conditioned reinforcer for many dogs!

- You can also try tethering your dog and practicing impulse control exercises. Secure your puppy to a strong and stable tether. After asking him to sit, begin clicking and treating for maintaining the position while you shift your weight from your left to right leg and back. If the dog is able to remain sitting while you do this, slowly begin to introduce larger movements, lifting your right leg and shaking it a bit, for instance. Gradually increase your criteria so that you are able to run past your dog, jump up and down, or wave the hem of a flowing skirt in his face while he sits politely, waiting for reinforcement. If at any point in the game your dog becomes overly aroused and nippy, reduce your criteria to the last point at which he was successful and consider splitting your criteria into smaller steps before proceeding.

- Practice initially with low-value treats. Once you complete the training steps with low-value treats, slowly begin introducing treats or toys of higher value. When you introduce a new or more exciting reinforcer, temporarily reduce criteria and go back to the beginning step. Don't be surprised if your puppy becomes "nippier" temporarily when you introduce each new, higher-value reinforcer. A puppy may take kibble politely 100% of the time but still snatch with his teeth for a coveted bit of roast beef. These setbacks are only a temporary part of the learning process; each time you introduce a new reinforcer, your dog should proceed from bite to polite more quickly than with previously introduced reinforcers. The dog is beginning to generalize the skill of generalizing!

- After you have practiced with a number of treats and toys, try altering your delivery. Present an open palm with the reinforcement initially. Many puppies will not bite an open palm, but will bite at a piece of food clasped between the thumb and index finger. When you are ready, move on from the open-palm approach to practicing all of the mouthing exercises holding the treats between your fingers.

- When you deliver the treat to your dog, be careful not to jerk your hand away quickly, since this can elicit a chase response. Instead, move the treat toward your dog's mouth rather than having him snap at your rapidly retreating hand. Use a cheap pair of gardening gloves in the initial stages of training if your hands are very sensitive!

Worth the effort

While training your puppy not to nip or bite may sound like a lot of work (and, to be fair, puppy-raising is definitely a lot of work), it is one of the most important things you can teach your dog. Bite-inhibition training saves lives; it helps dogs and people stay safe together and enjoy each other more thoroughly.

Puppy training should focus on preventing behavior problems in the adult dog—and no behavior problem is more dangerous for dogs and people than biting. Any dog may bite if it senses danger, feels trapped, or experiences pain, among many other reasons. Early and extensive bite-inhibition training provides the confidence of knowing that if your dog ever finds himself in a provocative situation, it's significantly less likely he will cause serious damage with his teeth.

The Need to Gnaw: How to Prevent Puppy Chewing

by Rebecca Lynch

What do pet stores sell? Toys for dogs to chew on. Bones for dogs to chew on. Treats for dogs to chew on. Are you seeing a theme yet?

Dogs enjoy having things in their mouths; they like to chew! It makes them happy. It's fun. It relieves stress and boredom. Dogs explore their world with their nose and mouth—it's just what they do. So why is it baffling to people when their puppies chew up their shoes?

Some people feel that their dogs chew their shoes out of spite. *"Fifi was mad at me because I went to work and left her home, so she chewed up my favorite shoes!"* Although I am sure that Fifi is really smart, I doubt that she has the mental capacity to think, *"I am mad at Mom because she left me here all day. I know that she loves those running shoes, so I am going to chew them up because I know that will make her mad. I'm going to show her!"*

Reality

The more likely scenarios are:

- Your puppy may be bored, and chewing relieves boredom.
- Your puppy may be teething, and chewing relieves discomfort.
- Your puppy is stressed. Shoes are loaded with our scent, and an owner's scent is comforting to a dog. Chewing something laden with an owner's scent makes a stressed dog feel better.
- Puppies like to chew, and if there were no toy or bone handy… there were shoes just lying there!
- Your puppy needs more exercise.
- Your puppy may have a nutritional deficiency or intestinal parasites. Talk to your vet and examine closely what you are feeding your dog.

- Your puppy needs more attention. Some dogs will pick things up and run with them simply to get attention.

Of course, there may be additional reasons, reasons that will only be discovered when we learn to speak with our dogs.

So what is the best thing to do when a dog is chewing on our stuff?

A dog can't chew it if he can't get to it

Some people feel that a puppy "should know better," but puppies don't know better. Chewing is a normal stage of puppy development, just like the normal toddler stage of touching things and putting things in their mouths.

Parents know that toddlers go through a stage where sticking fingers in the light socket is great fun. A parent could follow the child around, smacking hands and yelling. Or, a parent could purchase the childproofing plastic pieces to insert into the sockets, knowing that in a few months the child will no longer be interested in the sockets.

It is the same with puppies. It is much easier to put your shoes (and anything else chewable) away. The great thing about keeping your shoes out of sight is that your puppy will never learn that chewing shoes is enjoyable. Once your puppy passes through the chewing stage, you can leave shoes out without fear of destruction. So, if you can pick it up and put it away, do so! That way there will be no crying over lost shoes!

Abundant alternatives

Since dogs love to chew, they need something to satisfy that urge. Be sure to offer your pup lots of alternatives besides your shoes (they are stowed away in the closet, right?). Pet stores are overflowing with items dogs can put in their mouths. Stock up and leave chew toys wherever your puppy will be—be generous! It's smart to manage a stash of toys that can be rotated to keep play exciting!

Interesting options

There are many toys out there made for sticking yummy things inside. Kongs are fantastic! Made of hard, durable rubber, they are hollow so that you can stuff them with peanut butter, canned dog food, cream cheese, or any other tasty treats that you can fit inside. Buster Cubes, Treat Mazes,

Chapter 4 – Basics for Puppies

Roxxters, Kong Wobblers, and a whole slew of other toys are designed to hold kibble that will fall out piece by piece as your dog rolls the toy around to play. You could feed your dog's entire meal in one of these toys. Bonus: your dog gets mental exercise while he eats his breakfast.

Sterilized femur bones (the white bones you find at the pet store) also make great chew toys for most dogs. I prefer these bones to the ones with the brown, yucky flesh still on them that can harbor salmonella and other bacteria. I don't recommend rawhide because it is processed with nasty chemicals (such as bleach, lime, and formaldehyde) and is very unhealthy for your dog. Of course, don't give your dog any cooked bones from your dinner. Cooked bones can splinter and pierce your dog's GI tract.

Supervision, supervision, supervision!
If your dog is a little carpet shark chewing everything in sight, don't let him out of your sight. If you can't watch your puppy directly, confine him to a crate or X-pen. Each time your puppy gets to practice the behavior of chewing, that behavior becomes more ingrained and harder to change in the future.

Make a trade
Nobody likes a thief. If your dog has something and you walk up and take it away, that is what you become. These exchanges create a dog that, 1) runs and plays *Catch Me if You Can!*, or, 2) swallows things quickly as soon as he sees you coming. The former is annoying and the latter is dangerous. Having been a vet tech for several years, I can tell you that dogs can and will swallow some pretty amazing things—and not all of them come out OK in the end. Owners have spent thousands of dollars removing various items from inside their dogs. Sadly, not every dog lives to chew another shoe.

Next time you see your puppy chewing on your shoe or running off with your underwear, don't run and snatch the item out of his mouth. Reach down and pick up one of the many toys that are now scattered around your house. Make a trade—toy for the forbidden item. You will get your property back and the puppy will learn what is acceptable to chew.

There is another great side effect to trading with your dog. If you trade treats or toys for forbidden objects, your dog will start to *bring* forbidden objects to you to see if you want to trade. Instead of running away from you with that tissue you dropped, your dog will be more likely to pick it up and bring it to you.

To look at the trade option from a human perspective, think about this scenario. If I walked up to you and said, "Gimme $20 now," took your money, and walked away, you would not be happy. You would think I was a thief and a bully and would avoid me next time you had any money. But if I walked up and said, "Gimme $20 and I will give you this $50 bill," you would hand over the $20 really quick. Next time you had a $20, you might seek me out to see if I wanted to trade. You might even bring me $50 to see if I'd trade you for $100!

Teach the cue "drop it"

"Drop it" is an essential cue for all dog owners, and it is really easy to teach. When your dog has something in his mouth, give the cue "drop it" and place a yummy treat on his nose. Your dog will drop whatever is in his mouth in order to eat the treat. If he doesn't drop it, it means that the treat you are offering is not as rewarding as whatever he has in his mouth. Try again with something tastier. If your dog has something in his mouth that is his, give the cue, present the treat, and, when he is finished chewing, give him back his toy. Your dog learns that the cue "drop it" means good things may happen.

You can also use your clicker to teach "drop it." Tug toys are fantastic for this exercise.

1. Get your puppy engaged in playing with a tug toy.
2. When your puppy has a good hold on the toy, stop moving the toy. Completely freeze.
3. The moment your puppy gives up tugging and looks up to say, "What gives?" click, and then reward with a treat and/or resuming the game of tug.
4. Once your puppy learns that spitting out the toy starts the game again, he will let go pretty quickly. That is the perfect time to add the verbal cue. Say "drop it," then freeze.
5. Click and reward for letting go.

Chapter 4 – Basics for Puppies

Play nice

Don't allow your puppy to learn to be destructive with his toys. I can't tell you how many people I have talked to who say their dogs will eviscerate any plush toy in about 3.5 seconds. If a dog decides to perform an operation on your couch, it won't be pretty. Instead, from the start teach your puppy how to play nicely with his toys. If you see him starting to rip something open, walk over calmly and make a trade with another toy. If he does not get to practice destroying things, he will not learn how fun it is!

Exercise your dog

A tired dog makes a happy owner! Exercise can help relieve stress and boredom. If your dog is tired and content, he will be less likely to chew. Exercise can be mental or physical. If it is a rainy day or you are not physically able to walk your dog or play a game of fetch, exercise his mind instead of his body. Treat-dispensing toys and training sessions are fantastic ways to tire your pup mentally.

Diet detail

Is your dog getting a balanced diet? If your dog is not consuming his nutritional requirements, he may be trying to "supplement" his diet. Talk to your vet and/or analyze your dog's food at dogfoodanalysis.com. Discover what you are feeding your dog—you may be surprised at what gets put in a bag of kibble!

Scent your dog's toys

Dogs navigate the world with their noses. Place a tiny dab of vanilla extract on each of your dog's toys. Your dog will learn quickly that things that smell like vanilla are fair game. I recommend vanilla because most people have it in their kitchen, it will not harm your dog, and it is pleasant to smell.

Chew on this

Remember, your puppy is not chewing your shoes as part of an evil master plan to get back at you. Your puppy is simply being a dog. There are many ways to help you and your puppy survive the chewing stage. Grit your own teeth, plan ahead, hide your shoes, stock up on toys and treats, use your clicker training skills, and wait out your baby's developmental stage.

5

Basics for All Dogs

Every trainer is different and the needs of each household are unique; however, there are some basic skills and behaviors that are helpful for almost all dogs. Does your dog pull your arm off when you walk around the neighborhood? Does he bark in the crate for hours? Does your dog knock down visitors with his enthusiastic greetings? Each of the articles in this chapter covers a different but essential skill for a well-trained dog.

How to Crate Train Your Dog 138
by Casey Lomonaco

Teaching "Off" with Positive Reinforcement 143
by Joan Orr

How to Teach Your Puppy Not to Jump 150
by Sarah Stoycos

How to Teach Loose-Leash Walking 154
by KPCT

What Squirrel? 10 Techniques for Training with Distractions 157
by Casey Lomonaco

Happy Together: How to Train Successfully in a Multi-Dog
  Household 163
by Irith Bloom

Five Training Tips for Old Dogs 171
by Lori Chamberland

How to Crate Train Your Dog

by Casey Lomonaco

Life in most families is both joyous and hectic—which means that the family dog is often under-stimulated and underfoot—a situation that can lead to big trouble. One measure that can ward off trouble is sensible and thoughtful use of a crate. A crate can provide a relaxing, enjoyable, and safe haven for your dog during periods of hustle and bustle. While there are many techniques for getting your dog acclimated to and loving the crate, please remember that the best gifts to give dogs during joyous or hectic times are not "presents" but "presence." Dogs need you to make time for them. Even though you are busy, a dog still needs mental and physical stimulation to be well-behaved. The crate is not meant to be a replacement for meeting your dog's basic needs.

If you have not yet purchased a crate for your dog, you will want a crate that is big enough for your dog to stand up, turn around, and lie down in. If you do have a crate, how can you get your dog to like it? The techniques and games described below will work with dogs that are unfamiliar with the crate as well as with dogs that have determined that crating is an aversive experience.

Surprise—Santa came to your crate!
The first technique is really easy. When your dog is not looking, hide amazing treats and yummies inside the crate. Hide a bully stick, a marrow bone, a stuffed Kong or Goodie Bone, pieces of kibble, meatballs, or hot dogs—whatever your dog likes. Imagine your dog's surprise when he saunters by the crate to be greeted with enticing aromas that beckon him to enter.

At first, leave the door open while your dog is in the crate. Once he is going into the crate readily, begin closing the door for brief periods of time while he consumes his bully stick, marrow bone, or stuffed Kong, letting him out when he is finished.

The "lock-out"
I really like this exercise. When your dog knows that really yummy things magically appear inside his crate occasionally, it's time to make the exercise

a little more interesting. Put treats inside the crate and lock the door. When this happens, the dog will often run to the crate, staring at the door. If the item is especially appealing, the dog will often start pawing at the crate, as if to say, "Hey, let me in there!"

Well, OK, dog. If you insist.

Mealtime

Perhaps the easiest way to create positive associations with the crate is to make it the place where your dog gets his dinner. In addition to feeding his regular dinner in his crate, make the crate a place where lots of fun things happen—use food-dispensing puzzle toys, stuffed Kongs, and more.

Movie night

Grab a great movie, a bowl of popcorn, and your dog's meal ration for the evening. Sit next to your dog while watching the movie, dropping a piece of kibble (or popcorn) into the crate when he is relaxed and quiet. Practicing crating and relaxation while you are at home will prevent your dog from viewing the crate as a predictor of your absence.

Shape the entrance

If you want your dog to enter his crate on cue, there are a few ways to teach that behavior.

> **Capturing:** If you play "lock-out" enough, you may be able to capture this behavior. Click your dog when he goes into the crate, toss a treat outside the crate to reset for the next repetition, and repeat until your dog is running to the crate reliably. At this point, begin shaping for the down position.
>
> **Shaping:** "Free shape" the entrance by clicking your dog for small steps in the direction of the goal behavior. First click for looking at his crate, then stepping toward the crate, then sniffing the crate, one paw inside, two paws inside, four paws inside, sitting in the crate, and, eventually, lying down in the crate.

Remember, "Don't name it 'til you love it!" Avoid adding a cue until your dog is giving the behavior you like reliably. If you want your dog to lie down in the crate, wait to add the cue for "go to your crate!" until he is entering the crate and lying down.

Using a mat: If you've already taught a solid "go to mat" behavior, crate training is often as easy as putting the mat in the crate and asking your dog to go to his mat. Incidentally, you can also use a well-taught "go to mat" behavior to get your dog on the scales at the vet's office.

Using a target stick: If your dog follows a target stick, shape the crate entrance with a target stick. This works especially well with wire crates, hard-sided plastic crates that have ventilation holes on the side, and soft-sided crates with a zippered opening on top. If you prefer, use a target disc instead of a target stick.

Shaping zen

Once your dog is going into the crate reliably, it's time to start teaching him to relax in the crate. I call this technique "biofeedback," and it has worked wonderfully with my young Saint Bernard puppy. He can be crated quietly for hours at a time, even when surrounded by unfamiliar dogs and people, while I teach classes, attend seminars, or assist at Karen Pryor Academy workshops. It's a relief to have a dog that not only goes into his crate but actually sees his crate as a cue to relax.

What does "biofeedback" involve? Quite simply, it means clicking for relaxation. Here's my basic list of "relaxing" things to click for:

- Blinking
- Yawning
- Licking lips
- Resting head on paws
- Sighing
- Rolling over onto back hip
- Lying on side
- Lying belly up
- Stretching

Because my own dogs get quite excited when they hear the click, I used a verbal marker for this behavior—a low, slow, calming "yes." I tend not to use high-value food reinforcers for this behavior, since they can create too much excitement. I use a low-value reward, like kibble, eye contact, or a light scratch behind the ears.

Wait to get out of the crate!

I don't usually use treats to teach this technique. When your dog is in the crate in a sitting or down position, begin opening the door slowly. If the dog starts to stand or rise out of position, close the door quietly and wait for him to resume the position. His butt on the floor of the crate is your cue to open the door.

For dogs that are used to bolting out of the crate, it may take them a while to get used to the new rules of the game. Your dog may get frustrated and bark, whine, or paw at the crate door to get out. Ignore this behavior; wait for the behavior you want. Once your dog remains in the position with the door wide open, work on building distance and distractions. Occasionally reward the release with a treat, scratch, opportunity to greet a favorite person, or a favorite game.

More hints

Here are some additional crate-training tips you may find helpful:

- Put your dog in his crate only after he has been exercised and has eliminated outside recently.
- The crate should be placed in a living area so that the dog does not associate the crate with social isolation. Your dog will likely enjoy his crate much more if he's in the living room than if he is crated in a dark, damp, back corner of the basement.
- Practice crating both while you are at home and while you are away from home. When your dog is crated and you are away from home, avoid leaving him with toys that he could rip to pieces and choke on.
- Calming aids in and around the crate may be helpful for some dogs. Some clients have had great success using DAP (Dog Appeasing Pheromone) plug-ins near the crate. I often play *Through a Dog's Ear* while my dogs relax in their crates. On occasion I dilute some lavender essential oil in distilled water and spray it on crate bedding.

- Should your dog have a bed in his crate? Only if
    - he is reliably potty-trained
    - he does not chew on bedding, fabrics, and so on
    - he does not have a penchant for de-stuffing pillows, stuffed animals, and so on
- If your dog whines in the crate,
    - ask yourself, when was the last time he went potty? If you think he might need a potty break, wait for the briefest instant of quiet, open the crate door, and take him out.
    - and your dog has recently eliminated and is not hungry or thirsty, ignore the whining. Wait until your dog offers a behavior you like (15 seconds of quiet, lying down, sitting) before releasing your dog. Quiet behaviors are the key to opening the crate!
- If your dog injures himself trying to get out of the crate, seek the help of a qualified behavior professional immediately.
- Crates are sanctuaries. Dogs should not be bothered while they are in their crates. Do not allow children (or inebriated adult party guests) to harass dogs while they are in their crates.
- Crates are great potty training tools for most dogs. Crates tend to be less useful as potty training tools working with puppy mill dogs that have spent their critical stages of development in crates surrounded by their own filth and feces.

Crates: Rewarding for both dogs and owners

Crates are not cruel. Introduced correctly, a crate becomes a dog's sanctuary. For a dog, it can be like having his own bedroom. Traveling with your dog or attending a performance event, it's especially nice to be able to bring that "bit of home" along. It offers comfort and a feeling of security. Crate training has so many benefits that it is definitely worth the small investment of time it takes to teach your dog to love the crate. Crate training is a gift for the entire family.

Teaching "Off" with Positive Reinforcement
by Joan Orr

Self-control is one of the most critical skills a dog needs to learn and a skill that is required multiple times a day. We expect our dogs to refrain from picking up something forbidden when it appears within reach. Some examples that come to mind include dropped medication, chicken bones, the hamster, dead birds, Granny's hearing aid, Susie's favorite stuffed toy, the last remaining baby soother...

Many people train "off" as a command with its associated threat: "Leave it or else." The trouble is, once the dog has swallowed the light bulb (I am not making this up), or the $3000 hearing aid, the ensuing "or else" does not do much to remedy the situation. It is not as if you can dock the dog's allowance or extract an IOU to pay for the costs of his transgression. Experienced clicker trainers, especially those whose training goals require an exceptional degree of reliability (those who work with guide dogs, service dogs, bomb detection dogs, and so on), know that training cues rather than commands produces a dog that can be counted on even in very difficult situations.

Cue vs. command

It is important to understand the difference between a cue and a command. A command implies a threat: "Do it or I will make you." A command is given before the behavior is learned, and it can be enforced if the dog does not comply. For example, a trainer may teach "sit" by pushing down on the dog's rump while saying sit, repeating the word and action over and over until the dog figures out that the word sit goes with the action of sitting, and that sitting fast enough will prevent the rump pushing. In the early stages of this kind of training, the dog associates the command "sit" with all kinds of stimuli and with actions that have nothing to do with the dog sitting on its own.

"Off" is commonly trained as a command by placing a temptation near the dog and holding him back, or tugging on his leash and saying "off" in a stern tone of voice. If the dog does manage to grab the prohibited item, the command is repeated while the item is forcibly removed from the dog's mouth. This method is stressful for the dog, and he may not learn much. In many cases, the command approach may place the trainer at risk of being bitten, too.

A cue is completely different from a command. There is no threat implied with a cue. A cue is like a green light that tells the dog that now is the time to execute a behavior for the chance of reinforcement. A cue is attached to a specific behavior only after the dog is offering the behavior on his own. The "sit" cue, for example, is only given once the dog has learned to sit, and, therefore, the cue is not associated with anything other than the act of sitting. If the dog does not respond to a cue, a trainer knows that further training is required. The trainer does not assume that the dog is intentionally misbehaving and must be forced or helped to do the behavior.

Getting the behavior

A common and very reasonable question about teaching cues is, "How do you get the dog to sit or demonstrate the goal behavior in the first place, so that you can click/treat and eventually add a cue?"

There are many ways to get behavior without using any force or coercion. Using "sit" as the example, one of the easiest ways to get a dog to sit is simply to wait for it to happen! Capture the sit with a click followed by a treat. After two or three accidental sits followed by a click and treat, the dog will get the idea to offer a sit deliberately. Alternatively, you can induce a sit by holding a treat over a dog's nose and moving it back over his head until he sits. A dog can also be taught to touch a target with his nose, and then the target can be used to induce a sit.

Regardless of the method used to get the dog to offer a sit, the cue is not added until the dog offers the sit without any prompts or lures. The cue should be associated with a freely offered sit, so that the dog associates the cue "sit" with the action of sitting, free from other stimuli. The clearer the association is between the cue and the action, the better the dog will learn the cue.

Chapter 5 – Basics for all Dogs

Steps to "off"

How do you get the dog to offer the "off" behavior so that you can click/treat and eventually add a cue?

One popular method is to hold a treat in your closed fist and allow the dog to sniff, lick, paw it—whatever he wants to do to try to get the treat. Keep your fist closed until he backs off for just a fraction of a second, then click and open your hand to give him the treat. Alternatively, you can click when he backs off, and give him a better treat from your other hand. Avoid the temptation to say anything—no scolding or otherwise telling him not to pester your hand. The dog learns best if he figures it out for himself without fear of reprisal.

If the dog is too frantic to get at the treat, use something less tantalizing to start. If the dog loses interest and does not try to get the treat, use something more tantalizing.

Raise criteria gradually so that the click/treat comes only when the dog is deliberately moving his head back several inches from your hand. Raise criteria again so that the click/treat comes only when the dog makes eye contact with you after moving away from your hand. Gradually require longer periods of eye contact, until the dog backs off from your hand and maintains eye contact for three seconds. Now is the time to add the cue "off."

Show the dog your fist containing the treat. When he looks away from it and toward you, say "off," click, offer the treat, and say "take it." Teaching opposite cues in pairs like this is a really effective approach. From now on, always say "take it" when you give a treat after the dog responds to the "off" cue.

Practice with increasingly smelly treats. Add difficulty by holding your fist in different ways: out to the side, higher, lower, on the ground, on the table, and so on. Once you have a reliable cue response (the dog looks at you right away and maintains eye contact when you hold out your fist and say "off"), it is time to increase the difficulty again.

Hold a low-value treat in your fist so that just a little of it shows. Try giving the "off" cue. If the dog backs off and gives you eye contact, click and treat. If he licks at the treat, ignore him and repeat the steps described above.

The dog may get some satisfaction from licking at the treat, but will give up eventually in favor of winning the chance to eat the whole thing (or the better treat from your other hand). Do not give the cue until the behavior is once again solid. When the dog will respond to the "off" cue with a little of the treat showing, increase the difficulty by using a tastier treat.

Practice in different locations with increasing levels of distraction until the dog responds to the "off" cue when you offer food partially exposed from your closed fist under any circumstances.

Making it harder

If you have reached this point, when you give the dog the "off" cue he will back off from your fist containing a partially exposed high-value treat and give you three seconds of eye contact. The behavior is reliable even when you show him the fist placed in any position, and when you give the "off" cue in any location inside and outside of your house—no matter what is going on around him. You are ready to make it harder. The next steps should go quickly, since the dog now understands the "off" cue.

1. Hold a treat tightly between your thumb and forefinger. Ask your dog to sit. Show him the treat and give the cue "off" before he gets a chance to get up and come to investigate. If you do not think he is ready for this, separate yourself from him with a fence or baby gate so there is no chance of him snatching the treat. Give the cue "off" and click/treat when he looks at you.

2. Gradually increase the duration of the eye contact until you are back up to three seconds.

3. Increase the difficulty incrementally as before by using bigger and better treats, by holding the treat in different positions, and by training in different locations.

It may be tempting to try offering a treat in your open hand or placing a treat on the floor to see if the dog will respond to the "off" cue, all the while ready to cover the treat if the dog tries to grab it. This is not a good idea, and you run the risk of having to start all over if the dog snatches the treat. You do not want to teach the dog that it is a race to get the treat and if he is fast enough he might (and probably will) win. Your goal is to have a dog that

Chapter 5 – Basics for all Dogs

looks at you calmly, waiting for direction if temptation appears, and not a dog waiting with anticipation to race you to the treat. Your dog needs to be firmly convinced that if temptation comes along, the best way for him to win is to ignore temptation and to look at you for guidance.

"Off" with more valuable items—even your shoes!

Until now there has been no chance for the dog to do anything more than (maybe) lick at the treat. By this point in the training he will have no interest in trying to go for the treat, since looking away from the food and at you has won him a click/treat every time. It's time to move to training "off" with items that are on the floor or table, or otherwise more available to the dog.

1. Start with a neutral item that your dog will not care about—a small box is a good example. Let the dog sniff the box to see that it is of little interest.

2. Ask the dog to sit. Place the box on the floor out of reach, give the "off" cue, and click/treat when the dog looks at you.

3. Push the box closer and repeat. Increase the difficulty by repeating this process with objects of greater and greater interest to the dog. The more interesting the item, the farther you need to place it from the dog to start. Try putting a treat or toy in the box to make it more interesting, without giving the dog access to the treat or toy.

4. When you are ready to use the dog's favorite toys or your best leather shoes as training objects, guard against mistakes by putting the object under a clear plastic tub, on the other side of a baby gate, or out of reach with the dog on leash. Use a leash to prevent the dog from moving close enough to the temptation; the leash should not be used to tug or correct the dog. Ideally, you're increasing the difficulty for the dog in small enough increments that he will never bother to go to the end of the leash and the leash will remain loose at all times during this training. Be creative—come up with ways to prevent the dog from making mistakes and grabbing the item, while at the same time giving him the best chance to succeed in responding to your "off" cue.

5. Once you have progressed through an array of objects on the floor, table, and counter, and the dog will reliably respond to the "off" cue even with high-value items, repeat the process using food. Start with the food at a distance and covered, and move toward uncovered food at close range, raising criteria in baby steps as before. By this time the dog will most likely have become conditioned and will intentionally ignore any temptation by looking away from it and toward you, even before you give the cue. Training will go very quickly at this point.

Do it your way

You may structure your training differently from what is described in this article, since these instructions and examples are only meant as a guide. Keep in mind that the goal is to make it as easy as possible for the dog to get it right and to win a click/treat.

Establish a very strong reinforcement history with the "off" cue. The more times you click/treat, the more reliable the behavior will become. At the same time, set things up so that the dog does not get a chance to snatch the treat and earn reinforcement for an undesirable behavior. Avoid situations where you need to race the dog to cover the food or use physical force to stop him from getting it. The best way to avoid these problems is to raise your criteria in baby steps, and to develop a strongly offered behavior or a strong response to the "off" cue before increasing the level of difficulty.

Some trainers add the cue early in the process and some wait until the dog shows the ability to back off from a high-value treat in plain sight. This is a matter of personal preference and individual training style, and also depends on the personality of the dog. Some dogs do better with direction and some dogs do better if they figure it out on their own. If the dog shows signs of frustration—barking, lying down, scratching, yawning, or excessive lip licking—then you have made things too difficult. The dog cannot learn well when he is stressed and anxious. Reduce your criteria, make it easy for the dog to win a click/treat, end the session, and start your next session at a point where you know the dog can succeed.

Invest for the future

Teaching "off" with positive reinforcement may seem like a lengthy process, requiring more time and effort than simply giving the dog a good yank and yelling "off" at him. Certainly, careful step-by-step training without shortcuts is more time-consuming than any quick-fix method. Reliability comes with consistency, raising criteria in baby steps, and establishing a deep reinforcement history.

Training with clicks and cues is fun for you and the dog and helps build a strong bond of trust. Each cue that you teach lays a foundation for future training; the dog will learn each subsequent cue more quickly than the last. The time and effort you put into training "off" and other cues will pay off over and over. You'll enjoy life with a well-adjusted, reliable dog that looks to you for guidance when temptations appear.

How to Teach Your Puppy Not to Jump
by Sarah Stoycos

It's the rare and fortunate person who adopts a puppy that doesn't jump up to greet everyone within a two-mile radius. Unless a puppy is particularly shy, there is nothing more exciting than meeting people or, better yet, greeting people she already loves. Jumping to greet is a very logical behavior for puppies. It gets them closer to our faces and it elicits our attention. It is our job to help puppies understand that we would prefer that they keep their little paws on the floor.

Don't jump!

As with extinguishing any undesirable behavior, curbing jumping is a two-part process:

1. Don't allow the unwanted behavior to pay off; and
2. Be sure that you reward a desirable behavior that is incompatible with the undesirable behavior.

Keep in mind that your definition of a payoff may not be the same as your puppy's. The intention of jumping is to get our attention; therefore, just looking at a jumping puppy is a payoff in her mind. Shouting or pushing away is also a form of attention and, as we know, bad attention is often better than no attention at all! The more excited you get, the more excited your puppy becomes.

Many people teach a beautiful "off" behavior where the puppy jumps, the person says "off," the puppy goes to the floor, and then the puppy is praised or rewarded in some way for getting off. Mission accomplished—the puppy has received attention for jumping! Soon you will find yourself with a puppy that jumps so that you'll say "off" and reward that beautiful off. You still have a jumping puppy in the end. To satisfy the first part of the process of eliminating the reward for jumping, puppies need to be ignored each time they jump. No shouting, no pushing, and no looking = no attention. Turn away and ignore your little kangaroo.

Chapter 5 – Basics for all Dogs

Instead try…

For most puppies, ignoring the jumping is not enough. Because we tend to focus on what our puppies are doing wrong, we forget to let them know what they are doing right. Puppies need something else to do in place of the jumping, something that will get them the attention they so desperately crave. They need extra information to overcome the thrill of wildly greeting the approaching person.

Sometimes it's possible to teach a puppy to sit in order to receive attention, but this is asking a lot of an excited ball of fur that can barely contain herself! Even if we drop our expectations a bit, it is still possible to be successful in teaching a puppy to greet politely. Having four paws on the floor is entirely incompatible with jumping, so why not reward that?

The key is to reward four paws on the floor *before* the jump actually takes place. Once your puppy has jumped, she has practiced the undesirable behavior (practice makes perfect) and you are no closer to your goal. As soon as someone approaches your puppy, start clicking and treating your puppy for keeping paws on the floor. Start out with her on a leash so that she can't get away and jump accidentally. At the start of the interaction, click and treat frequently, but as your puppy gains some semblance of self-control, you may slow down the rewards.

Next: Master timing, increase difficulty

It's essential to begin rewarding before the approaching person is too close to your puppy, otherwise the puppy will jump before you have a chance to click and treat. Ask the visitor to kneel down with your puppy and interact with her quietly. As the person kneels, you may discover that it helps to continue clicking and treating until the puppy is calm, even with a person on the ground much closer to her. After you've practiced for a while, you will be able to watch for your puppy's body to tense up in anticipation of jumping. Be sure to click and treat before she launches herself into the air!

Soon you should see your puppy choosing to sit. Shortly after that, she may begin to catch herself just as she is about to jump. Keep pre-empting that jump with clicks and treats for four paws on the floor. Always place the treats on the floor. It's important that your puppy learn that all good things come from down low. With a little practice, you'll find that you have to go out of your way to approach excitedly in order to create a situation that is likely to result in a jump. What a great problem to have!

In training, keep making the task more difficult, little by little, by making the situation more and more exciting. Soon your puppy will have those paws on the floor all of the time. If at any point your puppy manages to jump, simply turn away and ignore her, then start over, making it a little easier for her to succeed. Gradually build the level of excitement.

Team training

One of the challenges that puppy parents face is an approaching person who loves having an adorable little puppy jump on him. Let's face it, when you are walking a puppy you are a magnet for people who want to interact with your adorable pet. We all hear: "That's OK, I'm a dog person. I don't mind." Rather than trying to address this claim, ask your puppy's new friend to help you train her. It's easier to get the necessary buy-in if the person you encounter feels that he is being included in the training process rather than restricted from interacting with your irresistible puppy. If he complies, he receives the reward of playing with your puppy. Positive reinforcement works on people, too!

Welcome home

Remember to reward your puppy for not jumping on you or other members of your family, too. Consistency is the key to your success. Be sure that every greeting is treated as a learning opportunity. Entering a room where a puppy is waiting, there is often a flurry of happy activity—as though your puppy has been alone for the past three days instead of only three minutes! Whenever you enter a space where your puppy is waiting for you excitedly, be ready to click and treat for those paws on the floor. If your puppy is behind a baby gate, click and treat paws on the floor until your puppy is calm enough for you to enter. Practice going in and out of the room, clicking and treating for paws on the floor over and over again so that your puppy can practice offering you this good behavior. If you reward her each and every time for staying down, your puppy will eventually choose not to jump at all.

Puppies that are crated will usually zoom out of the crate as if making a jail break. Jumping soon follows. Help her to exit calmly. Click and treat your puppy for sitting in the crate before you let her out. When you open the door, immediately click and treat for all four paws on the floor. Do the same in any situation that is likely to cause your puppy to jump. The better you are at clicking and treating before a jump has occurred, the faster your puppy will learn.

Practice creates progress

There is one other exercise that you can do with your puppy that can help her stay calm enough to remain on the floor in an exciting situation. Practice moving around quickly so that your puppy is excited enough to jump on you. Just as she is about to jump, stop moving and click and treat before she jumps. Start out moving slowly, and gradually increase the level of excitement until you are able to run around the room with your puppy without her jumping on you when you stop. You now have a puppy that can go from 100 mph to 0 mph in one second flat!

By keeping her paws on the floor throughout all these exercises, your puppy will not only be rewarded with treats, but she'll get the attention she craves. Staying on the ground calmly will soon be her default position. With time and practice, the treats will no longer be necessary every single time your puppy (soon-to-be larger dog) greets someone. In fact, staying on the floor will become her first choice. Give it a try. It's a win-win for everyone.

How to Teach Loose-Leash Walking
by KPCT

Oh, my aching arm! How can you get your dog to walk without pulling? We are masters at allowing our dogs to drag us down the street. The most-asked question at obedience classes and private consultations is "how can I get my dog to stop pulling on his leash?"

As far as dogs and leashes are concerned, we want to arrange things so that loose leashes "pay off" and tight leashes don't. Historically, trainers encouraged folks to act like a tree the moment their dog began to pull on the leash. This method does work nicely with puppies, but it just doesn't work for the adolescent or older dog that has learned to pull you around.

The following method requires *first* that all or most reinforcement will come from behind you, and *second* that you will toss the food on the ground—not far—so the dog has to look for it.

Let's play

Loose-leash walking is going to begin as a game. Here are a few simple steps you will train *before* you do any walking with your dog:

1. Put your dog's leash on and just stand still. When your dog releases the tension on the leash, click and show him the treat in your hand. Let him see you place the treat on the ground by the outside of your left foot. Once he's eaten the treat, move behind your dog to the end of the range of the leash so it is taut and stand quietly. When he moves to release the tension, click. Show him the treat and place it by your left foot. You don't care about eye contact. What you are teaching is that releasing the leash tension gets clicked and treated. Do this a number of times.

2. Continue to stand now that your dog is not pulling. Now you will click for eye contact. After the click, treat by your left foot. Remember after he has finished eating the treat to move back to the end of the leash.

Chapter 5 – Basics for all Dogs

3. Again, just standing with your dog on a loose leash and looking at you, toss your treats right past your dog's nose to about three feet away. When your dog eats the treats and comes back to you looking for more, click and treat by placing the food by the outside of your left foot. Move and repeat.

4. Again toss the treat right past your dog's nose. When your dog finishes eating it and turns around to come back to you, you turn your back and start walking. (Just take a few steps in the beginning.) When you dog catches up to you, but before he gets past your pant leg, click and treat. Repeat.

Note: Make sure when you toss the food it goes right past the dog's nose.

This is the warm-up. Now that you have the dog following you for a few steps it is time to start walking and reinforcing behind or next to you.

Training on the move

Your dog is on leash. You turn away from him and start walking. Your dog follows. As the dog catches up to you and is coming up next to you—maybe even makes eye contact—mark (click) and drop the treat next to your left foot. Don't keep moving and be sure the first few times that you let the dog know that you have food in your hand. Once he's finished his treat, start again. Show him the treat and then turn and take a few steps away from him, walk till he catches up, drop the treat next to you or a little behind.

Note: Dropping food next to your side or a little behind helps the dog to stay close to you. It prevents the dog from anticipating and forging ahead. So drop the food behind you, or even let the dog take it out of your hand behind your back. Don't drop the food so far away that the dog has to drag you to get it.

Start again. Begin to walk in such a way that the dog is at an angle beside you or is behind you. As the dog catches up, drop the food behind you (or next to your pant leg). Once the dog has eaten the food and is coming back toward you, start walking away from him again. Try for more steps before dropping food. Timing is everything! Don't let the dog get in front of you. If he does, pivot away, wait until he catches up but is next to you or slightly behind you (or his nose is at your pant seam), and drop the food.

Now it's your job to increase the number of steps before dropping the food behind you. Never drop food if your dog has gotten in front of you. Work toward walking more steps before rewarding. You can vary this exercise and reinforce while he is next to you if you wish, or toss the treat way behind you so the dog has to hunt for it and then reinforce him for catching back up to you.

Keep it up

As your dog gets better, and you can now walk quite a distance without forging and pulling, don't fail to reward intermittently. For your dog to walk without pulling he has to believe (because you rewarded him) that there is a better chance of good things happening near you than in the wide world. Use the long line if you have to control your dog and are not taking a walk. Remember, if you never let the leash get tight, your dog won't learn that he can pull you. What he doesn't know won't hurt him or you!

There are important benefits to walking your dog—dog walkers live longer!

What Squirrel? 10 Techniques for Training with Distractions

by Casey Lomonaco

For trainers of all skill levels, proofing a behavior for reliability despite strong environmental distractions is one of the most elusive training goals. But hope is on the horizon. Here are 10 techniques that can set up both you and your dog for successful distraction training.

1. Start small
2. Raise the rate of reinforcement
3. Raise the value of reinforcement
4. Shrink the stimulus, creating distance
5. Increase your speed
6. Cue an alternative known behavior
7. Play your way past distractions
8. Use Premack
9. Practice to achieve perfection
10. Set criteria effectively

Start small

Training proceeds more rapidly if dogs are set up for success. The fewer opportunities your dog has to rehearse incorrect responses, the higher the percentage of correct responses you will see as the behavior develops.

When you are training your dog to respond reliably to your cues despite distractions, start small. If you have taught your SDIT (service dog in training) to sit in your living room, chances are slim that he will be successful if your next practice session takes place midday at a local farmers' market! Introduce new distractions gradually.

Make a list of potential distractions for your dog and rank each on a 1–5 scale. Let 1 be a very mild distraction (music playing in the background, perhaps), and 5 a more serious distraction (deer running past just 15 feet away). Remember that distractions are cumulative—multiple level 1 distractions in a given environment can really add up quickly!

If your dog is unable to respond to a cue in a new environment, temporarily lower your criteria. If I am working on a name response in a new environment and my dog does not respond to the cue for her name, I go back to clicking for eye contact. When I get the focus behavior reliably, I resume use of the cue.

Raise the rate of reinforcement

Increasing the rate of reinforcement can be an effective way to keep your dog's attention despite environmental distractions. Increasing the reinforcement rate means temporarily lowering other criteria for correct responses. For instance, if you have been teaching polite leash walking in a low-distraction environment and your dog averages twenty paces for a single reinforcement, training in an environment with new distractions you may need to temporarily reduce your criteria so you are reinforcing your dog every four steps. In a significantly more distracting environment, you may need to click every single step initially, and then gradually increase criteria for distance according to your dog's success.

Raise the value of reinforcement

Use better stuff! As my business partner, Steve Benjamin, says, "Your reinforcement has to smell and be more appealing than that dog's butt." If in a new environment your dog won't respond to a low-level reinforcement like kibble, try something better—steak, hamburger, liver, cheese, or whatever he likes best.

Shrink the stimulus, creating distance

Shrinking the stimulus by manipulating distance brings a highly effective behavior modification technique, desensitization, to your distraction training plan. Desensitization means that you are 1) exposing the dog to a stimulus (a distraction, in this case) at a level that does not evoke the undesired response (ignoring your cue, in this case), and 2) gradually increasing the intensity of the stimulus as the dog grows comfortable at each successive level of exposure. If your dog cannot respond reliably to a cue 5 feet away from a sidewalk where someone is jogging, he may be able to respond 50 feet away from the sidewalk. Start where he is successful and move closer to the distraction incrementally once the dog is successful 80% of the time at the current exposure level.

Increase your speed

My chow mix, Mokie, loves a good run or jog. It is much easier for me to keep her focused around distractions if we move past them together quickly. If we are working on a heeling behavior and she is distracted by a squirrel across the street, we have more success if we begin moving together at a fast pace rather than if we walk slowly. Once I can keep Mokie's focus at a fast pace (a run), I try the same behavior at a jogging pace. When she is responding reliably at a jog, we practice at a regular walking speed. Finally, once she is reliable at a regular walking speed, we practice the same exercise at a slow pace.

Cue an alternative known behavior

One of the behaviors I find most useful is both of my dogs' ability to follow a target for an extended distance. Working on reactivity with my St. Bernard, Monte, I find that "follow the target" is a great way to keep him focused around distractions. If his nose is glued to my hand, he cannot stare at the barking and lunging dog across the street.

Of course, if I'm using the "follow-the-target" behavior to elicit a heeling response around distractions, I'll need to have already conditioned for a reliable "follow-the-target" response for the necessary distance and environmental components.

Play your way past distractions

In the presence of distractions, many dogs find play to be a higher-value reinforcer than food rewards. For these dogs, playing your way past distractions can be much more effective than increasing food reinforcement value. Many dogs would turn their nose away from a lovely steak around bicyclists but would gladly tug their way past the same distraction.

I like playing your way past distractions, increasing the rate of reinforcement, and increasing the value of reinforcement because all of those strategies include an element of classical conditioning. Make the dog feel better about being in the presence of a distraction by consistently and repeatedly pairing the distraction with that particular stimulus.

Use Premack

The Premack Principle explains how a higher probability behavior can be used to reinforce a lower probability behavior. Unknowingly, many parents use Premack with small children at mealtime: *"If you eat your broccoli, you may have ice cream for dessert."* The higher probability behavior (eating dessert) is desirable to the child, so he may well offer a lower probability behavior (eating broccoli) first.

In dog training, Premack is used in much the same way. One of the maxims of reliable recall training is that you should not, at least in the very early stages, call your dog away from something he likes (play with a best doggy pal, for instance) or to something he doesn't like (a bath, nail clipping, grooming).

But a truly reliable recall response means you can call your dog away from any situation and feel confident that he will respond to your cue willingly and happily. Maybe a dog doesn't want to stop playing with his doggy friend, but if that doggy friend is running toward traffic, you need to keep your own dog safe. If you cannot call your dog away, his life is on the line.

For situations like this, Premack can be very effective. To call my dog away from play I can click when he responds to my cue, feed when he arrives at my side, and then release him back into play after the response. In this scenario, the dog receives three reinforcements:

- The conditioned reinforcer—the event marker itself (the click) is the first reinforcement.
- Primary reinforcement A—the food. In Karen Pryor's book, *Reaching the Animal Mind,* a primary reinforcer is defined as "anything the animal needs and wants badly enough to work for [...], from oxygen to tennis balls."
- Primary reinforcement B—the opportunity to engage again in play. Mokie loves playing with Monte or with her best friend at class, Leila. For Mokie, the opportunity to re-engage in play with Monte or Leila functions as a primary reinforcer.

This is powerful stuff—three reinforcers for one behavior! These reinforcers also mitigate or negate what for some dogs could be an aversive—being expected to disengage from an enjoyable, inherently reinforcing activity like play, chasing prey, or sniffing the ground.

Chapter 5 – Basics for all Dogs

Practice to achieve perfection!

It's really true: practice makes perfect. There is no fast, easy, "get-rich-quick" shortcut. Consistent training, lots of practice in new environments with new distractions, and a solid reinforcement history for the correct behavior are essential. When trainers are clear and consistent with criteria, and make wise decisions about lowering or increasing criteria, reliable cue response is only a matter of time.

Not sure how to raise criteria effectively and appropriately? I really like Jean Donaldson's technique called Push-Drop-Stick (PDS). PDS is an easy way to assess your dog's ability to succeed in any given training environment.

> **Set criteria effectively: PDS (Push-Drop-Stick)**
> Select your current criteria. For example, you'd like your dog to target your hand on cue 20 feet away from the distraction of another dog/handler team jogging past.
>
> 1. Count out five treats.
> 2. Cue the behavior five times. Each time your dog responds to the cue correctly, click and deliver a treat.
> 3. Each time your dog responds incorrectly, do not click or treat. Set the treat aside as a "counter."
> 4. Repeat until you have no more treats.
> 5. Count the number of treats set aside.
> 6. If you have one or no counters set aside, your dog is at least 80% reliable at the current criteria level. Push—raise your criteria. Take one or two steps closer to the distraction and repeat.
> 7. If you have three or more counters set aside, your dog is at 40% reliability or lower. At this low reinforcement level, many dogs may get discouraged and give up on the training game. Temporarily Drop—lower your criteria, moving a few steps away from the distraction, and repeat the PDS protocol.
> 8. If you have two counters set aside, your dog is 60% reliable at the current criteria level. Stick—do not raise your criteria yet. Do another repetition of PDS and reassess your dog's progress.

Remember that behavior is in a constant state of flux. I have days when I feel as if my timing is spot-on and other days when I get discouraged because my timing is slow or off. Dogs have days when they perform well in a given environment, and other days when they are more easily distracted.

PDS is a quick (often less than one minute) tool you can use to establish baseline performance for any given session in any given environment. It allows a trainer to make "on-the-fly" adjustments to training plans in order to set dogs up for success as much as possible. Dogs need to practice being successful rather than being set up to practice making mistakes. Those mistakes will only have to be cleaned up in later stages of training.

Start training!

These ten techniques should help you and your favorite dog achieve distraction-training success, with PDS providing a quick way to track the training results. None of the techniques are meant to be mutually exclusive; handlers are encouraged to experiment and to be creative in combining the techniques in the context of distraction-training sessions. Try them all and see which ones work best for you and your dog.

What are you waiting for? Turn off the laptop, grab your clicker and your dog, and start implementing these strategies today!

Happy Together: How to Train Successfully in a Multi-Dog Household
by Irith Bloom

If you have more than one dog (or more than one clicker-savvy pet) in your household, you may find it challenging to manage training at times. There are strategies, though, that can help make it easier to train in a multi-dog household.

Note: In this article, any dog that is actively being trained is referred to as a "working" dog, and any dog that is not being trained at the moment is referred to as a "non-working" dog.

Multiple dogs, multiple handlers

The easiest way to get around the challenges of training multiple dogs is to have as many handlers as there are animals. Each dog gets individualized attention and training proceeds like a training class, with multiple dog and trainer "teams." Each team works on its own task and at its own pace. Some clicker trainers worry that in this situation dogs won't know which click to listen for, but in practice dogs generally learn quite quickly which click is for them.

Management tools for non-working dogs

A relatively easy solution for when there are more dogs than trainers is to manage the situation by physically separating the dogs. There are a few different ways to accomplish this.

Doors: Just about every home has at least one interior door. Put yourself and the working dog on one side of that door, and the other dog (or dogs) on the other side. Every few minutes rotate which dog is training in the room with you. Some non-working dogs might become over-anxious while waiting for their "turn" to train. To help mitigate this problem, place food dispensing toys or a remote feeder in the room with the non-working dogs.

Crates: If a dog has been trained to enjoy being in a crate, that dog can be crated when not working. Assuming the dogs have solid "go-to-crate" and "wait-to-exit-crate" behaviors, it's easy to send one dog into the crate while you work with the other, and then switch dogs. Give the dog in the crate a stuffed food toy, or drop treats into the crate periodically as you train the other dog. Note that forcing a dog into a crate is not a good idea. Make sure to teach your dog to be comfortable in the crate, to enter it willingly, and to wait in it until released before you try to use the crate as a training management tool.

Baby gates/X-pens: You can also separate non-working dogs by putting them on the other side of a baby gate or inside an X-pen while you and the working dog train. If you have many dogs, it may be easier for you and the working dog to be inside the X-pen while the non-working dogs remain outside. Regardless of the exact arrangement, as you train the working dog, toss treats to the non-working dogs occasionally.

Tethers: Another option is to tether the non-working dogs. If all the dogs being trained are relative novices, this is often the easiest solution. Simply clip a leash or tether to the collars or harnesses of each of the non-working dogs and attach the leashes or tethers to the knob of a locked door or another relatively immovable object. Place a comfortable mat of some kind (a dog bed, a towel) right next to the base of the tether so the non-working dog has a pleasant surface on which to relax. As you train the working dog, periodically drop treats on the non-working dog's mat.

Stationing

Stationing is a term used by people in the exotic animal field that refers to teaching an animal to go to, and stay on, a home base of some sort. For dogs, mats make great "stations." Here's one method for teaching a dog to station on a mat (there are many others).

1. **Choose and lay out a suitable mat.** Select a mat that is made of a comfortable and, ideally, non-slippery, material. It should be large enough for your dog to lie on with some room to spare. Place the mat so that there is space for your pet to step on and off in different directions.

Chapter 5 – Basics for all Dogs

2. **Get your clicker and treats.** Position yourself a short distance away from the mat. Count out five treats and get your clicker ready.

3. **Watch your dog closely for any behavior directed at the mat.** It's not reasonable to expect your dog to move spontaneously onto a mat without any prior training, so begin the training by watching for any behavior directed at the mat. Your dog might glance at the mat, turn his head toward the mat, or even take a step toward the mat. Click and treat (C/T) any mat-directed behavior until you feed all five of the treats you counted out. Then take a short break.

   It's important to click and treat frequently to keep the rate of reinforcement high when shaping, so be sure to reward even subtle mat-directed behavior at first.

4. **Do more training sessions, gradually raising criteria.** Continue with short sessions of about five C/Ts each, gradually requiring more and more overt mat-related behavior from your dog as the sessions progress. When your pet begins to walk over to the mat, start tossing the treats away from the mat after you click. This repositions your pet far enough from the mat to walk over again during the next repetition.

   Train for no more than five or ten minutes at a time before you take a longer break. Your dog gets to set the pace, so it's okay if it takes a few sessions before your dog actually begins to walk over to the mat.

   Pick the mat up off the floor between training sessions to eliminate opportunities for your dog to interact with the mat without earning a C/T.

Here's a typical progression you may see while shaping your dog to go to a mat:
- Dog looks in general direction of mat.
- Dog looks directly at mat.
- Dog takes one step toward mat.
- Dog takes more steps toward mat.
- Dog steps onto mat with one paw.

- Dog steps onto mat with more paws.
- Dog sits on mat.
- Dog lies down on mat.

5. **Add a cue.** Once you get to the point where your dog goes over and lies down on the mat as soon as you place the mat on the floor, you can begin to add a cue for the behavior (you can also wait until later, but this timing tends to work well). Pick a phrase such as "go to your mat," and begin saying it as your dog walks toward the mat. Click and treat as usual for correct behavior.

    There are several different ways to add a cue for a "go to mat" behavior. One easy way is to say the cue when your dog is more than halfway to the mat, so that you are almost certain your dog will go to the mat and lie down on it. Gradually back up how early you say the cue until you say it before the dog actually starts moving toward the mat.

    If you really want good stimulus control and you are at the point where you are saying the cue before your dog goes to the mat, do not C/T when the dog goes to the mat unless you have cued the behavior.

6. **Build duration.** Whether you have added a cue or not, once the dog is going to and lying down on the mat reliably, begin to train for duration by withholding the click for an extra fraction of a second after the dog's belly hits the mat. After you click, be sure to toss the treat away from the mat, so the dog has to walk over to and lie down on the mat again. Gradually increase the length of time you wait before you C/T so that the dog will remain on the mat until you C/T even when you wait several minutes. You can also teach your dog a release cue by saying a release word (such as "release") just before you C/T. The sequence then becomes:

    - You cue "go to your mat" (if you are using a verbal cue).
    - Dog goes over to mat and lies down.
    - You wait however long.
    - You cue "release" and then immediately C/T.

Chapter 5 – Basics for all Dogs

7. **Add distractions.** It takes time to build a stationing behavior that is solid even in the face of distractions. Laura VanArendonk Baugh gives a lovely example of how to teach behavior in the presence of distractions in "Help, We're Being Invaded! How to Train Polite Greetings" (see p. 190). Bear in mind that a major distraction your stationed dog will have to deal with in your multi-dog household is another dog being trained.

Training time should be fun for everyone

Whatever method you use to keep the non-working dogs out of the way as you train the working dog, it is important to ensure that everyone is having fun. One easy way to do this is to share the bounty of treats.

Each time you click the working dog, quickly give a treat to the working dog and then immediately toss a treat to the non-working dog(s). If the non-working dogs are in another room with a remote feeder and the remote works through your door, push the remote button after each click to dispense a treat in the other room, or set the remote feeder to dispense treats at random intervals. Since dogs will quickly figure out that being in the non-working position means getting treats with no effort, you'll find that they really love being in the non-working role.

Promote harmony

When you are handing out treats but no clicks are involved, it is a good idea to either establish a regular treat-giving order (so Fido always gets his treat before Spot gets hers), or to use each dog's name before giving each dog a treat (say "Fido," and then hand Fido his treat, and then say "Spot" and hand Spot her treat). Regardless of your routine, be sure to give treats only to dog(s) that have been polite about waiting their turns.

Training behaviors that several dogs will do together

Training dogs one at a time is a great way to teach them to do behaviors on cue when they are on their own. Some behaviors will be called for when other dogs are around, though. Polite leash walking, also called loose-leash walking, is an excellent example. Even if you train each of your dogs to walk beautifully on leash when alone, you may find that when you try to walk two or more of your dogs together you wind up being pulled in all directions.

BETTER TOGETHER

> **Who are you talking to anyway?**
> When you give a cue in a multi-dog household, make it obvious to the dogs if the cue is intended for one dog or for everyone. In cases where a cue is for one dog only (for example, when you want to send a dog to his station), indicate the dog you want by making eye contact with that dog or by saying the dog's name. Click and treat only for a correct response from the dog you addressed.
>
> To address a cue to everyone, simply call out the cue, or precede the cue with "doggies" or "everyone" (or whatever word you like). Click and treat each dog that responds appropriately. Clicking just the first dog that responds and then treating each of the dogs in turn works in certain cases as well. Dogs tend to figure out quickly when you are cueing them individually and when you are cueing them as a group.

To prevent this problem, it's important to proof group behaviors so that each of your dogs learns to do the behaviors properly even in the company of your other dogs. As with all other training, you can achieve this goal by raising criteria gradually. Here's an outline of one way to train polite leash walking for multiple dogs.

1. **Teach each dog individually how to walk politely on leash.** Dogs are not born knowing how to walk on leash. A good first step is to teach a dog that staying close to you earns clicks and treats. One way to maximize the odds that the dog will stay close to you is to start in an environment like a bathroom, which is so small that the dog has nowhere else to go, and click and treat the dog whenever the leash is in a loose J-shape. From there, gradually progress to larger rooms, and then practice around your entire home. Once the behavior is solid indoors, begin to practice in the back and front yards, and, finally, on the sidewalk and in other environments where there are many distractions. It can be helpful to set up fake distractions for your dog indoors to prepare for the transition to the more exciting outdoors.

   Practice until you can go many yards without a click or treat while the leash stays in a nice J-shape, first in relatively boring environments, and then in more exciting environments. Each time you

Chapter 5 – Basics for all Dogs

change environments, go back to clicking and treating for a J-shaped leash while you are standing still, and build back up from there. If you find your dog cannot stay by your side, you're probably raising criteria too quickly.

2. **Begin working with two dogs at once.** Once at least two of your dogs have learned to walk politely on leash individually—even in exciting environments—you can start walking them together. Have a different handler for each dog, at least initially, if possible. As always, it's important to make things easier in other ways now that you have added a big distraction (the other dog) to the environment, so start out in a relatively boring place and click and treat for a J-shaped leash while you are standing still, and then after a single step, and so on.

   Practice until both dogs are able to walk politely, first simply in each other's presence and then while walking side by side while each handler clicks and treats. Graduate to having just one handler hold both dogs, and build up again until the dogs can walk together nicely for extended periods in a boring environment. Then go back to two handlers, this time in a more exciting environment, clicking and treating for relatively easy behavior at first. Gradually raise criteria until a single handler can walk both dogs together outdoors while the leashes stay in a J-shape.

3. **If you have more than two dogs, work every possible combination of dogs separately before you walk them all together.** Repeat step 2 with every possible combination of dogs. For example, if you have three dogs (let's call them Fido, Spot, and Rover), practice with Fido and Spot, then with Fido and Rover, and finally with Spot and Rover, until each pair of dogs walks well together. Only then should you try to walk all three dogs at once. When you do advance to walking all three dogs at once, it's best to start with three handlers. Work each possible pair with one handler while a second handler walks the third dog. Only then should you put all three leashes in the hand of a single handler. The same principle applies if you have four, five, or more dogs: work each pair, then each trio, and so on.

Not just for polite leash walking!

The principles described above can be used for any situation involving multiple dogs, including greeting visitors at the door, staying on mats during meal times, and waiting for permission to go through doors, to name just a few. When training these kinds of behaviors, remember to increase criteria gradually, and make everything else easier each time the environment gets harder or a new dog gets added in.

Consistency is the key to success

The key to having a happy multi-dog household is teaching all of the dogs a routine. Whether that routine involves taking turns being stationed while other dogs are trained, waiting politely to be given a treat, or going on walks individually in a certain order, the more consistent the routine, the more smoothly the household tends to run. This principle applies to households with more than one type of pet, as well as to households with multiple dogs.

Five Training Tips for Old Dogs
by Lori Chamberland

One day I woke up and my Labrador, Zam, was old. It happened that quickly. Suddenly his eyesight and hearing weren't that great anymore. Overnight, the old man developed a repertoire of new-found naughtiness: barking, begging for food, and demanding attention whenever he wanted it, thank you very much. He couldn't see or hear very well, and nuisance behaviors that never existed before suddenly cropped up; now was hardly the time to cut back on his training. Quite the opposite. But, I had to make some adjustments to the way I trained. Here are strategies I have used, and continue to use, to help Zam age gracefully and to keep his mind engaged.

1. Put behaviors on visual and verbal/auditory cues

One of the things I'm glad I did a long time ago was to train visual and verbal cues for Zam's most frequent behaviors: sit, down, and recall. Adding a new cue to a known behavior is simple to do and has come in very handy for us.

For example, until recently I had been calling Zam in from the backyard and reinforcing his coming back to me. When he started to "ignore" my calling him, I realized eventually that what I'd fluffed off initially as "old-man selective hearing" was actual hearing loss. Oops.

I started using his visual recall cue instead. I'd trained this cue 12 years ago and really hadn't used it since. But, a clicker-trained cue is a lasting cue, and the visual cue was no problem for Zam. He started coming right away, and with much greater speed than before. It was almost as if he were saying, "Why didn't you show me that's what you wanted in the first place?"

Zam reacted the same way to the visual cues for his "sit" and "down" behaviors. I use his visual cues now and he has no trouble responding. If you take the time to add visual and verbal cues to your pet's most important behaviors, that effort could be well worth it someday.

2. Practice carrying your dog, or desensitize him to a harness

When Zam's sister Scout (no longer with us) became physically unable to climb stairs quite suddenly, I was very grateful that I had conditioned the dogs to being picked up and carried long ago. Scout had to travel up and down stairs, and there was no time to desensitize her to being carried. I was thankful I had already done that work.

With Zam, I practice picking him up and putting him into and taking him out of the car frequently, even though it's not necessary yet. I practice carrying him short distances so he won't panic if I ever have to carry him.

If you have a large dog, it's not always possible to carry him or her. There are assistance harnesses with handles that allow you to lift a dog's hind legs. This tool is a good thing to condition the dog to accept long before you ever actually need it!

3. "Un-minimize" your cues

At Karen Pryor Academy we stress the importance of minimizing cues—that is making them as "clean" and subtle as possible while still being salient to the animal. Until recently, Zam's cue for spin had been faded to just a subtle flick of my right or left index finger (depending on which way I wanted him to spin). One day when I gave him his cue for spin and got a blank stare in return, it occurred to me that maybe Zam couldn't see the cue. When I made the cue "bigger" and more perceptible to him, he got it right away. I now use my whole hand and forearm in a circling motion as a cue for spin.

Here is another example: I had faded Zam's nose-to-hand target to just one finger. I'm now going back to using the whole hand as a target since I noticed Zam poking his nose at my finger but "missing" it (which, by the way, is adorable).

If a dog's eyesight is starting to fail, you may notice him not responding to visual cues as well as before. Try more exaggerated movements and see if that helps.

4. Condition a tactile bridge

What if your dog's eyesight *and* hearing are going (like Zam's)? You still want to be able to mark and reinforce the dog for certain behaviors. Now what?

Enter the tactile bridge (or marker signal). If your dog can't hear the clicker well and can't see well, you can condition a specific type of touch as your new "clicker."

Acknowledging that Zam may not be able to hear at all someday soon, and knowing that his vision is definitely compromised, I wanted another way to "click" him. I hate to reinvent the wheel if someone has already come up with a useful idea, so I did what any good trainer would do: I walked down the hall to Ken Ramirez's office and asked, "Ken, what do you use for a tactile bridge?" Ken uses a quick double-tap on the dog's shoulder. There we go! A new marker signal.

Tap-tap. Feed. Tap-tap. Feed. Repeat.

5. Remember, targeting is your friend

Zam isn't ready to get out of bed! Another thing about old dogs is that they balk sometimes. "I don't want to go in the house right now." "I don't want to get out of my bed right now." "I don't want to move from my favorite spot right now."

The reasons behind balking can be varied. Maybe the dog is tired, sore, cranky, or all of the above. While you should be sensitive to these possible causes and give your old dog more time to do what you're asking, there are some times when you need to move your dog and don't have all day to do it.

A well-trained and handsomely reinforced hand target can get you out of almost any situation in a hurry. This is true for dogs of all ages, but I certainly find myself calling on the trusty hand target a lot more often these days with my senior dog. It's such a simple behavior and one that's been reinforced so frequently throughout Zam's life that he's more than happy to do it.

Old dog, new approach

Training an older dog requires some adjustments, but with a little patience and planning you can ensure that your dog's golden years are comfortable and happy.

6
Socialization

Your training may be progressing well, but when it comes time to meeting another dog or new people, your well-trained dog may suddenly start exhibiting unexpected behavior. Does your friendly dog suddenly bark as if he wants to attack the new dog or person? Is your dog so enthusiastic that he overwhelms other approaching dogs or people? It is important to begin socialization training early and to understand when *not* to socialize your dog. This chapter explores how to deal with and prevent over-excited, unruly, or even aggressive introductions and meetings, how to introduce puppies to older dogs, and how to prepare your dog to meet the veterinarian or groomer.

What to Expect: Introducing a Puppy to Your Adult Dogs 176
by Laurie Luck

Overly Excited Greetings: The Good, the Bad, and the Ugly 182
by Nan Arthur

Help, We're Being Invaded! How to Train Polite Greetings 190
by Laura VanArendonk Baugh

Don't Socialize the Dog! 197
by Laura VanArendonk Baugh

Spa Day: How to Train Your Dog to Love a Bath, a Brushing, or
Even a Mani/Pedi 204
by Colleen Koch

What to Expect: Introducing a Puppy to Your Adult Dogs

by Laurie Luck

Getting a new puppy is exciting—at least for the humans in the family. Sometimes the dog of the house doesn't think the pup is a welcome addition, however. Many people believe that adding a puppy to the family will be harmonious and that their current dog will be a good dog "mommy" or "daddy." They are disappointed when that doesn't happen. Often, expectations are unrealistic, but in most cases, what the human family members see instead of those expectations is completely normal.

Knowing in advance what to expect can help families, and the existing dogs, make the process of introducing a new puppy to the household as easy as possible.

What to expect

I've had the unique experience of welcoming 15 puppies into our house over the last 12 years. As puppy raisers for a service dog organization, on average my husband and I welcome a new pup each year. The new pup arrives when he is about 8 weeks old. He is away from his littermates, mama, and his familiar surroundings for the very first time.

We have three dogs (permanent family members), and each new puppy addition has taught us more about how adult dogs and puppies integrate. We're working on puppy #15, and here is what I've learned so far:

- None of my dogs has ever welcomed a puppy with open arms (paws).
- All of the dogs growl and snap and move away from the pup.
- None of the dogs has ever hurt a puppy.

These observations are pretty normal. Year after year, every new puppy has had the same welcome from my dogs. While the occasional dog will delight in welcoming a pup into the house, in my experience most dogs don't open up the "welcome wagon" when a new pup enters the family.

Chapter 6 – Socialization

Communication skills

Puppies are just learning how to communicate with one another. Usually, pups have only had experience reading their own littermates and mother. Their communication skills are still developing, and they don't know the "rules of the road" when it comes to interacting with new and different dogs.

Puppies even have different play styles than adult dogs. When you compare the way puppies play to the way adult dogs play, the differences are vast. Dogs follow a prescribed set of rules. There is a certain way to greet one another. There is a specific way to invite play. There is a way to stop play. There is an entire manners structure that adult dogs ascribe to, and it makes their social interactions predictable and enjoyable. There is a shared language between dogs, and adult dogs are fluent in that language.

Puppies don't follow the rules that the adult dogs depend on for good, solid doggie communication. Puppies don't even know that rules exist! When littermate puppies play together, the only rule is *Don't hurt one another.* I've watched a gleeful puppy jump on his sleeping littermate's head with reckless abandon. Upon waking, that littermate joyously engages in play with the head-jumper. With that kind of feedback, it is easy to see why puppies don't understand that the world has rules.

When a pup arrives at a new home without another pup in sight to play with, naturally he picks the next closest thing: the adult dog. The pup does what he has done with his littermates—launches on the head of the sleeping adult dog. "What a rude awakening," says sleeping dog! And the snarl that comes from the adult dog is wholly unexpected and startling to the new puppy. Occasionally, if the snarl isn't enough to deter the puppy from re-launching himself onto the sleepy dog, a full display of teeth along with the most guttural growl you've ever heard will convince the pup to cease and desist.

Hear this

According to our adult dogs, puppies have really poor social skills and have lots to learn. Our adult dogs have been valuable teachers to the puppies we have hosted, and we are grateful to them. The first lesson the puppy learns is where the lines are drawn. There are a lot of DON'Ts that our dogs teach the puppy:

- DON'T jump on my head.
- DON'T steal the toy I'm playing with.
- DON'T put your face in my bowl when I'm eating.
- DON'T walk on me.
- DON'T bite my ears or my tail.
- DON'T sit on me.
- DON'T bark in my face.
- DON'T come any closer.

As long as the adult dogs' behavior is appropriate (they don't connect with the pup, for instance), everything is fine, and the pup begins to learn the new rules of this new house. After about three weeks, some play between the adults and the puppy begins, although with two of our three dogs it takes maybe four or five weeks before they will choose to play with the pup.

Set up for success

For a harmonious household, you want to set up both the puppy and the dog for success.

> **Supervise!** Supervision is essential. Because the pup doesn't have the same set of social skills as the adult dog, I'm around for all of the interactions between the two. I want to be there to help guide the puppy toward appropriate social efforts and to keep the peace for the adult dogs. I also want my adult dogs to know that I'm there running interference for them; they can count on me to keep the puppy from becoming too much of a nuisance. The more I supervise, the fewer opportunities the dogs have to snap, bark, or growl at the pup.
>
> Too often, the adult dogs in the house are expected to take whatever the puppy can dish out. That's akin to expecting patrons of a restaurant to accept a stranger's child crawling under and climbing on their tables! Those expectations set up the puppy for trouble. The puppy won't learn the vital social skills he'll need to navigate the doggy world he lives in. It's also not fair for the dogs that live in your house. The adult dogs may accept it for a short period of time, but then the puppy's behavior reaches

a tipping point. In those circumstances, the dog may strike out with more force than he would have if he had been allowed to tell the pup to knock it off much earlier in the process.

Use crates, gates, and pens. I like to put either the adult dogs or the puppy in the crate, behind a gate, or in an exercise pen (X-pen) for some quiet time. Imposing periods of predictable, scheduled, and consistent separation between the puppy and the adult dogs goes a long way toward a harmonious life together. Puppies tend to be persistent and energetic. They don't give up quickly and may pester an older dog for much longer than the dog would allow. By setting up scheduled separation opportunities, both the pup and the dog are getting the breaks they need from each other.

Establish an escape route. It's essential for both the dog and the puppy to have an escape route and a "safe house." I taught my dogs how to move away from an annoying puppy early in our service-dog-raising years. I called out "kennel" if my dogs were beginning to become annoyed by the puppy. They would run to their crates, and I'd put a frozen, stuffed Kong inside and close the door. The dogs could enjoy a special treat and be rid of the annoyance. Very quickly, they began self-crating when they had enough of the puppy. I reinforce that decision to self-crate almost every time with the delivery of a frozen, stuffed Kong.

Avoid punishment. Growls are a form of communication. Because puppies have immature communication skills, they frequently miss the more subtle signals your older dog shows, and the dog may need to resort to growling. Resist the urge to correct your dog for growling. Growling may be what the puppy needs in order to recognize that the dog doesn't want to interact. If you find yourself correcting either the puppy or the dog, supervise more instead and use the crates, gates, and pens as ways to manage the interactions between the two.

Click and treat

You can teach your dog to tolerate the new puppy using the same clicker training principles you use to teach your dog to sit and lie down. Think about what behavior you'd like to see from your dog that isn't too hard to accomplish, and reinforce the behavior you like. Doing anything *other than growling* at a puppy might be a good behavior to click and treat. If your dog ignores the puppy instead of snarling, reinforce that! Ignoring is better than snarling, right? Just as in obedience class, after your dog is reliably ignoring rather than snarling, raise the bar and expect a little bit more from your dog. You might reinforce tolerance next. Say your dog doesn't growl or get up and move if the puppy lies down beside the adult dog. Reinforce that!

Using the clicker can help an older dog understand what behavior you would like to see from him in relation to the new puppy. A healthy side effect of using the clicker to ease the transition is that the pattern creates a happy association with the new puppy for the existing dog. When the new puppy comes around, the older dog will get the opportunity to earn clicks and treats.

Remember that it is your responsibility to the existing dog to keep the puppy far enough away that he can't annoy the existing dog. It's up to you to ensure that the existing dog is able to get clicked and treated easily, so be sure to use tethers, crates, and gates to help your dog earn a click. Continue to click and treat appropriate behavior from the existing dog until he's tolerating appropriate puppy antics.

As the older dog gets more comfortable with the puppy and tolerates appropriate puppy interaction, I often change the criteria. I click the existing dog for making the decision to excuse himself from the situation voluntarily. I would much rather that my dog simply walk away from an exuberant puppy than escalate his behavior to match the puppy's.

I won't put the existing dog in a position where he resists his natural "doggie nature" to endure unpleasant puppy interactions *just* to earn a click and treat. I ensure that the existing dog is enjoying the interaction and is patient and tolerant because he's beginning to enjoy the interaction with the pup, and not just enduring it for the sake of training.

Using the clicker to reinforce appropriate behavior, along with limiting the pup's access to the existing dog, translates into setting up both for success. Manage the situation and provide clicker-trained guidance as to what's appropriate—for both the pup and the existing dog.

Warning signs

Not every dog likes puppies. Some dogs don't tolerate puppies at all and may have over-the-top reactions that could harm the puppy. It's important to keep a watchful eye on the interactions and intervene when body language and communication escalate to an unsafe level.

If during the process of escalation the puppy yips or squeals, and your dog escalates his response even more, definitely intervene. Dogs well versed in dog-dog communication understand that a yip or squeal is the equivalent of the pup crying "Uncle!" and should back off from the pup. If you see the opposite—the cries of "Uncle" lead to increased agitation in your older dog—separate the two immediately.

One big (happy) family

After what seems like an eternity but is really only about three weeks, you'll begin to notice some signs of harmony between the dog and the puppy. If you have done your part helping the dog and puppy develop their communication skills, this is the beginning of a fabulous friendship—or at least a peaceful co-existence. Not all dogs love each another, so don't be disappointed if your dog doesn't fall head over heels in love with the new dog in the house. There is enough love for both, and comfortable cohabitation is a fine accomplishment.

Overly Excited Greetings: the Good, the Bad, and the Ugly
by Nan Arthur

When someone mentions a "spaghetti western," my mental picture is of an actor's lips moving out of sync with the words coming from the film's audio. Watching dogs go crazy on the end of a leash while they are trying to greet other dogs or people is akin to watching an old spaghetti western. The dog and the handler are out of sync with one another.

When this crazy greeting behavior ensues, it is clear that the dog and handler have different agendas. It doesn't matter if the displays come from 10-pound Fifi or 100-pound Fido. They are highly embarrassing and leave many humans wishing they had a "meet you in the streets at noontime" showdown solution to make all the barking, bucking, and bravado stop. They just want to enjoy being with their dogs.

Along with the embarrassment of these displays come safety issues. Anyone who has had to restrain, hold, or wrestle a big dog that is lunging, whining, barking, or spinning has worried about his or her own safety and/or the dog's safety. This even occurs with some small dogs that seem to have super powers when they get excited about meetings.

It takes an understanding of the good, the bad, and the ugly of these displays before you can begin a program to change the unwanted behavior. Consider carefully where your dog's behavior falls before beginning any behavior modification program, and examine the following categories and suggestions before moving forward.

The good
If you live with a wild greeter, you might find it hard to believe that most positive reinforcement dog trainers love to hear from clients whose dogs are overly excited and behave outrageously when they see other dogs or people they want to greet. Trainers like this type of enthusiasm and are passionate about working with these dogs because the behavior is still in a very

Chapter 6 – Socialization

repairable state. Excitable dogs just want to have fun. With a program that helps them relax and learn to focus, and that provides coping skills, it's pretty easy to override the gusto with a good outcome.

The exercises below will help build solid foundation skills that offer a dog a variety of options that divert attention from triggers when he faces something exciting. Working with a trainer to build foundation skills is optional if you have good clicker skills and are willing to take the training time to ensure that the behaviors are strong and well practiced. Consider a trainer if you don't have the time or the skills.

The bad

Unfortunately, far too often trainers are called after something has happened that pushed a dog over the edge of excitable into what appears to be more hostile behavior. A situation that can begin with a friendly dog that feels frustrated by leashes and other equipment—and a handler who is upset, yelling, and/or dragging the dog away—sometimes ends up as reactivity.

That's because the dog can link his frustration to other dogs or people. When this pattern continues, it can create reactivity and the potential for aggression each time the trigger (other people/dogs) is presented and the dog feels frustrated. This level of behavior should be addressed with rehabilitation and guidance from a professional trainer. Look for a trainer who understands how to use positive methods and who can incorporate the foundation exercises as well as other customized training that helps counter the unwanted behavior. Once your dog has some skills, you may be able to work with your dog on your own.

The ugly

It is natural for people to want to take their dogs out and do things with them, but societal pressure to have "Lassie" (the perfect dog) on the end of the leash creates stress for handlers. Unfortunately, when handlers seek help, sometimes they're told to "correct" the dog for outlandish displays of friendliness. When a dog has been punished too often for a very normal behavior, eventually he may associate that punishment with other dogs or people, since it only happens when other dogs or people are present. His greetings may turn into ugly displays.

Another potential "ugly" result can occur when high-energy dogs greet other dogs too enthusiastically. The greeting can trigger some dogs to attack to "correct" the rude behavior. The attack, in turn, can lead your dog, the over-friendly greeter, to learn defensive behaviors that can develop into aggressive displays fairly quickly if there is no intervention and the excessive greetings are allowed to continue.

When overly friendly greetings turn into aggressive behaviors, the road to a positive ending is much longer and more intense to travel. At that point, not only is behavior modification needed, but a relationship of trust must be repaired. Working with a professional who has a strong background in behavior, and possibly working with a veterinarian behaviorist, might be the wisest course.

What happened to my dog?

As you teach your dog new behaviors, it is also essential to look at the roots of the unwanted behavior. In other words, where did it start?

Many people point directly to puppy classes as the starting place for their dogs' wild displays. When puppy classes allow too much free-for-all play, and where puppies play with such intensity that all of their attention must remain on each other for safety, puppies learn to ignore their owners and invest their energy into even more intense play. This beginning can set up a lifetime of overly excited greetings toward other dogs, leaving owners following along like glorified pooper scoopers when their dogs see other canines.

Some puppy classes are structured this way in the name of socialization, but modern, scientific-based trainers understand that it is important to teach puppies to be attentive toward their owners and to learn how to be relaxed and calm around other puppies or dogs before they are encouraged to play. Then, with a spotlight on attention and calmness, puppies can be allowed short play sessions with other puppies—keeping the interactions very brief until they learn how to keep their impulses in check.

Another situation that encourages wild greetings is permitting street play, allowing dogs to meet and play when they are out on walks. Dogs can learn quickly to demand a visit with other dogs they see while out on walks, or with people if dogs are allowed to pull toward a person they want to meet and receive attention from. Dogs learn that if they make enough of a fuss to visit with other dogs or people, they might be rewarded with a meet and greet. The meetings can be even more problematic if the dog is large enough to pull or jerk his owner to the action. When that happens, the dog not only learns to use his strength but is also reinforced for doing so, which makes the behavior stronger (no pun intended) with each success.

Of course there are many other reasons that dogs display high-spirited greetings: the need to submit to other dogs, lots of attention from owners, and the jubilation dogs feel about seeing other dogs. Each piece of your own dog's history should direct your training. The exercises below can give your dog foundation skills that improve his ability to focus attention on you when you are near other dogs or people.

What to do

When a behavior persists over a period of time, there is only one reason for it to continue in spite of the efforts to curtail it: the dog believes it is the correct answer to receive reinforcement. In other words, it works! What the dog wants or sees as reinforcement can be anything from the handler's attention, to an actual excited greeting, to moving some distance away from the greeting area (something an unconfident dog might want and so would behave wildly to compel the handler to move on to avoid an embarrassing scene). Rest assured, dogs continue unwanted behaviors because there is a "payoff."

Equipment can play an important role in how well your dog behaves around other dogs or people. Switching to better equipment can be an easy fix, but your equipment is only as good as the training that goes along with it. So, if your dog pulls to get to another dog or person all the while choking and coughing, not only do you risk causing permanent tracheal damage, but your efforts to discourage the behavior are not working. It's time to consider other options.

Switching to a front-clip harness can relieve pressure from the neck, help your dog relax, and give you more control if your dog does try to pull. A harness is not magic, however, and dogs need to learn how to walk with you in the new equipment before you introduce triggers. You need groundwork. If your dog's history of pulling on leash is an extensive one, you may want to work with a trainer who understands how to build solid foundation behaviors for leash walking before you try to take behaviors on the road.

Two of the exercises I have found to help most in solving the problem of the overly excited greeter are automatic eye contact and "get it." If both of these behaviors are taught to fluency, you will be able to give your dog a different focus and teach him to check in when distracted rather than act on impulses.

"Get it"

The simplicity of this exercise is also its beauty. You'll train your dog to find treats on the ground in response to the verbal cue, "get it." It's really as simple as it sounds. If you follow some basic rules, your dog will be on the way to a newly trained behavior that has many benefits.

The main goal and, ultimately, the main benefit of the "get it" game is to divert your dog's attention away from things that might distract him or trigger the unwanted behaviors. Use food rewards that are extremely powerful in the beginning stages of training so that the behavior becomes strong right from the start—strong enough to override any distractions.

Consider food rewards that are your dog's absolute favorites. These may include, but are certainly not limited to, cut-up hotdogs, small pieces of cheese, diced cooked chicken, small pieces of steak, Red Barn roll, kibble, cream cheese, and other small training treats. Have a variety of food in the mix so that your dog will get excited to discover one of his special treats. Hoping that the next treat will be that special chicken or that hotdog helps keep your dog in the game (gambling, if you will). Pea-sized treats are best, but be sure to adjust (reduce) your dog's portion size at meals when you use a lot of training treats.

Training "get it" for its many benefits

There are other benefits to the "get it" game apart from diverting your dog's attention from distractions. The "get it" exercise is actually a classical conditioning exercise (the Pavlov's Dog effect). It leads the dog to try a naturally calming behavior (sniffing) that is then highly reinforced as the dog finds the food on the ground.

Chapter 6 – Socialization

So, with the "get it" game not only will you create a positive association between the environmental stimulus that excites your dog and a reward, but your dog will become calmer. Calm is desirable, first of all because the natural inclination of a pet owner is to maximize a pet's emotional well being. And, with a calmer animal, an owner is best positioned to address a behavior situation rather than simply react to it. One more plus to note is that the natural calming behavior, sniffing the ground, is a signal to other dogs that everything is OK; they can relax, too.

Start right—with gear and treats!
Begin with your dog on-leash, since you will be using this exercise in public where your dog will be wearing the harness and leash. It's important for your dog to learn the game with his "travel attire," so always practice with the necessary equipment. Start your training in a low-distraction environment (inside) with lots of breaks between sessions so that your dog has time to process each step of the exercise.

Have a number of high-value food rewards in one hand and the leash in the other. Drop a random number of treats as you say, "get it." The goal is to be able to cue "get it," and your dog's nose starts toward the ground immediately.

In the early stages, make the treats an obvious reward by dropping the food just in front of your feet. Then, drop the food to one side, then to the other side, and, finally, drop the food behind you so that your dog has to move behind you to find the rewards. Mix up the number of rewards you use each time—sometimes one, sometimes ten—so that your dog never really knows what is coming and gambles by staying in the game in case the next reward is ten pieces of chicken!

When your dog goes behind you to find treats reliably, keep that position strong by doing the majority of the training behind you. In this way you can block your dog's view of worrisome or exciting things and take the pressure off of your dog to make a decision about what to do next. You are giving your dog permission to "clock out" and decline the job of being greeter to the world. With your dog behind you, you have a few seconds to assess a situation and decide if you need to move to a less distracting environment.

Since you want to take the "get it" behavior on the road, your goal is to train to fluency (85% or better success rate in at least 20 locations around your home is a good rule of thumb) so that the behavior becomes generalized and strong. Once your dog has mastered the behavior at home, start to add distractions such as people walking around the room. Step outside to practice, but always keep your dog on leash. If at any point your dog is unable to "get it," be sure to go back to a less-distracted environment, raise the reinforcement rate with a more rapid delivery of treats, or use higher-value rewards.

Trainer's tips
- While training "get it," do not cue your dog with the leash. "Get it" should be a calm, relaxed behavior that doesn't include your dog hauling you around by the leash. Keep your leash with enough slack to form a "U," even if it means following your dog around to ensure that the leash remains loose. This exercise should be one your dog chooses to do, not one that is cued by the leash.

- Be prepared to up the ante with even better food rewards or a higher rate of reinforcement (more and faster presentation) when you take the show on the road. Plan to be more interesting than the environment. If you find that you can't, don't train. You will be wasting time and treats if your dog is so aroused or worried that he can't think.

- If your dog is distracted but not reactive, try raining treats over your dog's head to see if that draws his attention away from the stimulus. Practice raining treats at home, however, so that it's not an irritation to your dog if you try it in public!

- Don't consider your training a failure if the behavior falls apart. It is simply information for you to use the next time you work in a new area. Improve or strengthen the behavior with lower-level distractions before moving on to bigger and more exciting things.

- Always be ready to take a break from training if your dog seems confused or stressed. Training sessions should be short, no more than 10 minutes long. Training a few times a day will cement the behavior in just a couple of weeks.

Chapter 6 – Socialization

Automatic eye contact

A dog offers automatic eye contact when he knows to check in with his handler the second a distraction appears. This is the second behavior to train when you are working with a dog to decrease overly excited greetings, and it is best taught with a clicker. See Aidan Bindoff's "Paying Attention—A Training Exercise for Puppies and Dogs" (p. 40) for tips on how to get started and Alice Tong's "Reducing Leash Reactivity: The Engage–Disengage Game" (p. 298) for a more advanced application..

By teaching your dog how to check in with you when faced with a distraction, you are starting to teach your dog how to do that same check-in when faced with other dogs or other people. Keep in mind that when you add new distractions to training, there should be enough distance between your dog and the distraction for your dog to continue checking in. If the dog cannot maintain the check-in behavior, you are too close to the distraction and need to increase the distance between you and the distraction.

Putting it all together

Building on "get it" and automatic eye contact, the next step is to transfer the two behaviors to leash-walking outside of the home. The final goal is to teach your dog to walk beside you and check in when he sees a distraction, any distraction. If you are patient and positive, following instructions, you can reach that goal in just a few weeks.

Use "get it" when you are not confident your dog will be able to check in with you. Mastering automatic eye contact will soon override the need to use "get it," but do not be afraid to use "get it" any time your dog gets excited and you would like to offer him the opportunity to relax.

To get to where your dog can walk with you calmly, checking in as necessary, you will need to practice in many controlled situations that don't offer surprises. Find neutral dogs and calm humans to help you work through the different levels required to get closer to triggers. These helpers shouldn't be distractions that add to the problem! Enlisting friends who are calm, finding relaxed dog companions, and even consulting a trainer can really help to build your dog's skills.

All of this planning and careful, fun training will get you back in sync with your dog so your Spaghetti Western days will ride into the sunset.

Help, We're Being Invaded! How to Train Polite Greetings
by Laura VanArendonk Baugh

The last quarter of the year is a rough one for dogs. In October, monsters, fairies, movie stars, and cartoon characters appear in the streets, claiming the sidewalks and even approaching the house. Mom and Dad can usually buy them off with candy, successfully deflecting their intrusion, but it does rattle a dog. Then in November, a swarm of hungry relatives packs into the cramped kitchen. They dine splendidly before settling in with the television, as children pursue the dog around the house. By December, St. Nicholas has to use the chimney, because anyone appearing at the front door is subject to a flurry of frantic barking and jumping!

From a dog's perspective, this rash of home invasions is simultaneously exciting, alarming, and irritating. Unfortunately, once a dog has slipped into a frenzy, it's difficult or impossible to get calm, thoughtful behavior again. The job of trainers and responsible owners is to prepare dogs beforehand so that such challenges are, well, less challenging.

What's the problem?
What is reasonable and acceptable greeting behavior for dogs? Humans become accustomed to certain situations, finding it hard to see problems with, let alone alternatives to, those situations. Sometimes it's only when everyday situations are magnified by holiday stresses that a situation comes into focus as a problem. Greeting visitors at the door is one such situation. Substitute a human child, or even an adult, for the dog to assess the subject's behavior.

- Would you allow your toddler to ram repeatedly into your guests' legs? Leap at them and pull their clothes?
- Would you look kindly on a friend who, sighting you at a distance, charged at you and launched at your chest, knocking you backward?

Chapter 6 – Socialization

- Would you consult with a businessman who, upon introduction, ignored your outstretched hand and instead began hugging and kissing you?
- Would you think it acceptable to isolate your child in a back room when guests came because he couldn't say hello properly?

It's easy to see that these behaviors are inappropriate, even ridiculously so. Yet we accept them from our dogs, because we don't know they are capable of better behavior—or we don't know how to teach them otherwise.

It is to your advantage to teach your dog to greet others calmly, rather than charging ahead in excitement. It doesn't take much imagination to see how a mid-sized dog could easily injure an elderly relative, but risk isn't limited to large dogs and frail humans. I've had clients who were knocked down stairs, who broke a wrist stumbling over dogs underfoot, or who were forbidden to visit their grandchildren when accompanied by their dogs.

Teaching appropriate greeting behavior is important for the dogs' safety as well. That frantic, excited greeting is often mistaken for aggression—or simply recognized as inappropriate social behavior that needn't be tolerated—by other dogs that then react defensively. I see more dog scuffles caused by rude greeting behavior than by anything else.

Define the goal

I love it when a client tells me he wants his dog to stop jumping on guests. Clicker trainers know it's far more efficient to teach the dog a desirable behavior than to try to teach him to stop an undesirable one.

Trainer: "You want him to stop jumping? What do you want him to do?"

Client: "I don't care—just no jumping!"

Trainer: (I produce my patented wicked smile.) "Hmm. Not jumping could include barking insanely, running about the room, chewing on my pant leg, peeing on my foot… Are all of these behaviors okay with you?"

Usually the answer is no.

Trainer: "What if we teach him to sit to meet people?"

When the focus is on the problem, it's difficult to define the desired behavior. I ask clients to describe what the dog should be doing instead. I tell them that if at that moment they can't give a clear picture of the correct behavior, then they should walk away, because they don't have anything to train yet. Responding to a "bad" behavior without teaching a replacement "good" behavior will only create conflict.

Of course, there is a variety of acceptable greeting behaviors; choose one that suits both your dog and your situation. An anxious dog may benefit from a mat or crate that has been conditioned as a reassuring "security blanket" that you can place as near to or far from the door as needed. The mat is a good option for most dogs, but it's great for worried dogs! A low-threshold dog may need an acceptable outlet for his excitement if it won't be suppressed easily. I find many of these dogs benefit from having a toy to hold, something that lets them channel some energy orally. Even at age five, my hair-trigger Laev picks up a toy to greet new arrivals so that she can keep her paws on the floor or sit to greet. Without a toy, there's a chance she'll jump on the guest. It's like steam in a kettle; the pressure has to go somewhere!

It's much, much easier to train a specific behavior than a vague one. Choose the type of greeting you'd like your dogs to present to guests. Sit in front of them? Lie down near the door and wait to be approached? Decide on one correct response and train for that, rather than permitting different behaviors at different times. It's harder for the dog to know what's expected if he is variously rewarded for sitting, standing, lying down, and trotting around the room quietly (even if you would be satisfied with any of these behaviors).

Make a plan that starts with the basics

You can't expect to overturn a lifetime habit in a few haphazard minutes; you'll need a systematic approach. Break down the training plan to achieve the goal you have in mind. Let's use the goal of asking a dog to sit to meet a guest as an example.

Start with the basics. Many frustrated owners complain that their dogs don't sit to meet guests when they are excited. But, upon testing, we find that the dogs don't know the cue "sit" reliably, even without distractions. It's pretty simple to capture or, if necessary, lure a sit. Keep in mind that you will

Chapter 6 – Socialization

need to generalize this behavior—a dog that has learned to sit facing you in the kitchen may not realize that you mean the same thing when he's facing away from you (toward a stranger) in the front hall! You'll need to practice sits in a variety of places.

A different kind of stimulus package

For many dogs, the first challenge is being in the room with the door! You may think of "someone at the door" as a simple event, but there are components here that may be individual triggers for your dog's excitement:

- The proximity to the front door
- Owner reaching for door handle
- "Click" of door latch
- Squeak of hinges
- "Pop" of air seal when door opens

And that's not even mentioning the obvious triggers: a car in the driveway, knocking on the door, or the doorbell.

When I train, I start these distractions at the smallest possible increments. (Someone generously called me the Queen of Splitting the other day, and I could think of no greater clicker compliment!) For many dogs, these exercises start at a completely neutral door with no history of visitors—how about a pantry or closet door?

- Cue "sit," knock once on the pantry door, click/treat. Letting the dog watch you make the sound, and taking the training completely out of the front-door context, focuses on the single criterion of holding the sit during the trigger noise and does not lump several potential triggers together.
- Cue "sit," knock twice on the pantry door, click/treat.
- Build up to vigorous knocking on the pantry door. By this point, the dog should be entirely relaxed and happily expectant when you knock.
- Cue "sit," grasp the pantry doorknob, click/treat.
- Cue "sit," turn the knob, click/treat.

- Cue "sit," pop the pantry door latch, click/treat.
- Cue "sit," open the pantry door an inch, click/treat.
- Cue "sit," open the pantry door as if for access, click/treat.

All of these steps can be broken down into even smaller steps if necessary. Remember to click only the solid, reliable sit you want to keep; if the dog is shuffling or excited, drop to a lower level of distraction and review. Kathy Sdao describes suction cups on the dogs' paws as a metaphoric goal—"tap-dancing" in place is a sure sign of arousal and impending failure. Remember to take frequent breaks (5–10 reps at a time is usually plenty) and be sure that your treats or other reinforcers are valuable to the dog. The "paycheck" should make self-control worthwhile in the face of exciting visitors.

When the dog's behavior is solid with an unimportant door, that's a good start toward desensitizing. It's also teaching that knocking or the doorbell provides an opportunity for the dog to earn reinforcement, and is not a cue for a whirlwind of arousal. Next up is to extend the training to the entry door. Remember to review previous criteria as you introduce this new criterion, the front door.

- Cue "sit" in the front hall, click/treat.
- Cue "sit" in the front hall, reach toward the door, click/treat.
- Cue "sit" in the front hall, touch the doorknob with one finger, click/treat.
- Cue "sit" in the front hall, grasp the doorknob, click/treat.
- Add knocking, the doorbell, a family member outside, a neutral stranger outside, a cheery stranger outside, and so on. Add each element one tiny step at a time.

Occasionally someone protests these training increments, "But he's totally fine in the kitchen—why do we have to take all these steps? It's not until someone's coming in that he starts misbehaving!"

Training starts well before the mistake becomes apparent. The early steps let the dog figure out exactly what you want. While you may think "calm down at the door!" is perfectly obvious, an enthusiastic welcome may seem more natural to a dog. More importantly, the multiple steps establish a reinforcement history.

Many dogs have never had a successful experience at the front door. They don't even try to figure out what an owner is asking there, because they don't believe it's possible to find a "right answer." Defining a contract, asking the dog only for something he's capable of doing and that will be worth his while, is an invaluable training foundation.

Even with the many baby steps, clients report so much more progress in a single hour's lesson than in months or years of trying to fix the problem behavior more directly. Splitting may feel longer at first, but splitting works much faster!

Progress at your dog's pace

The single most common problem I see in training successful greeting behavior is that the humans skip ahead to the final steps, assuming that's appropriate since the dog is doing well. One owner told me that mat training didn't work after all. I'd seen her dog going quite readily to settle on the mat after their initial training, so I asked what she meant. She explained that her dog had indeed been doing fine, so she'd sent the dog to the mat when her Thanksgiving guests arrived—all 17 of them! Of course the dog had bailed off the mat. There are quite a few steps between learning to settle in an empty room and staying there while 17 food-bearing people enter! Be sure to continue the training in small increments. If the dog makes a mistake, simply back up and review, or consider whether you can break a step down even further.

Remember, too, that this is hard work, especially for enthusiastic dogs. Reinforce generously and often.

Capitalizing on the holidays

If your house receives many trick-or-treaters, Halloween is a great opportunity to practice greeting behavior, but only if you've already done your foundation work. It's often best to have two handlers, one to click and treat the dog and one to wrangle and treat the sugar-crazed kids. If your dog starts to tire and make mistakes—this behavior is difficult after all—quit early and put him away in a safe place for the rest of the night. If your dog is startled by a costume, let him flee to a safe place. Pressuring him to stay will only create distrust in your foundation work, making future training more difficult. It's better to move away and start over. Never force your dog to remain near something that frightens him, especially if a child is involved.

After consistent reinforcement for the behavior you want, your dog will find it's not worth his time to bark or jump—he can get attention and more for offering polite behavior instead! Your dog has learned to recognize old triggers as new opportunities. Because you trained for the behavior you want and broke it into small steps, the dog believes he can be successful.

Add some tempting savory smells to your criteria, and you'll be ready for Thanksgiving. By Christmas, your dog will be greeting your guests with a stocking in his mouth!

Chapter 6 – Socialization

Don't Socialize the Dog!
by Laura VanArendonk Baugh

Really? That title is a typo, right? A professional dog trainer would never advocate against socialization, would she? Well, maybe!

The problem isn't with socialization itself, but with many people's understanding of socialization. Socialization is vital for proper mental and social development in dogs, and it needs to be offered properly. Mistakes in socialization, even if intentions are good, can backfire and may even produce an overly shy or overly aggressive dog.

When *not* to socialize a puppy

Good socialization introduces a puppy or dog to something new, maybe even challenges the dog a little. Good socialization provides a positive experience for the dog. *It was a weird floor surface, but we were able to play cool games on it. That guy had the strangest hat ever, but he knew how to play the target game for treats!*

It's all about showing a puppy new things and letting the puppy "win" in the challenge presented. But too often people think only of showing the puppy new things, without taking care that the puppy feels very successful. In fact, sometimes what people intend as helpful socialization creates more problems than it prevents.

As an example, consider the well-meaning but potentially dangerous recommendations to "Touch his feet and ears a lot so he gets used to handling," and "Play with his food while he's eating so he learns that is okay." Without specifically making sure that the puppy enjoys both the interaction and outcome, these actions can sensitize a dog to handling and food approach.

Any time a puppy is not actively enjoying the socialization experience (at least by the end—it's okay if he learns to overcome a short challenge), there is the potential for doing more harm than good. Refer to the checklist (p. 201) for key points to a good socialization experience.

When *not* to socialize an adult dog

What if you have an adult dog? Maybe you made some socialization mistakes, or you inherited a bad socialization legacy along with the dog. In either case, socialization experiences aren't as they should be. Is there hope?

Yes, of course there's hope! But mistakes happen in the name of socialization with grown dogs, too. I get a lot of phone calls that run like this:

Dog owner: "Hi, I'd like to sign up for a class."

Trainer: "Great! Are you interested in a group session or private training?"

Dog owner: "We want a group class. We want the socialization."

(Note: This phrase is the most poisoned of cues for a professional trainer. It indicates either a dedicated dog owner trying hard to do everything right, or an owner in denial regarding potentially dangerous behavior.)

Trainer: "Yes, socialization is very important.… Can you tell me exactly what you're looking for?"

Dog owner: "He just needs to get used to other dogs."

Trainer: "What does he do now around other dogs?"

Dog owner: "He pulls really hard, barks, jumps, won't listen.… Sometimes his hair stands up. So we know he needs socialization."

Trainer: "Okay. He sounds like he gets pretty worked up? Tell you what, let's do a private session…"

Dog owner: "Oh, no, we don't want private training—he's great at home. He needs to learn to be around other dogs."

Truth

Yes, that dog needs to learn to be around other dogs. But he's probably not going to learn well in a group class. A dog with an over-the-top reaction is a dog too aroused to think clearly, process information, and retain knowledge for later. In short, *that dog is not going to learn, and I'd be wasting your time and money if I took that dog in a group class!* Not to mention putting other dogs at risk of a bad socialization experience.

Recently I had a client who did not want to waste time on a foundation lesson, who wanted to have the first lesson in the trigger situation. I explained that this was equivalent to taking a brand-new student driver onto the interstate and then trying to explain gear shifts, turn signals, and left and right pedals—all at 65 mph. It's essential to have skills under stress; therefore, you have to learn them before you're under stress.

So my client took a few weeks to practice the basic skills first. In her second session she was utterly amazed as her large mastiff-type dog, a dog she could no longer walk due to the strength required to restrain his reactive lunging, lay quietly on a mat and responded to cues. He was aware of a second dog, but stable and focused. Yes, it was worth it.

Learning happens in a mind that is still engaged. It's important to start teaching the dog new behaviors while he is still under threshold—and that's not going to be in a room with five other new dogs.

"Pet" peeves

Not everyone recognizes the necessity of a foundation and of incremental steps. Instead, well-meaning owners, often thinking they're doing the right thing in "socializing," put their dogs (and other humans and dogs) in unfair situations—and sometimes even in danger.

Where does this seem to happen the most?

- popular walking/running/biking trails
- dog parks
- pet fairs and festivals
- community events

Most of these environments violate key points of the good-socialization checklist: the dog has no escape route and he cannot choose to leave and return of his own volition. Many people won't leave the trail mid-run or go home from the street fair after only 20 minutes if the dog is overwhelmed. So, the exposure continues and the dog gets more aroused. By the end he is really confirmed in his reactions.

Other people attending a community event did not sign up to rehabilitate a troubled dog; they came to enjoy a social outing. Putting a stressed dog in their midst neither helps the dog nor enhances attendees' enjoyment. At best, it only confirms public opinion that dogs are often nuisances and should be banned from public areas. At worst, it creates more problems for the dog and puts others in danger.

While I am a clicker trainer, look for positive alternatives, and wholly advocate non-violent solutions, I am rapidly approaching an unwelcome point. If I have to intervene again to prevent a dog fight or a bite to a child while a dog owner explains that he or she is deliberately putting the dog in an overwhelming situation "to work on socialization," there's a good chance I will need bail and an attorney!

If you are not willing to retreat if your dog needs it, do not take the dog with you. Period. If your dog is too aroused and cannot recover, your training isn't yet ready for the scenario. You need to quit before you create more problems. End of discussion.

Here's the positive!

There are better ways to socialize your puppy or adult dog than to jump right in to group classes or wander far and wide searching out crowds of people and other animals. Successful training techniques prevent or solve problems instead of creating them. Appropriate socialization training proceeds with steps, and ensures that the dog is ready to progress each time.

As illustrated by my client and her mastiff above, private training classes offer a fantastic head start to socialization training. In a situation like the one with the mastiff, or any situation where an owner is looking to improve socialization skills responsibly, a good trainer will suggest a private session. At that initial or evaluation session, the dog starts learning new ways to interact with his environment and his human. Most importantly, he learns how to interrupt his own arousal. The next step is to teach him to choose relaxation in the presence of his triggers (other dogs, humans, and so on.). These skills have to be learned before they can be used.

You can go, but where?

Not to rule out field trips altogether, though! There is plenty of room in a socialization training plan for outings as long as anticipation and care are part of the package. So, where to go?

Match the scenario to the dog's current skill set. Has the dog ever been to a public event? If not, starting at the street fair with new asphalt substrates, a thousand people, several dozen food vendors, other (possibly stressed) dogs, music from the dance troupes, and the roar of engines from the car show is probably not a good choice for an outing. How about starting with the neighbor's cookout, where you can introduce your dog to fewer people and then pop him back home after he's had a good time?

> **Socialization Checklist**
> - Does the dog have an escape route? (Can he move away from the motorcycle or the funny hat or the other dog?)
> - Is the dog using the escape route repeatedly or is he reluctant to come back to the challenge? (If so, the challenge is probably too challenging!)
> - Is the dog coming back of his own volition? (That's a good thing, as it means you are keeping the challenge level with his curiosity!)
> - Are you using food to lure the dog back? This is very common, but in my opinion it's a mistake. This demonstrates not the dog's comfort level, but the magnetism of the food. I sometimes see dogs drawn into an uncomfortable location by food, focusing on the food to avoid seeing the scary parts. When the food is gone, these dogs look up and "suddenly" have a fear reaction. I use lots of food in training, of course, but food is for rewarding, not bribing!

When I take a dog out to socialize, particularly if I know it will be challenging for that dog, I make sure my schedule is clear of anything but that dog. If you really need to cover all of the fairground's antique booths before you go home, the dog shouldn't go. If it's more important that you keep a steady running pace than that your dog has a chance to self-assess and relax after a close bike encounter, the dog shouldn't go. That doesn't mean you can't ever run with the dog. It just means that you'll have to do some runs where you're willing to put dog training before your own training in order to get a great running partner for years to come.

At other times I will go somewhere for a longer period, but with the option to retreat as necessary. My car can be a secure and safe place for a dog trained to relax comfortably in his crate. The car is protected from heat or cold and strangers, and can act as a base from which the dog can make forays into socialization experiences. Obviously, this is not an option for a dog that doesn't regard his crate in the car as a haven, or with a car that isn't safe.

What to do?

Once you've picked a good field trip, assess your dog's skills. What behaviors is he really fluent at right now? Sit? Target? My definition of a dog "knowing" a behavior is that I can slap $50 on the counter and say "Watch this!" and he'll perform promptly on the first cue to win my bet. If you don't have a $50 behavior yet, that needs to be taught before you venture out. There's no profit in trying to train a new behavior in a new environment.

The $50 behavior is your "canary in a coal mine." As long as that behavior is healthy, you're working beneath the dog's threshold. When that behavior begins to degrade—you ask the dog to sit, and he does it slowly, or he does it facing away instead of facing you as usual, or he displays some other variant you don't usually expect—be cautious. The dog is challenged. It might be time to back off for a while or change tactics.

Next, choose your goals for the outing; these will vary widely by dog and by situation. Would you like your pup to relax while bicycles pass, recognizing they're just background noise? Or do you need your shy dog to feel more comfortable passing or meeting strangers on the sidewalk? Has your dog seen gentlemen with big beards and ladies with long skirts?

What about other dogs, cats, horses (rural residents or urban police mounts), skateboards, motorcycles, and other things not normally found in your living room? Will your dog be meeting or just observing?

Out in the environment, start by asking for your "canary" behavior, and perhaps others, reinforcing generously. You want the dog to think that new environments are fun and pay well! Now watch for your dog catching interest in something or looking to explore. Go with him, verbally encouraging him gently and reinforcing appropriate behavior with petting or treats. (Remember the points from the socialization checklist!)

If the dog is hesitating, let him make a step or sniff forward, and reward that by tossing a piece of food to the ground in front of him. Don't use the food to lure him. Not only does luring disguise his natural behavior beneath the eating behavior (so that it is harder to read what the dog is feeling), but the dog was frozen when the food appeared and so freezing has been reinforced. If you start out luring, even as your dog grows more comfortable he will be less likely to move forward or explore his environment on his own. (If the dog is in distress, rescue or distract him, of course! But that is management, not training or socialization.)

When the dog is visiting with a stranger or sniffing the bicycle, know when to quit. Call back your pup before he gets too excited and displays frantic behavior, or before his courage fails and he finds himself facing more than he's ready to face. Stop at the peak of his experience! Call him back (don't pull) and reinforce coming to you. If you don't have enough of a recall yet, drop a series of treats and lead him back to you.

Get creative

While socializing should definitely include socializing with people, it should also include a lot more: floor textures, strange noises, different types of weather, odd smells. These experiences should all be a part of your socialization goals. Nearly anything can be turned into a great socialization experience for a puppy!

Sometimes necessity is the mother of all sorts of inventions. I drove across several states and was tired when I checked into my motel, but my 8-week-old puppy had slept much of the trip and was full of energy and enthusiasm! I filled the motel tub with an inch or two of water and floated several handfuls of kibble, creating a fun game for her. Simultaneously she could burn energy in a great play session, explore the properties of water and controlled splashing, and have an enjoyable experience in a bathtub. (It was an easy cleanup and I left no mess for the cleaning staff.)

Socialization success

If your dog needs socialization, please provide it in the doses he requires. Your dog will make much faster progress with a series of baby steps than with any overwhelming preliminary experiences. If you don't seem to be making progress with your dog's socialization training, consider professional help. You'll have more success with a good training protocol than just hoping things get better. With a good trainer, you certainly won't make things worse accidentally. In the end, you'll be the one knowing when, where, and how to socialize your dog.

Spa Day: How to Train Your Dog to Love a Bath, a Brushing, or Even a Mani/Pedi

by Colleen Koch

Imagine a life where your dog loves being groomed. When you pull out the brush or nail trimmers, your dog comes running—just as if you opened a new bag of treats. How would that make you feel?

It is never too late to train your pet to love being bathed or brushed. With a little time and patience, you and your puppy, adult, or senior dog can look forward to sharing relaxing grooming time.

Be sure of your strategy: Attitude, time, reward

All grooming interactions should be positive experiences for both the groomer and the one being groomed. Any time you are thinking that training for a good grooming experience is a chore is not a good time to practice. Wait until you are in the right frame of mind so that the training time is positive for both you and your dog.

Short training sessions are always the most productive. If you notice your dog is reluctant to participate, then you are probably going faster than your dog would like. Slow down and use a higher-value treat or reward to make the time more comfortable for your dog. There is no rule that says you have to trim every toenail every session.

Train (and practice) in small steps that emphasize fun and rewards. When I start to train a new behavior, I like to use my dogs' favorite treats. However, once my dogs understand what I am asking them to do, I start to decrease the value of the treat.

The mani/pedi: Staging and tools

Many people are afraid of trimming their dogs' toenails. They are worried that if they trim the nails too short, the nails will bleed or it will hurt the dog. This is an especially common fear if a dog's nails are black, since then it is more difficult to locate the blood supply to the nail, called "the quick." The blood supply is more visible with clear nails than with black nails. But, if a dog is trained to hold still when the nails are trimmed, then the risk of cutting the nails too short decreases.

If your dog has long hair, first train your dog to allow you to place a stocking over the toes. This will let you trim the nails without getting the hair caught in the nail trimmer. Remember that even training your dog to accept the stocking cover should be attempted slowly and should always be fun. If your dog does not enjoy this part of the routine, it is not very likely that the nail trimming will be enjoyable either.

There are quite a few styles of nail trimmers, including guillotine, scissor, and powered nail trimmers. It is important to find the type that you are most comfortable using. My favorite non-powered nail trimmer, and my tool of choice for many years, is the scissor variety that looks a lot like a tree pruner. I feel as if I have a lot more control and can make super-thin slices of nail. Recently I have come to prefer the powered Dremel because it allows me to make the nails very smooth and rounded. All three of my dogs were initially afraid of the sound of the Dremel until we did some training.

Mani/pedi: Training overview

The best way to train your dog to accept and be comfortable with nail care is with clicker training, specifically shaping. Shaping occurs when you click and treat for progressive behaviors that lead to the ultimate behavior goal. To shape a behavior, it is important to break down the process into very small steps. For nail care, the dog must learn the following small steps, in order:

- Hold still and offer a foot.
- Place the foot in your hand.
- Place the foot in your hand while the nail trimmer is in your other hand.
- Accept the nail trimmer moving progressively closer to the foot.
- Accept the nail trimmer touching the foot.
- Accept the nail trimmer touching the nail.
- Accept the nail trimmer tapping on the nail.
- Accept the nail trimmer trimming the nail.

If you use a powered trimmer, first shape the behaviors with the trimmer turned off. With any trimmer, first shape the behaviors without actually trimming the nails. Make the dog very comfortable with the entire process. Your dog should enjoy the presence of the nail trimmer long before any nails are trimmed. When that is true, you can train/shape all of the steps above, including any sound and/or vibration of the trimmer, and then move on to actually trimming nails.

Note that, like you and me, some dogs will prefer one type of trimmer tool over the other. I find that if a dog does not care for the scissor type, the dog will be fine with the Dremel, and vice versa. You can train your dog to accept your preferred tool—it will just take a little more time and patience. View it as more quality bonding time!

Mani/pedi: Ready, set, go!

Here's the message to convey: *The nail trimmer means good things.*

Regardless of the type of nail trimmer you choose, the first step is to create a positive emotional response to the nail trimmer. Bring out the trimmer and then feed your dog. Your dog will learn that after the nail trimmer appears, a meal appears. It is important that the nail trimmer (something bad) is presented prior to the appearance of the food (something good) so that the trimmer predicts food—and not the other way around. You don't want your dog to anticipate a nail trim each time you bring out a meal or treat.

Once a dog associates the nail trimmer with food, then bring the nail trimmer a little closer. If your dog stops eating, it means the anxiety level has increased. Slow down the training process—move the nail trimmer a little farther away until your dog can accept the trimmer's presence while he eats. Your dog is learning that the nail trimmer is an opportunity for reinforcement.

When your dog is comfortable eating in the presence of the trimmer, get out your clicker and some really good treats! Start to shape the nail trim, following the small steps outlined above. The first goal is for your dog to hold still in the position where you are most comfortable trimming the nails. Don't worry if you decide later that the position you trained your dog to hold still in is not comfortable for you; you can change it later. Once your dog looks forward to a nail trim, simply reshape the dog's position so that it is comfortable for you. It is important to find, start with, and maintain a position that is comfortable for the dog, however, in order to move forward successfully with training.

Train for a very short time—offer 5–10 treats for no more than 5 minutes at a time. Try for a high rate of reinforcement, since the high rate keeps your pet interested in the new "game." When you are clicking at a rate of 15 clicks per minute, you know your dog really understands what you are training and the specific behavior you desire. When you reach this point, you can ask for the next step in the shaping plan.

When your dog can hold still in the presence of the trimmer, the next step is getting your dog used to the sound of the nail trimmer (the click of a traditional trimmer or the whirr of a powered trimmer). Click and treat when the dog remains still during the sound of the trimmer. This is a good opportunity for you to practice your own technique, clipping a small amount of a pasta noodle "nail" at a time. Use any spaghetti or macaroni noodle. For thick nails like those of a Basset hound, try elbow macaroni!

Start trimming the noodles at a distance from your dog and click and treat the dog for standing still. For Dremel-type nail trimmers, turn the tool on low. Remain at a distance from your dog. The distance should be determined by the dog: how close can the noise be for the dog to still eat a treat? How close can the tool get before the dog will not eat a treat? Be sure to start where the dog is comfortable and taking treats.

(Your dog will probably think you are a bit crazy at this point. All he has to do is stand still and let you touch him with the nail trimmer, or watch as you trim noodles nearby, and he gets clicked and treated!)

If the dog moves closer to the sound of the Dremel or holds still as you approach, click. I like to let the dog choose to come closer to me with the Dremel, and then shape the hold still behavior.

Move on to each of the shaping steps above as you and your dog are ready. If the dog moves away, remain quiet and wait until the dog returns to the position you want, and then click and treat. Keep the rate of reinforcement high as you go through this process. Remember to keep training sessions short and to stop at a success point, even if you have to go back a step in the shaping plan.

Trimming those many nails, step-by-step

Here is some specific advice for a few of the nail-care training steps:

Moving the trimmer (in this case, a powered Dremel) closer and closer to the nail:

- Move the trimmer all around the dog's body. You want the dog to get used to standing still while you lean over him and while the sound of the Dremel comes from behind and beside him.
- Eventually touch the bottom of the Dremel to the body of the dog, ever so lightly. Once the dog is used to that, increase the duration of the touch and then start to move the Dremel over the body.
- When the dog is standing still reliably while the Dremel moves over its body, start to move the Dremel down a leg.
- Touch the top of the dog's foot while the dog is standing still and click and treat that stillness.

Touching the foot and nail:

- Place the Dremel bottom on the big foot pad first, then click and treat.
- Hold the foot as you would for a nail trim and touch the nail with the bottom of the trimmer.
- Barely touch the tip of the nail with the Dremel. Do this very briefly so that you can be successful.
- Work on duration. If your dog doesn't mind a quick touch with the Dremel, repeat daily to keep up your skills and the dog's. To work on duration I like to use the A, B, C method. Instead of counting one one thousand, two one thousand, etc., I recite the A, B, Cs. This way I feel more precise with my timing. If I get to "F" before the dog moves, the next time I go only to "E," and then maybe to "C," then back to "F" and so on. Ping-ponging back and forth starts to increase duration.

When the dog holds still during any of these nail care steps, it is a clickable moment, since the goal of this clicker training project is to trim your dog's nails by yourself. To do this successfully, your dog must be a willing partner and not require any type of restraint. When it all "clicks," you will have a fun spa day rather than a challenging chore.

Now we're stylin'!

Like nail care, brushing your pet should be relaxing for both you and your dog—quality bonding time. Like us, most dogs have preferences for brushes. A brush has to be the right combination of soft and comfortable, but it also must be the proper tool for keeping your dog's luscious locks mat-free.

To train your dog to enjoy being brushed, use your clicker and favorite food treats. Or, use favorite toys or playtime as reinforcers. Keep things fresh and exciting.

If your dog has a hard time sitting still and wants to go, go, go, then holding your dog down to brush him will result in a very frustrated dog, a dog that will try all he can to avoid you and the brush. That is not exactly a scenario conducive to a well-coiffed dog or to quality bonding time!

If you are starting with a dog that would prefer to leave town when you bring out a brush, then a little classical conditioning is in order. Just as with the nail trim, by pairing the brush with a meal or playtime, you can change his perception of the brush. Have your dog target the brush, and then click and toss the toy. Repeat just a few times; stop the game before your dog wants to stop. Training sessions like this short one can be repeated several times a day.

Use the following steps to shape brushing your pet. Remember, in shaping it is important to include all the little steps in between even if, like some people, some dogs like to skip steps!

- In the presence of the brush, the dog holds still.
- The brush can approach the dog.
- The brush can touch the dog—gradually add duration without actually brushing.
- The brush barely moves, but gradually builds up to one stroke of the brush, then two strokes of brush, and so on.

There are areas where dogs are a little more sensitive to brushing. It is especially important to go slowly and to make the brushing highly rewarding for the dog in these circumstances. Touch the brush in the sensitive area and then brush in the area the dog loves.

Each step above is a clickable moment, but not all treats have to be food. When I am training a dog to be brushed, I like to use toys and play time. I often throw a ball or toy (good if your dog likes to retrieve). One brush then click/toss ball, two brushes then click/toss ball, one brush then click/toss ball, and so on.

If a dog learns that good things happen when he is brushed, he is more likely to allow and even enjoy a full brushing. At first, every brush should prompt a click and a ball throw or a toy tug. Eventually, increase the number of times you run the brush over the dog's coat (increased duration) before clicking and treating.

Start the brushing routine before the dog grows a thick or long coat, or before the coat gets matted. If a dog is trained to accept brushing early, and when it is a comfortable experience, the dog is much more likely to enjoy the brushing process.

If your pet is matted, and does not enjoy brushing, have your pet groomed or shaved professionally so that you can start the training process on a positive note. From there, you can prevent the mats from forming.

Splish splash, we're training a bath!

If your dog does not like taking a bath, it can be a nightmare to give one. Once again, make the process enjoyable when the pup is little. Many times clients will tell me, "He's OK with a bath—he just stands there." My question is, will the dog take a treat (or favorite toy) when you are bathing him? If the answer is no, then your pup is not too happy with bath time. There are a lot of really good dogs out there that put up with taking a bath. But I want the time I spend with my pets to be enjoyable for both of us. Taking time to make a bath a positive experience pays large dividends for the future. Once again you need to change the dog's perception.

First visualize your bathing set up—what is there that is appealing to the dog? By design, sinks and tubs are made of slick surfaces that do not provide

Chapter 6 – Socialization

traction for our four-legged friends. People think that this lack of traction gives us the advantage since the dog can't get traction to jump out. That is true, but not having traction also makes a dog nervous and fearful, and those are not the feelings you want your pet to have about bathing. Making the tub comfortable with a non-skid mat, small rug, or a bath towel can go a long way toward decreasing your dog's anxiety. This is an excellent opportunity to teach "go to mat." The mat can be placed in the tub area, and eventually in the tub.

Make the bath area a place where good things happen. Regardless of where you bathe your dog, the kitchen or the bathroom, watch to see how close your dog will get to that area. If you are standing or sitting there, click and treat any movement closer to the dreaded tub! The area now becomes an area of opportunity. Feed some of your dog's meals in the bathing area to reinforce the idea that the tub is a great place.

The process for training baths is very similar to training nail trims. The dog's part is getting into the tub and standing still. Use targeting so that you can get the dog to face one way or the other in the tub—it makes it easier to clean both sides of the dog. The dog must get used to the sound of the water as well.

Shaping getting into the bathtub

Break down into the smallest steps possible the process of getting into the tub. This helps the dog be successful.

- Look at the tub.
- Walk toward the tub. If your dog is really fearful, break down this step into very small steps—one step in the direction of the tub, then two steps in the direction of the tub, and so on.
- Touch the tub.
- Nose in the tub.
- One foot in the tub.
- Two feet in the tub.
- Three feet in the tub.
- Four feet in the tub.

Next, have the dog stand in the tub for short periods, gradually increasing the time. Feel free to feed your dog in the tub.

For dogs that are bathed in the sink, click calmness as you pick them up. Work gradually toward lowering the dog into the sink: pick up the dog near the sink and then put down the dog, pick up and move closer to the sink before putting down the dog, and so on. Each time, be clear about moving away from the sink; moving away is a reinforcer. Finally, slowly lower the dog into the sink.

When the dog is comfortable in the dry tub, it is time to add just a little bit of water. I do this at first with the dog near but not in the tub. That way the dog can get used to the sound of the water. Start with the water just dripping and then increase the speed the water comes out of the faucet. Repeat the process with the dog in the tub—don't get the dog wet but get him used to the sound of the water.

Next comes the actual bath!

The bathing process should proceed at a pace that is comfortable for the dog. By following gradual steps, you have established a very good foundation. Remember that if your dog is fearful of baths, if you start squirting, spraying, or dumping water on him, he will most likely become fearful again. Progress slowly. Just get your dog's feet wet and see how your dog responds. Then get his legs a little wetter, then the body. Finally, carefully wash the head, ears, and neck of your dog. Gradually increase the stream of water coming from the faucet into the tub.

You might not choose to use shampoo during the first bath session, because the goal is to stop the process before your dog gets upset. If you start shampooing, you are obligated to rinse, and this increases the time in the tub considerably. Maybe pretend to lather up and do a follow-up rinse. That way you are setting up everyone for success.

If you want to blow dry your pup, you can train that as well. You would use the same process that you used for the nail trim. Here, the shaping steps would be:

- Introduce the presence of the blow dryer.
- Turn the blow dryer on at low speed.

- Move the blow dryer closer and closer.
- Try blowing on the dog for short increments of time.

Cute, clean, calm—and clickable

Keep in mind that if your dog is older and/or has always hated being groomed, any of these training goals will take a little longer to achieve, and will require a lot more patience.

Ultimately the goal is to change everyone's perception of grooming. Ideally, both pet and owner come to look forward to the grooming time as time together. The common denominators for successful nail trimming, grooming, and bathing are taking your time and going slow—your dog should always set the pace. If you keep this in mind, you'll set yourself and your dog up for success.

When your dog is comfortable with all aspects of grooming, that type of care becomes a treat—a true spa day for the dog that you love. And, when your dog looks forward to a spa day, maybe it's time to treat yourself to one, too!

Solving Problems

Even the best-behaved dogs can develop behavioral problems. It happens to the best trainers. You can prevent some problems by being aware of them in advance and solve others by implementing clear problem-solving strategies. Don't wait until you're faced with these issues to think about them. Read these articles in advance so that you are prepared and won't have to spend so much time problem solving.

Ten Reasons Your Dog May Develop Behavior Problems 216
by Sarah Dixon

The ABCs of Barking 221
by Kiki Yablon

How to Put an End to Counter-Surfing 228
by Aidan Bindoff

How to Prevent Door-Dashing 231
by Casey Lomonaco

How to Keep Your Dog Calm When the Doorbell Rings 238
by Nan Arthur

How to Train a "Crazy" Dog!... 247
by Laura VanArendonk Baugh

Desperately Seeking Snoozing—How to Help Your Dog Relax........ 252
by Nan Arthur

Separation Anxiety: When Alone Time Makes Your Puppy Panic 260
By Terrie Hayward

Ten Reasons Your Dog May Develop Behavior Problems

by Sarah Dixon

Did a new dog join the family this year? Are you aiming to start off with fine habits and manageable goals? Is this the time to tackle your dog's problem behaviors, the ones that have had you perplexed?

A solid foundation in positive training gets you off to a great start, either with that new puppy or with your older dog. But training has to be more than just a foundation, especially if there are any undesirable canine behaviors on the scene. Consider the whole picture when it comes to behavior problems, and review the most common reasons a dog "behaves badly." Understanding the common explanations for behavior problems is the first step in solving and preventing those problems.

Reason #1: Not enough exercise

Dogs need physical exercise to be happy, and on-leash walks around the block are not usually sufficient. Activities like off-leash runs, running with you, fetch games, chasing a pole toy, or dog–dog play/daycare for social dogs are more appropriate exercise choices.

Reason #2: Not enough mental stimulation

Often-forgotten mental stimulation is essential for a well-balanced dog. Mental exercise can be just as tiring as physical exercise; someone who works at a desk job can be as tired at the end of the day as a landscaper. Using your dog's daily rations for food-enrichment activities or for a bit of training as often as you can will go a long way toward tiring your dog mentally. Something as simple as hiding your dog's meal or spreading the food in the yard can be an enrichment activity. Dogs love to forage or work for their meals.

Reason #3: Health problems

Health problems cause behavior issues more often than people realize; health issues are often missed. Think about it—if you are not feeling well, you are probably going to be cranky or not yourself. Your dog is the same

Chapter 7 – Solving Problems

way, except a dog does not have words to tell you. Health issues that can change your dog's behavior include arthritis, hip dysplasia, luxating patellas, sore teeth, thyroid problems, epilepsy/seizures, ear infections, digestive issues, skin or environmental allergies, yeast infections, hearing loss, eyesight loss, and cancer. If aggression or another behavior issue shows up suddenly, contact your vet. There is a good chance one of the above health complaints, or something related, could be causing your canine to be cranky.

Reason #4: Genetic issues

Sometimes behavior issues have genetic causes. Behaviors that range from aggression to hyperactivity can come down to what your dog inherited from its parents. If you are buying a puppy, it is imperative to find out if the parents have positive temperaments. If they do not, the chance of your puppy having a poor temperament is very high. Sometimes, with good socialization, you can override poor genetics, but often, even with the best socialization program, there are behavior issues if your dog has lost the gene pool lottery. Genetic issues tend to show up very young and are difficult to treat with behavior modification.

Reason #5: Inconsistent environment

If you sometimes let your dog jump on you because you're wearing casual clothes, but at other times punish him for jumping, how fair is this to your dog? Dogs do not know the difference in clothing! This pattern, or lack of pattern, is confusing to them and can cause anxiety. Being inconsistent can strengthen any undesirable behavior by putting it on a random reinforcement schedule. If you want your dog to not do something, be consistent by making that clear to him in a kind manner. If your dog jumps, for example, take time to practice sitting with positive reinforcement (providing something your dog likes such as treats or play immediately after the behavior) and ignore your dog completely if he jumps. Ignoring your dog means no talking, touching, or eye contact, since all are forms of attention and can reinforce behavior you don't like. Cross your arms, turn your back, and ignore your dog until all four paws are on the floor.

If your dog has a behavior problem, look to yourself—how do you respond? There is an excellent chance you have been reinforcing the behavior with attention and may have actually trained your dog to perform that behavior. Another example of a reinforced bad behavior is barking. Dog barks, you yell, dog thinks you are barking along—look at the attention I got! Dog barks more, you scold more, dog barks more, and on and on it goes.

Having a consistent set of boundaries and consistent rules in your house helps your dog understand that the environment is predictable. It also shows your dog that you provide guidance, leadership, and access to all the good stuff. Take the time to teach your dog rules using patience and positive reinforcement. Putting an end to jumping, or training to eliminate any other undesirable behavior, takes patience, consistency, and knowing what to ignore and what to reward.

Reason #6: Misunderstanding "normal" dog behavior

Normal dogs bark, pull on leash, eat poop, roll in dead things, jump up to greet, guard food and bones (to a degree), growl when they are threatened, chew whatever they can get their mouths on, pee and poop wherever, nip, protect property or their family, herd, and chase—and sometimes kill—small animals. All of these "nuisance" behaviors are perfectly natural parts of a dog's repertoire and vary depending on breed. Find a dog breed that is compatible with your lifestyle. It's simply unfair to get a mastiff and be shocked when he barks at strangers approaching your home. These dogs have been bred for thousands of years to be guard dogs. Siberian huskies and northern breeds may not be reliable off leash and may kill small animals. Border collies might herd your children. Dachshunds are known to bark a lot. These traits are due to natural canine behavior or are the result of selective breeding to perform a job. Sometimes you can train an alternative behavior, and sometimes you cannot. It depends on how genetically hardwired the behavior is.

Reason #7: Changes in routine

Changing the routine can be stressful for your dog and may cause your dog to act out. Just like us, dogs need a sense of security. Drastic changes in the environment or routine can really throw them off, causing anxiety that is commonly expressed as problem behavior. Moving to a new house often causes a lapse in house training, among other issues. A change in your work schedule can confuse your dog, and a new pet or child joining the family can also be stressful. In all of these cases, be patient with your dog and guide him through the struggle with kindness while he adjusts to the changes.

Chapter 7 – Solving Problems

Reason #8: Changes in diet

Switching your dog to a poorer quality or less suitable diet may also cause him to act up. Diet has a huge influence on behavior (going back to #3, health influencing behavior). Switching your dog's diet to something that is of poor quality or that doesn't agree with him may change how the dog acts. Always feed your dog a high-quality diet, and change foods gradually over a week or so.

Reason #9: Poor socialization or negative socialization

Socialization is the process of providing your puppy positive, controlled exposure to other dogs, people of all types, sounds, surfaces, and new experiences. Dogs need to be socialized to the human world starting as young puppies and continuing throughout their lives. The period from 3–16 weeks of age is the most critical socialization period. This time lays a foundation for a well-balanced dog. If a puppy doesn't get proper socialization during its critical period, it can grow up into a shy, fearful, or aggressive adult. A well-run puppy class can be a fun way to kick-start your dog's socialization skills.

Even a dog that has been well socialized can develop behavior problems after negative experiences. Being attacked by other dogs or teased by children when out in the yard are occurrences that can affect your dog's behavior negatively. A poor experience at the vet, training class, or groomer can do the same. Be selective about where you take your dog to socialize and which professionals you trust to handle your dog. I would also advise against leaving your dog alone in the yard when you are not at home, since you never know what could happen.

Reason #10: Fear periods or adolescence

If your normally fearless puppy suddenly turns shy one day, don't panic. It is normal for puppies to go through several fear periods as their brains develop. The first generally occurs somewhere around 8–12 weeks of age and another period occurs around 5 or 6 months of age. Depending on the breed and bloodlines of your dog, your dog may experience more or fewer fear periods. Do not panic; just let your puppy go through this phase. You may want to avoid going to the vet, training class, groomer, or new places for a week until your puppy is back to his normal behavior. If during a fear period something frightens your dog, it imprints very strongly. So, rather than trying to work through a fear period, it might be best just to let it pass.

Adolescence starts at about 6 months of age and usually continues to 12 to 18 months of age. Adolescence is when most dogs are turned over to shelters. This is a period when puppies start testing their world and their boundaries. A previously "good" dog may become a nightmare. Continued obedience training, maintaining structure and boundaries, patience, and skilled management are all essential practices during this phase. Management means setting up the environment so that the dog doesn't get a chance to do "naughty" things, and includes techniques like crating the dog when you cannot supervise directly.

Target to change

Understanding common potential causes of problem behavior in dogs can make it easier to sort out what is happening with your own challenging canine. Eliminate each of the various origins of change, if possible narrowing down to a trigger for the undesirable behavior your pet is exhibiting. With more detailed information, you will have a better chance of eliminating the frustrating behavior quickly. Of course, if your dog's behavior problems are severe, look for a reputable trainer to help you.

Chapter 7 – Solving Problems

The ABCs of Barking
by Kiki Yablon

Barking happens for a reason. Sounds obvious, right? It didn't always, according to applied ethologist Julie Hecht, writing in the spring 2013 issue of *The Bark*. At the turn of the century, barking was widely thought to be "simply an item on a dog's daily checklist: 'Take a walk, have breakfast, bark.'"

Nowadays there's a small but growing body of research about why dogs bark, what they might mean when they do, and who understands that meaning. Researchers have concluded that dogs have different barks for different circumstances, that dogs respond differently to different barks, and that humans as young as 10 years old are pretty good at deciphering barks, even when they can't see the dog.

But there's a gap between what scientists care about and what owners of barking dogs care about. Plug "stop barking" into Google and on just the first page of more than half a million results you'll see ads for a "bark eliminator," a "dog silencer," and an "ultrasonic bark control." Next time you're held captive in an airplane seat, thumb through SkyMall to see devices like these pictured alongside remedies for life's other little annoyances, like electronic cellulite smoothers and replicas of the One Ring. How likely do you think it is that such solutions take into account why a dog might be barking?

Clicker training takes a different approach. You may never truly know why a dog barks, but relying on the principles of behavior analysis, you can make a pretty good guess. With that information, it's possible to change behavior in a way that improves the quality of the dog's life as well as the owner's.

The goal of the training described here is to reduce excessive barking in a given situation, not to eliminate barking from your dog's repertoire. It's unrealistic, and unfair, to expect a dog never to bark. Many of my clients, when asked to consider it, actually appreciate some of the barking their dogs do. Barking can warn that a stranger is on the premises, announce that it's potty time, or express excitement at the prospect of a ball flying into a lake.

If your dog's barking is part of a larger pattern of fear or aggression or has begun suddenly with no major environmental changes, or if you truly cannot identify a pattern in your dog's barking, consult your veterinarian to rule out medical causes before embarking on a training program. Barking primarily while left alone may be a sign of separation anxiety and also should be brought to your vet's attention as soon as possible.

A postal cue

So what's your dog trying to tell you? Despite your best efforts, your dog still doesn't speak English, and you're not fluent in Dog. But barking is behavior, and the cool thing about behavior is that it's functional. Dogs—and humans, and rodents, and fruit flies—behave to make things happen, to gain sustenance or pleasure, or to avoid or escape unpleasantness or pain. To make an educated guess about why a dog might be barking, you can start where the behavior analysts start: look at what happens right after the barking. As an example, let's consider a dog that barks ferociously whenever the mail carrier comes to the front porch.

Why bark at the mail carrier? Perhaps the mail carrier is a stranger? Perhaps the mail carrier always closes the mailbox with a loud bang? Perhaps the dog did not see a person in a dark, bulky coat during his critical socialization period? Perhaps the dog was kicked by a mail carrier when he was a stray? You could speculate forever.

But the most relevant answer for training purposes is that the mail carrier always goes away when the dog barks. The mail carrier likely doesn't see it that way—he just has other mail to deliver. But as far as the dog is concerned, the consequence of barking, 99 times out of 100, is that the mail carrier leaves. The removal of something that the dog hopes will go away is reinforcement, specifically negative reinforcement.

A key tenet of behavior science is that past consequences—the C from this article's title—drive future behavior. What causes the dog to bark at the mail carrier day after day is not that the mail carrier comes to the porch. It's that he always leaves after the dog barks. The mail carrier coming to the porch—the event that occurs before the barking—is the antecedent, the A in the title. Antecedents don't cause behavior, but they set the stage for it by predicting a consequence. A green light doesn't cause you to step on the gas—it tells you that now would be the best time to do so. You do it because the green light predicts that you can move forward safely. When you teach your dog to sit using reinforcement, the cue "sit" is a green light. This green light tells the dog that if he puts his butt on the ground, you are likely to throw the Frisbee.

The environment also provides cues constantly—and many of them seem to be cues to bark. Becoming aware of how environmental cues influence your dog's behavior will help you change how your dog responds.

Make the ABCs work for you

To change behavior—the B in the title—adjust the antecedents, the consequences, or both. Another option is to arrange things so that a different B will produce the same C.

Put the mailbox on the front gate instead of on the porch—no footsteps, no barking to remove the footsteps. Teach "sit," cue it right after the footsteps, and turn the footsteps into a new cue to sit. Make the footsteps predict a rousing game of tug, cueing the dog to look for you or a toy. Change the consequence for barking to steak and then make the steak contingent on coming to find you after a few barks. Potentially, there are as many creative applications of this approach as there are humans.

There are three main components to any plan for changing behavior:

1. **Manage the environment.** The first step is to prevent the dog from getting more practice in the unwanted behavior. With each round of practice comes another chance at reinforcement, and behavior that's reinforced will be repeated. If your dog spends all day barking at people walking by the house when you're at work, and they all oblige him by going on their merry way, you're going to have a hard time making a dent in the barking by training when you're home.

   Training means making the behavior you want more reinforcing than the behavior you don't. Good management—or what behavior analysts call antecedent arrangement—is critical to setting up both you and the dog for success in training.

   Sometimes management alone is plenty. Do you simply want your dog not to bark at every living creature that walks past the house while you're watching a movie? Try closing the blinds, putting frosted window film on the bottom half of the windows, crating or tethering your dog with a stuffed Kong, or gating the dog out of the room with the window.

2. **Manage the reinforcement.** Problem barking tends to fall into two broad categories: barking directed at the owner and barking directed at other things in the environment. Owner-directed barking is often reinforced by owner attention. Other-directed barking is often reinforced by distance.

   Consider barking for attention: Your dog barks at you. You respond by shooting your dog a look or by saying "no," but your dog continues barking at you on a regular basis. That probably means he finds that response reinforcing. "I barked at Dad, and he talked to me!" Or, maybe when he barks at you, you get up and feed him, or take him for a walk, or pick him up. Why wouldn't he try that again?

   The good news is that it's your choice whether this behavior gets reinforced. Tell yourself that your dog barking at you is a cue—a cue for you to take a deep breath, or look at your toes, or keep doing whatever you were doing.

   Note: If the dog is a puppy, or doesn't usually bark to get your attention, do some quick triage: Is it past time for a potty break? Is the dog sick? Is the house on fire? Yes, you will probably reinforce the barking by taking the dog out. But better to reinforce the first few barks than to wait for it to get louder and more persistent and then reinforce it.

   Describing techniques that control reinforcement for other-directed barking is a subject for a separate article. But one approach I particularly like is changing the reinforcement for the behavior to something you can control. A classic example, explained by Karen Pryor Academy (KPA) Certified Training Partner (CTP) Andre Yeu, is putting barking (and quiet) on cue. Another example is thanking your dog for barking.

3. **Reinforce something else.** Before beginning any training, you need to answer this very important question: What should the dog do instead? There are many good reasons for finding another behavior

Chapter 7 – Solving Problems

to increase via reinforcement. High among them are practical concerns. If your dog is awake, he's behaving, so why not train him to behave in ways you like? It's much more helpful to tell him what you want him to do. Another important reason to train a replacement behavior, perhaps the most important reason, is that a high rate of positive reinforcement is essential to behavioral health and happiness—for both you and your pets.

So taking a deep breath when your dog barks at you is not where the job ends. Merely ignoring a behavior is a hard way to get rid of it; it's frustrating for you and the dog and, for that reason, likely to fail.

When a behavior has worked in the past, and then suddenly doesn't work, it doesn't simply go away. First it tends to intensify, and when barking intensifies, it can be impossible to ignore—especially if you're on the phone, live in a condo, or have a headache. The dog barks longer and louder for the same reason you might kick a broken Coke machine. This phenomenon is known as an extinction burst. When you finally do react because you can't stand it any more, you have new problems: (1) You've reinforced a very strong version of the behavior, and (2) you've put the behavior on an intermittent schedule of reinforcement, also known as a gambler's schedule. The gambler's schedule creates behaviors that are persistent even when they're only reinforced occasionally.

While you're breathing deeply, you're not ignoring the barking. Instead, you're waiting for something you like better, an acceptable way for the dog to get your attention. For a great way to remember this process, refer to KPA CTP Caryn Self-Sullivan's tip, Stop, Wait, Watch, Reward. If you've taught your dog a repertoire of simple behaviors using positive reinforcement, it's very likely he'll try one of those next. When he does, be ready to reinforce him. Even better, look for or cue acceptable alternatives before the barking starts, and reinforce them proactively.

Pulling it all together

It's 5:30 p.m. You've just come home from work and plopped down on the couch. Your dog strides toward you, looking at you intently. You know that your dog tends to bark when he wants dinner, which is usually served around now. You have a multitude of options. Let's look at just a few:

1. Wait for your dog to bark. Get up and feed him to stop the barking.

2. Wait for your dog to bark, then try to ignore him. Break down and feed him just as he reaches fever pitch.

3. Wait for your dog to bark. Cue a previously trained sit. If he sits, click/treat and/or get up and feed him. You've cut the barking short, and reinforced a better behavior. Of course, you may have also reinforced the barking. Your "sit" cue is an opportunity for reinforcement, which makes it a reinforcer in itself. But if you cue "sit" after the first bark or two, at least you're reinforcing less barking.

4. Wait for your dog to bark. Take a deep breath. Wait for him to stop barking for a second. Click/treat. As soon as he's done eating, click/treat again before he can bark again. Continue until he is intentionally offering a few seconds of quiet. Get up and feed him.

5. Click/treat as your dog approaches, before he can bark. When he's done eating the treat, click/treat again before he can bark. Continue until he is offering a few seconds of quiet. Get up and feed him.

6. As your dog approaches, and before he barks, cue the sit. When he sits, click/treat, and then get up to feed him.

7. Get up as your dog approaches, before he starts barking, and feed him.

If you are consistent in any of these approaches, over time whatever behavior you reinforce will become the dog's new response to the cue his rumbling belly gives him.

Listen to the dog

Did you notice that all of the above suggestions end with getting up and feeding your dog? Your dog may love tug or fetch, but right now he's barking for a reason. That reason is pretty easy to divine when you think about the consequences his behavior has produced in the past. Your dog is also doing you the favor of telling you what would reinforce him most at this moment. As it happens, it was something you were going to offer anyway.

Chapter 7 – Solving Problems

Your dog was barking to express an unmet need or desire. Attend to your dog's needs and desires proactively and you may find he has fewer reasons to bark. Clicker training can help you teach your dog better ways to get his needs met when you haven't anticipated them. When your dog does bark, and sometimes he will, you'll have the tools to manage it in a positive way.

How to Put an End to Counter-Surfing
by Aidan Bindoff

Many dog owners complain that their dogs steal food from kitchen counters or even from the dinner table. A new term was even coined to describe this behavior: counter-surfing. If you're tired of losing your dinner to a sneaky pooch every time you turn your back, here's what you can do about it.

"Stop" strategies

Counter-surfing is unwanted behavior. In operant conditioning, there are three basic approaches to stopping unwanted behavior:

1. Punishment through a consequence that diminishes the unwanted behavior
2. Extinction (allowing the behavior to fade away on its own) through removal of the reinforcer that is maintaining the unwanted behavior
3. Training an alternative or incompatible behavior

The first approach, punishment, has its disadvantages. It is usually (but not always) unpleasant, and therefore not much fun for dog or owner. Judging an effective level of punishment can be tricky. Too much punishment can be damaging, and too little can be ineffective. Other behaviors may end up being punished unintentionally, sometimes causing the dog to simply learn to avoid an entire situation altogether.

If you punish your dog for counter-surfing, for example, your dog may decide that the kitchen was the source of the problem, and opt to avoid the kitchen altogether—which could cause a host of other issues. But by far the most common problem that occurs when punishing counter-surfing is that the dog only learns not to steal food when the owner is around. As soon as the owner leaves the room, watch out!

This leaves us with the remaining two options: extinction and training an alternative or incompatible behavior. If you are new to clicker training, find an index card, write down the following, and stick it to your fridge:

Chapter 7 – Solving Problems

- What is reinforcing this unwanted behavior and how do I remove the reinforcer?
- What would I like my dog to do instead of this unwanted behavior?

Remove temptation

The answer to the first question in this case is easy: FOOD. Recall the adage "opportunity creates the thief." Food left unattended on kitchen counters is simply too tempting and too reinforcing for the thieving dog. Each time your dog manages to find food on the kitchen counter, counter-surfing has been reinforced. Extinction of counter-surfing requires clean kitchen counters. Use storage containers, high shelves, and cupboards so that food is never left unattended within reach of your dog. Clean up countertop spills and tidbits immediately, since even a crumb can be enough to reinforce some dogs.

If you must leave food unattended, put your dog in another room and shut the door. There is no sense in providing opportunities for reinforcement when avoiding it is as simple as closing a door.

Try instead

So what would we like our dogs to do instead of counter-surfing? We could choose a specific behavior, such as lying on a mat in the kitchen, and in severe cases we could train and proof this single behavior to be reliable even when we're not in the room—and even when there is juicy steak lying all over the counters!

If the mat is your dog's normal bed, then he can be taught "go to mat" fairly quickly by capturing this behavior. Simply wait until your dog lies down on the mat on his own, then click and treat. If you toss the treat a short distance away from the mat, you will set up the next trial. When your dog is reliably going back to the mat to lie down, put it on cue.

Increase duration

Once you have the "go to mat" behavior on cue, start adding duration. Rather than clicking as soon as your dog goes to the mat, hold off a second before you click and treat. Gradually increase the time before you click, asking for slightly longer or slightly shorter duration.

Keep the mat in the kitchen or, if space is tight, just outside the door but still in view. When you have 30 seconds of duration on the mat, try asking your dog to "go to mat" the next time you prepare food in the kitchen. Click and treat (toss the treat to your dog on the mat) every 5 seconds at first, then start to build duration up again. Why lower the criteria to 5 seconds when you know the dog can stay for 30 seconds on the mat? This is a new training picture, and we've introduced distractions (food being prepared), so we have to lower our criteria to a point where the dog can—and will—succeed.

When your dog is staying on the mat while you prepare food for 30 seconds, try leaving the room. Only leave briefly at first, return, and if your dog is still on the mat, click and treat. Again, build duration slowly, at a rate where your dog will succeed.

Eventually, they'll know better

All that most dogs need to know is that there are plenty of opportunities for reinforcement for a range of behaviors that don't include stealing from the kitchen counters. When preparing food, make sure you reinforce nice behaviors such as sitting patiently or lying down on the floor or a mat. Be sure to leave the room briefly, just to return and reinforce these nice behaviors that are offered even when you're out of the room. At first, be sure to tidy food from the counters so that any counter-surfing is not reinforced.

By combining extinction with regular reinforcement of alternative behaviors, your dog will learn that the most reliable way to get food is to sit patiently, or lie down out of the way. Attempts at counter-surfing will not be reinforced and will eventually go away. If your dog has been reinforced for counter-surfing many times, or intermittently, then the extinction process will take longer—but it will happen.

Remember the two important questions raised above—what is reinforcing this behavior, and what would I like my dog to do instead? You can apply these questions to virtually any unwanted behavior: raiding the garbage can, barking at the door, jumping on visitors, even pulling on the leash. You hold the power to solve any one of these problems if you can answer these two simple questions and consistently apply the solutions.

Chapter 7 – Solving Problems

How to Prevent Door-Dashing
by Casey Lomonaco

Spring seems to be the ultimate door-dashing season, as sunshine returns to cure the cabin fever that plagues many humans and canines during the long winter months. In busy families, the front door seems to be in perpetual motion, constantly revolving and providing myriad opportunities for escape. Friends and clients who have dealt with the stress and worry of a lost dog due to an open-door accident utter a common refrain: "It was only open for a second."

Once a dog has dashed through an open door, the possibility of the dog being harmed increases. Recently, I heard about a friend's dog that bolted out the door (apparently a well-established habit) and ran underneath a car entering the driveway. The driver said she felt the dog roll under the tires! Thankfully, the dog did not sustain serious injuries. Nonetheless, the experience was terrifying for all involved and left the dog's owners wondering what they could do to prevent a recurrence. They realized that their luck would run out eventually if they didn't address the situation.

A lot of prophylactic management and a little careful training can go a long way toward keeping your canine best friend safe during spring—and for all seasons. If you are trying to prevent your dog from developing a door-dashing problem or if you are already dealing with a seasoned escape artist, installing new safety measures today will be an effort that is well rewarded with peace of mind.

Provide plenty of legal exploring opportunities
Many of the chronic door-bolters I see are desperate for more physical and mental exercise. These dogs are usually brilliant problem-solvers (making them great candidates for shaping games!) that love a good challenge. Frequently, they are very active dogs that need more structured activity. When dogs lack appropriate and adequate outlets for their natural need to exercise and explore their environment, they will seek these opportunities for themselves. "FINE! If you won't take me to the park, I'll walk!"

While exercise will not solve all problems related to door manners, I find that even my own dogs are significantly less concerned with activity near the door if they have enjoyed a nice long walk or hike that day; their "exploring and adventuring" muscles have already been well exercised. They've already had the chance to smell a hundred smells, and they already know how many dogs peed in the neighborhood today. At that point, the dogs are more than happy to work on a stuffed Kong or marrow bone so that my husband and I can run in and out of the house with groceries or with tools from a lawn and garden project, or welcome visitors into our home.

Manage, manage, manage

One of the most important things to know about door-bolting is that it falls into the extremely self-rewarding category of dog behaviors, alongside its cousins: prey-chasing, counter-surfing, hole-digging, diaper-genie-rummaging, toilet-water-drinking, litter-box-raiding, and stuffed-animal-humping. With all of these behaviors, remember one thing: Dogs get better at anything and everything they practice. This includes polite behaviors, like sitting, relaxing on a mat, or entering a crate on cue, but also includes unwanted behaviors like those listed above. Every time your dog escapes successfully, it becomes more likely that he will try to do so again in the future.

Management generally takes the form of tools (often, crates, gates, and tethers) that you use constantly during the training stages and as needed once you've installed the initial desirable behaviors. When you have completed the training, it is likely that you will no longer need to crate your dog so that you can slip out the front door to retrieve the mail. But, if you are hosting a party of a few dozen friends, not all of whom are well trained in the management rules of the house, it might be a good idea to keep your dog crated, gated, or tethered while your guests are arriving.

You may also consider, temporarily or permanently, using alternative exits to the home, if that is an option. It is convenient when owners of determined door-bolters have an attached garage or can enter and exit through a contained basement. These owners can invest in training if it is a priority, but already have a built-in safety mechanism, much like the double-gating system in place at nearly every dog park, created to prevent "oops" escapes. You may find that exiting through the back door creates less arousal than leaving through the front door. If so, choose to use that exit during the training process to make life a little easier for yourself. Be careful; dogs get wise to this trick pretty quickly.

Know your biggest challenges and have a plan in place. One common challenge for owners of door-bolters is bringing home groceries or bringing large packages inside. Most doors open out (are pulled open rather than pushed open). It can be challenging to block a dog from escaping, especially when your arms are full and your sight may be limited by the items you are carrying.

In a situation like this, an ounce of prevention may be worth a pound of cure. If a family member is home and you are bringing home more than an armful of groceries, consider calling ahead and asking that person to leash the dog or hang out with him in the backyard until you can get your packages inside and secure the door. If you don't expect a family member to be home and are planning a large grocery run or a run to the home supply store where you'll be purchasing many items, consider crating your dog before you leave. When you arrive home, you can unpack without worry. Welcome your dog out of his crate when you have secured the home and are able to give him your full attention for an effusive greeting.

Let the training begin!

Dealing with a door-bolting dog is like training any other behavior. The key factors are:

1. Prevent rehearsal of the unwanted behavior (management)

2. Identify an appropriate, desirable, alternative behavior (What do you want the dog to do instead?)

3. Teach the replacement behavior, making it a predictor of good things.

Doors are almost always exciting places for dogs. Who knows what adventures are on the other side? Most of the dogs that I know that bolt at the front door also bolt through other doors that are easier to control and present less of a danger if a mistake is made. Use that to your advantage. (Remember, you really want to avoid mistakes—practice makes perfect, so work to have your dog practice the right thing.)

In this exercise, I'll use the crate as the first door, but owners should think of as many doors as possible to practice at, so that your dog can generalize the behavior well. The more doorways you can practice this behavior at, the more solid the behavior will be. You can practice at

- The bathroom door (you know your dog likes to follow you in there)
- The bedroom door, if dogs are allowed to sleep in your room or on your bed
- The garage door
- Car doors (both getting in and getting out of the car)
- Gates at the dog park, if you frequent one
- The entrance to the training classroom, if you attend training classes with your dog
- The door to the backyard
- The door to the pet store
- Any other doors you can think of!

Step one: Install default behaviors

Decide what you want your dog to do when approaching a threshold. I recommend choosing a behavior for which stimulus control is not required (it doesn't need to be on cue), because you want this to be a default behavior. When this behavior is trained, you want at least one of the cues for the behavior to be environmental. I choose "sit" for my dogs, and eventually want the sight of a door to be a cue to put their butts on the ground and keep them there until instructed otherwise.

To begin installing a behavior like this, simply take a good portion of your dog's kibble and for a few days feed your dog any and every time he sits, whether you ask for it or not. As if by magic, you'll notice those sits happening a lot more frequently. Let your dog know that sitting earns treats in all kinds of environments—in the backyard, in his crate, out on a walk. The more times you can feed a sit, the better. You want to teach your dog that sitting is a VGT (Very Good Thing) because it makes Very Good Things happen for dogs!

You also want to install eye contact/a whiplash turn so that your dog knows what is expected of him immediately after crossing a boundary. Practice saying your dog's name in a happy tone of voice, immediately following with a number of super-yummy treats. Do this for a few days as well, in all kinds of environments, until your dog responds rapidly and happily when he hears his name!

Once your dog is throwing sits at you left and right and loves the sound of his name, it's time to move on!

Step two: Teach the butt button

The butt button is a magical button that exists on floors all over the world. This button, when pressed by a dog butt, makes all kinds of doors open miraculously. You and your dog will be learning a very important lesson together. The butt button is in place so that your dog can train you to move toward and open doors.

My recommendation is that you start this exercise with your dog in a crate, provided your dog is well acclimated to his crate. If your dog is not crate-trained, it's worth teaching, but you can skip on to the next step, Step three: on-leash practice, for now.

Sit in a comfortable space near your dog's crate, where you are able to see him easily. I recommend grabbing a magazine you like and browsing an article, using your peripheral vision to keep an eye on your dog. As soon as your dog sits, get up from your chair and begin approaching his crate. As you move, keep an eye on that wiggly butt. If it leaves the crate floor, do not say anything, exhibit no frustration, but quietly return to your seat and the fascinating article you were reading. Again, keep a close eye on your dog, and as soon as he presses the butt button, begin moving. Work in this manner until you are able to approach the crate and place your hand on the latch.

Throughout this exercise, you are only watching your dog's derriere. As long as it is on the floor of the crate, continue to slide the latch up and open the door. If at any point your dog stops pressing the butt button, close the latch, stand up, and wait for the butt to go back on the floor before you resume opening the door. Alternatively, you can return to your seat each time the butt comes up and start the exercise again. Eventually, you will be able to get the door all the way open and your dog's butt will still be on the ground—it's a miracle! Release the dog from the crate with a "let's go!" and immediately say his name when he leaves the crate. As soon as he whips his head around, jackpot by quickly dispensing 10–15 super-yummy treats.

Once your dog begins sitting to ask to get out of the crate and waits readily for a release, looking happily at you after exiting the crate, it is time to begin generalizing these behaviors to other doors.

Step three: On-leash practice

It's time to begin leashing your dog and practicing the same steps:

1. Wait for butt button.
2. Quietly and slowly begin opening door.
3. Continue opening as long as butt button is pressed.
4. Release with "let's go."
5. Cross threshold and, as you cross, say your dog's name in a happy tone of voice.
6. Get ready to pay off with something fantastic.

Practice at all of the doors mentioned above. Practice going in, practice going out. Practice before walks. Practice if your dog wants to go out to the backyard for a potty break.

You'll notice that some doors trigger greater arousal levels than others. To deal with these doors, do lots of practice at less exciting doors first. Practice with the very best treats at the very hardest doors. As your dog progresses through the training stages, you'll notice that he begins pressing that button faster and faster, even at new doors. You'll find yourself closing doors far less frequently, and then hardly at all, and then never. You'll notice that his whiplash turn/name response becomes faster and faster until you don't need to use it much anymore. Your dog will know that walking through a doorway is an environmental cue to offer you focus. At this point, you can choose to vary your rewards—sometimes with a treat, sometimes with a walk, sometimes with the freedom of removing a leash (if the environment is safe).

Chapter 7 – Solving Problems

Step four: Off leash?

Some doors will present more danger than others. Often, these are doors that open into potentially dangerous unfenced environments, and may include your front door and car doors. Manage those exits safely over your dog's lifetime by only allowing him to cross the thresholds when cued and when the leash is safely in your hands. Keep in mind that it is often easier to body-block a dog from bolting through a door that pulls open (moves toward you) than it is with a door that is pushed open (opens "out").

If there are other doors where it is safe to practice, begin dropping your dog's leash as you approach the door, releasing him through the door with a cue and saying his name as he crosses the threshold. Either reward him with treats as you gather up his leash and move along or unclip the leash and allow safe access to free exploring. This is certainly a "know-thy-dog" exercise and is not safe for all dogs or all situations. It is better to be safe than sorry when your dog's safety is on the line, so proceed with caution!

How to Keep Your Dog Calm When the Doorbell Rings
by Nan Arthur

The crowd gathers outside and is tense with anticipation as it makes its way to the paddock (your front porch). The field is lined up. Ding dong...

"And, they're off."

"Out of the gate is Fido, pacing ahead of Suburban Woman."

"From the back, it's Fifi, a long shot, but picking up the pace."

"Rounding the turn, it's Fido, with Suburban Woman picking up momentum, and Fifi a length behind."

"Down to the wire, it's Fido, but Suburban Woman is closing in!"

"It's Fido crossing the threshold, and the crowd goes wild..."

... and so does Suburban Woman who is trying to get Fido and Fifi to stop celebrating on her guests.

Are you Suburban Woman, loving but exasperated owner of Fido and Fifi? Does your home seem like the 5th at Santa Anita every time the doorbell rings? Wouldn't it be wonderful if your dog actually moved away from the door when the doorbell rang rather than crowd you for a position to greet, or "eat," the people on the other side? Wouldn't you love to have a dog that sits, lies down, or even runs to another room when the doorbell rings—instead of all the embarrassing things your dog currently does?

Rather than wishing and hoping your dog will just stop going crazy, or trying to wrestle your dog away from the door every time you have a visitor, place your bet on a sure thing by training your dog for this situation. With some effort and a commitment to practicing with your dog, completing this doorbell game will make you feel as if you have just won the Daily Double.

Chapter 7 – Solving Problems

The Doorbell Game: Getting started

Before you begin, decide where you would like your dog to go or what you would like your dog to do when the doorbell rings. If your dog has a history of jumping and behaving like a circus act gone mad at the sound of the doorbell, your goal might be to send him to another room, to a crate, or outside for simplicity or safety reasons. If your dog just barks, or pushes you out of the way to greet your guests, you might be able to train a "sit" or "down" after the doorbell rings. Your final decision should be one based on safety and realistic expectations. It wouldn't be reasonable to ask a dog that escapes, or has a history of nipping or aggressing when people come in, to sit or lie down as "scary" strangers parade past, but that would be a wonderful goal for a dog that is overly friendly.

Always train in a quiet environment. Make sure you have at least 10–15 minutes of uninterrupted time whenever you practice so that your dog has a chance to really absorb the information. Take your time, practice a few times each day, and remember that it could take several days or even a week or two before you obtain the desired results.

You will need a clicker-savvy and hungry dog, several levels of food rewards (from average to high-value treats), a treat pouch so your treats are readily available, and your clicker. Eventually you will need someone to be your "guest" and to help you ring the doorbell, but not until you have the foundation behaviors in place.

When you reach for the doorknob, it often triggers an already excited dog. His anticipation is high; someone is visiting or, potentially, intruding. You first must train your dog to calm down. Your dog's composed behavior will allow you to walk to the door unencumbered and inform your guests that you will be with them in a moment. Then you can cue your dog what to do before you actually open the door.

Calming the beast

If your dog pushes toward the door or jumps on you when he sees you touch the doorknob, gently step between him and the door, using your body to impede his movement. Step forward into his space, if necessary, to urge him to slide off of you. Take a deep breath to help him (and you) relax. Do not make eye contact or talk, since this often gets dogs more excited. Calmly walk a few steps back from the door to show that you are not opening the door. Dropping a few treats on the floor for your dog to find as he tries to figure out why you are not leaving will help your dog calm down faster. Eating helps to calm the adrenaline, which, in turn, helps your dog "think" again. Just be sure to drop the treats slightly away from the door to show him that good things happen away from the door.

Training your dog to move away from the door

The preliminary step in training this diversion exercise is to teach your dog to move away from the entry so that you have some room to get to the door without him crowding or pushing. Keep in mind that during the early stages of this training your dog doesn't have to do anything except move away from the door. Don't ask for a "sit" or other trained behavior just yet; you can add those later if that is the goal.

Invite your dog to come with you to the closed front door. Hold a number of treats in the same hand as your clicker (you want the other hand to be free) and take a deep breath. Reach out with your empty hand and touch the doorknob, turning so that you can observe your dog. Watch your dog carefully, since you will be looking for subtle movements during these early stages. At this point in the training, you won't open the door, but just touch or hold the doorknob.

Your dog is free to move around, but what you are looking for is any movement away from the door. Click and treat when your dog moves or backs away from the door even the tiniest bit. Click and treat several times while the dog is in that position, reaching out to feed him so he doesn't have to come close to you or the door in order to get his treat.

Repeat the exercise 8–10 times, walking to the door from different areas in your home (as if someone had just rung the doorbell) and reward your dog for any movement away from the door. Be sure to tell your dog, "all done," or another release cue, after each successful movement away from the door. Continue to practice holding the doorknob and then clicking and treating for movement away from the door. If you see that your dog has figured out that the click occurs when he scoots or moves away, you are ready to train the next step.

Chapter 7 – Solving Problems

If your dog continues to move forward toward the door when you reach for the doorknob, practice this foundation for a few more rounds, or even days, depending on your dog's reinforcement history of rushing the door. Take your time teaching this foundation exercise, since mastering this stage will help your dog stay focused when you do add the doorbell.

Adding the cue and movement away from the door

To teach your dog what to do after the doorbell rings, practice this next stage in several different steps. What you are teaching is that when you approach the door after the bell rings, a verbal cue will direct your dog to do something else—go to another room, go outside, or "sit" / "down" at a pre-determined station.

The goal of the foundation stage was to teach your dog some composure, as well as how to give you some space at the door. Once you have achieved that element, you can start to add the verbal cue, which tells your dog there is something you want him to do when the doorbell rings. However, you are still not ringing the bell just yet.

If you use a verbal cue such as "just a minute," you can both inform your guests that you will be right with them, taking the pressure off you to hurry and answer the door, and use the phrase as a direction cue to your dog to move away from the door and toward the area where you want him to go.

Use the average-value treats as you begin to add movement away from the door, clicking and treating for the initial movement. Switch to the high-value rewards once you get your dog to the area where he will be confined, or where you want him to be stationed in a "sit" or "down." Plant the seed that the best rewards come after he moves away from the door.

Once you have walked to the door, touched the doorknob, and announced the "just a minute" cue, turn and move away from the door, encouraging your dog to move with you. Say something like "good boy" or "let's go" as you pat your leg or gently clap your hands. The goal is to get 4–5 steps away from the door and then click and treat several times where you stop, using the best treats. Where you stop could be the final destination for dogs that will be stationed in a "sit" or "down" or an intermediate stop for those dogs that will need to be confined.

Confining your dog

For dogs that need to be confined, practice getting farther and farther away from the door until you reach the area where you will confine him.

When you are ready to practice confining your dog, keep in mind that you may need to go all the way into the area with him the first few times so that he doesn't think you are "tricking" him into getting locked outside or in another room. This is where the high-value treats come in.

Go all the way into the confinement area or all the way outside with your dog (another reason you need to tell your guests, "just a minute!"), and then have a click-and-treat party with the high-value rewards. Add lots of praise and fun talk. You really want your dog to think this is the most wonderful game in the world so that when you do add the doorbell, it is no big deal and your dog will start to head toward the confinement area. You can also do a food confetti party, by tossing lots of food around as you leave. Much later, when all training has been completed, you can offer a stuffed Kong, or a wonderful chew treat for your dog to work on as you leave him in the confinement area. If you are working with more than one dog, only do this if you know that the dogs won't fight over these treats.

Using a "sit" / "down" station

If you are going to work on a "sit" or "down," your dog should already be fluent in that behavior. You should have a mat or rug several steps away from the door so that your dog can be sent to that area. The mat acts as a visual cue for your dog and makes it much easier for him to find his spot each time. It also prevents your dog from sliding around if the area has a slippery surface.

Direct your dog to the mat or rug after the "just a minute" cue and ask for the sit or down. Begin to back away slowly so that you can observe your dog as you move toward the door to open it. The goal is to be able to return to the door as your dog remains on the mat.

Increase the distance between you and your dog in small steps, taking one step away and then coming right back to click and treat him. Next, try two steps, quickly moving back again to click and treat. Continue to add more steps until your dog can remain at the station and you can get all the way to the door.

As you work on increasing the distance, take breaks and then resume your training by going to the door from different areas in the house. Continue at this level until you can get all the way back to the door with your dog in place.

Opening the door

Once your dog can wait at the station, you can try opening the door as your dog remains in position. The first sequences should look like this:

1. Approach from different areas in the house.
2. Announce the "just a minute" cue.
3. Direct your dog to the station.
4. Walk to the door and jiggle the doorknob.

Did your dog remain in place? If he did, walk all the way back to your dog to click and reward, and then repeat several times before adding the next step: opening the door.

When you are ready to open the door, open it just a little, close it, and then go back to your dog to click and reward. Continue until you can open the door completely with your dog remaining in place.

Once you are able to open the door entirely, have a helper assist you by waiting outside the door as you open it. Have him or her walk in as you go back to your dog to click and reward.

When you try this "for real," ask your guests to come in on their own in the early stages of training so that everyone doesn't get congested in the entryway, making it more difficult for your dog to maintain his "sit" or "down." Keep in mind that you will need a very high-value reward and multiple clicks and treats for dogs that find the arrival of guests highly rewarding. In other words, be better than the environment with your rewards!

If your dog gets up at any point after you have stationed him in a "sit" or "down," it is important that you do not click and treat just yet. You don't want your dog to learn that he can get up, follow you, or greet people on his own, and still get a reward. He needs to learn that that the only way he gets to visit is to continue to sit or lie down.

If your dog gets up, your helper should stop and back up (going all the way back to the door, or even outside, and closing the door, if necessary). Gently block your dog with your body and direct him back to the station. After you have him back in place, smile and use your voice and praise to encourage him to stay put until you have made it all the way back to the location where you or your helper was when he got up. Once you get that far, walk back to your dog, and then click and treat several times. The dog will begin to learn that you want him to remain there and, for doing so, you will come back and reward him. If your dog keeps getting up, release your dog and train again after he has had a break. When you come back to training, make it easier by only taking a step or two in the early stages, or just have your helper stand quietly inside the threshold of the door if that is where your dog has difficulty. You can use a leash or tether to prevent your dog from moving too far away from the station until he better understands that the "sit" / "down" is the answer.

Practice these components many times throughout the day, until you can see your dog moving away from the door when you say, "just a minute" and until you are successful directing your dog back to his station. Since this is a difficult cue to train and learn, you may want to suspend any other training while you work on it.

Adding the doorbell

Before you move on to this phase, your dog should be able to demonstrate success with the foundation steps described above. When you say the "just a minute" cue, he should move away from the door and go all the way with you to his confinement area or his station. All you will need to do now is pair the verbal cue with the doorbell.

Your helper, stationed outside, will be the doorbell ringer. You can use cell phones, a walkie-talkie, or a baby monitor to communicate to your helper when to ring the bell again, since you will not be opening the door in the early stages of this doorbell training. After your helper rings the doorbell, walk up to the front door, touch the doorknob (your dog should now be staying back or moving away), and then say, "just a minute."

If after the doorbell rings and you move to the door to touch the doorknob, your dog doesn't stay back or move away, drop your criteria. Go back

Chapter 7 – Solving Problems

to work on touching the doorknob after the bell rings until you have your dog moving back again (without going to his confinement area or station). This backward slide sometimes happens with dogs that have a strong reinforcement history of rushing the door. No big deal—just show your dog that it's the same game he learned earlier, but this time the doorbell rings first. Again, be sure your dog is fluent in the foundation steps before opening the door.

As soon as the bell rings, say the "just a minute" cue and move to the confinement area or the "sit" / "down" station. Click and treat when your dog completes the behavior. Don't worry if your dog barks during this phase if he normally barks when the doorbell rings. You may always have a little barking associated with doorbell ringing before your dog moves to the confinement area or his station, but the barking often decreases as your dog learns what to do. Your dog may also run back to the door as you move away, but hold your ground and wait until he comes back to the area where you stopped before clicking and treating. Be sure to do a number of reinforcements when he does come back.

Practice ringing the doorbell and not opening the door. Keep repeating these same steps until you can see that the "just a minute" cue after the bell rings has your dog turning and moving toward his destination. If your goal is to confine your dog, be sure to do so.

Go back and invite your helper in after you have your dog in place in order to simulate someone actually coming in the house. To generalize the behavior to different people, enlist several helpers to assist you with this final stage, but be sure to explain that they may have to wait outside a few minutes as you work through the completion of this training.

When your dog is training to a station and is consistently moving there with ease after the bell rings, go back to the steps of just turning the doorknob, and then opening the door a little, and so on, just as you did before the doorbell was added. The only difference here is that the doorbell now comes before all the other pieces. Continue until you can open the door and your guest is able to walk past you and your dog.

Everyone wins the doorbell game

As you move from touching the doorknob to opening the door to ringing the doorbell and admitting guests, each stage of this training game builds on the previous learning. The various stages may take time for you and your dog to master; don't be afraid of backing up and starting a stage again. Enjoy the time with your dog—and the pleasure and treat parties along the way!

With continued practice, the constant race to the front door will be eliminated and the doorbell will no longer be like the starting bell at the Kentucky Derby. Your guests will wager that visiting you results in a big payoff, as each time they enter your home they are greeted by a responsive and respectful dog. You, your dog, and your guests all will have won the doorbell game!

Chapter 7 – Solving Problems

How to Train a "Crazy" Dog
by Laura VanArendonk Baugh

Call *me* crazy. I like crazy dogs.

I like over-the-top dogs, dogs that come bounding in biting at their leashes (or anything else they can cram into their mouths). I like rambunctious, nutty, go-getters that exhaust their owners. Those are my favorite dogs to train. Why do I enjoy these dogs so much? I find them to be surprisingly easy and rewarding. All of that dog energy can be channeled to our own purposes!

Most pet owners want to reduce the arousal their dogs show (and most dogs will calm progressively with age and training); some competition or working handlers want to keep the hair-trigger reaction, but with reliable, trained behaviors. Both ends are possible with clicker training.

A friend, a crossover trainer like myself, was bemoaning the superb enthusiasm of her young, unneutered, standard poodle. His habit of pogo-jumping was wearing her out. "I can't train him to heel until I can stop his bouncing," she complained.

"Not true at all," I protested. "Don't you dare try to stop that bouncing. You want that energy for happy, enthusiastic heeling. Use it!"

Channel the energy

How *do* you channel and use that energy? There are several principles I follow in channeling the energy of eager achievers.

- **Ignore the crazy stuff.** Owners of "crazy dogs" tend to see and focus on the obnoxious jumping, the leash biting, the lunging for enthusiastic greetings, and the persistent harassment to play tug or fetch. I see a dog asking in every possible way to engage with his human, a dog begging for the interaction of operant conditioning.

    Many compulsive methods require considerable time and effort to suppress unwanted behavior, all before starting to teach desirable behavior. With clicker training, you can jump straight into teaching a new behavior and disregard what you don't want, trusting that it will disappear shortly. If you are like me, the surplus excitement won't bother you. With clicker training, you'll get what you want soon enough!

- **Love that energy.** Enthusiasm carries into training making training that much easier. All the effort the dog is putting into bucking like a bronco on the leash will soon be thrown into eager downs and fast targeting. This makes the trainer's work simpler. You don't have to create new behavior, you just have to shape what's already occurring. And that's perfect for a lazy trainer like me.

- **Use the dog's own motivation.** With an average dog, you have to take time to find what motivates that dog—a special toy, a preferred treat? Crazy dogs are motivated by everything! That means you won't be stumped when the dog gets distracted or when you're caught without treats on hand. Simply use whatever is stimulating the dog in the current environment. More benefits for a lazy trainer! "You want to see that friendly new person? Fine, let's work for it! You can keep eye contact to earn this stick I picked up." Crazy dogs tend to tell you exactly what they want to work for at the moment. If you believe them—he wants to play tug, or meet a person, or chase a ball—they're eager to work for their reward.

- **Reinforcement is control.** Too often, owners have been told they have to "get control of" their dog by suppressing his natural energy. But energy has a critical mass; if suppressed and contained too long, it cannot help but explode into activity. This is why a dog that does not know how to earn a toy, for example, will grab at hands or clothing. The forcible condensing of fusion results in a supernova, and the same is true for crazy dogs. Suppression creates time bombs and the mere illusion of command. Channeling creates true control. A dog that knows it's possible to earn what he wants can control himself to get it instead of fighting with his owner or trainer. (Careful management of criteria is critical here.) If you try to fight the dog's natural exuberance, you will never really manage his energy. But once the dog believes he can earn his energy release, you have him forever.

Chapter 7 – Solving Problems

The dog wins—and chooses control

That's all very well in theory, but how does this work in practice?

The dog can always win. I start teaching a very basic concept—what the dog wants is available to him, but by my rules. You don't want frustration, you want analytical thinking. It's very easy for this type of dog to get locked into frustration and hectic behavior. You can establish right from the start that there's a way to win if he thinks about it.

Inherently, this concept includes impulse control. Rather than plunging about in a desperate scramble for what he wants, the dog can hold himself still and try to earn it. (If the dog and owner team need impulse control instruction right away, for safety reasons, it is possible to start there. Personally I prefer to jump right in to teaching a new behavior, but I don't mind being jumped on or scratched before the dog acquires the new behavior. Some handlers can't tolerate such risks, though.)

Here's how I teach very basic impulse control.

I show the crazy dog a treat, briefly, and then enclose it in my fist. The dog will probably attempt to poke it free, nudging my hand, pawing at me, nipping, and barking. (I usually start this exercise myself, as most clients don't have the experience to trust where this is going.) The average crazy dog is active and will not pause in his quest, but will actually pull back as if to pounce again. Right then, I click that quick movement and open my hand, delivering the treat or letting it drop to the floor. Then I repeat the process. Most dogs are backing up within a half dozen repetitions, though some take longer if they've been reinforced for obnoxious or pushy behavior. It's also possible to do this with a tug toy, but, in any case, practice your technique in advance—accidental nips and grabs are no fun!

Helpful hints

- **Split criteria.** Then, split it finer. And even finer! Failing to split criteria is the single biggest error made with crazy dogs. Trainers and handlers tend to "lump," failing to break behavior into achievable pieces. What would seem like an ideal increment for a more typical dog is really a tremendous leap for crazy dogs. When these dogs don't achieve success quickly, they load energy and release it in hectic and undesirable behavior. (It's at that point that some owners or trainers decide to use compulsion or coercion to control the dog.)

The thing to remember is that the dog can always win. If the dog knows there's a right answer and that he can achieve his click, he will not stop trying to get it. There will be problems only if the criteria are not appropriate or if all the pent-up energy is not relieved appropriately.

When I worked with my young dog, Laev, I taught stationary duration behaviors in quarters or eighths of seconds initially. I've worked with other dogs and taught them to tolerate a handler's departure with the slight movement of one shoe. Once the dog has the idea and develops the necessary self-control, you can increase increments substantially, and achieve the larger behaviors (a three-minute stay, for example). Always start small.

- **Provide an energy release.** Most people don't realize how stressful learning can be. Stress isn't necessarily bad. In fact, sometimes it's not distress, but eustress (a pleasant or curative stress). Stress does still take a toll on the dog, though. Many dogs indicate that they need a break by losing attention, wandering away, or sniffing. My favorite crazy dogs indicate fatigue by launching themselves at you or another attractive outlet, or by jumping, nipping and barking. There has to be a way for the dog to dump energy, and it should almost always be through movement. Play tug, prompt a favorite active trick, or simply move about. Place this release behavior on cue early in training and use it to release energy when the dog has been demonstrating a good deal of self-control or otherwise working hard. If the dog explodes energetically outside of the cue, that means the training has continued too long or you attempted an unrealistic jump in criteria. Adjust the training and try again.

- **Use active behaviors.** Passive behaviors are much more difficult for crazy dogs than active behaviors—the dogs have to contain themselves! Behaviors which involve movement allow a constant release of that mental energy and are less likely to lead to explosive outbursts. This is why a crazy dog can retrieve or search for much longer than he can practice his down stay, which seems to be a much less complicated behavior.

This is useful information for managing dogs in daily life. Is the dog stressed by an outside influence, perhaps a stranger or a rude dog? Instead of "sit and watch," as many teach, ask the dog for a heel, a spin, or a leaping target. The movement helps dispel stress much more efficiently and still provides the benefits of a focused behavior.

Is your crazy dog too enthusiastic at the door? Instead of teaching "sit" to greet, which is very tough for these dogs, teach the dog to fetch a toy and bring it to the new arrival, holding it in his mouth as he is petted. This gives the dog a place to channel his energy (his jaws) while also preventing mouthing or licking.

- **Be proactive.** The problem with crazy dogs is that they are faster than humans, mentally as well as physically. By the time you realize you've encountered a challenge, your dog might have evaluated several behavioral options and settled on what makes the most sense to her—something you probably do not want!

  At the educated end of the leash, your job is to instruct the dog about what will pay off best—well before that scenario arises. Dogs load energy too quickly to interrupt them once they're reacting (although they can learn that later). Catch them before they lose their focus.

In the end, crazy dogs show some of the most dramatic transformations, from happy, brash, and crashing maniacs to happy, enthusiastic, and focused partners. That's reinforcing for all of us.

Desperately Seeking Snoozing—How to Help Your Dog Relax
by Nan Arthur

It might seem that it would take voodoo, or something similar, to teach unruly, out-of-control, and/or overly enthusiastic dogs how to be calm and relaxed. For people who live with dogs that fall into these categories, there can be a good deal of frustration and anxiety; more often than not, these dog guardians are frazzled from searching for the "calm zone."

Owners of excitable dogs often feel as though they have tried everything to slow down their dogs—watching TV dog trainers, reading books, watching YouTube videos, hiring trainers, experimenting with different equipment, and more. Most of the time these efforts yield little or no success. Even professional dog trainers can feel overwhelmed if they have never had to put together a training plan for a dog that is "over the top," a dog that could be in jeopardy of losing his/her home. These trainers might also feel as though they have tried everything in their bag-o-tricks of obedience behaviors.

While living or working with dogs that are out of control, hyper, or "crazy" is not an easy undertaking, teaching those dogs skills to help them relax is a lot less work than you might imagine. It takes an understanding of some basic dog behavior, balancing exercise and rest, and investing a concentrated effort toward acceptable behaviors with the "calm zone" as the final goal.

Getting through the layers

Many dog professionals talk about realistic expectations when they are trying to problem-solve a behavior issue, but it goes much deeper than that for dogs that are reaching into the outer limits of exuberance. Understanding your dog's needs is a multifaceted process. Each layer needs to be examined before you try to set training goals for your dog.

When considering a training and behavior modification program it's important to think about what is "normal" for the age and breed of the dog. For instance, expecting a border collie to be a couch potato at the age of 15

Chapter 7 – Solving Problems

months is like asking a Formula One driver to slow down during a race—neither is likely to happen.

Beyond realistic expectations there are many other considerations, including the amount of time you have to devote to working with your dog to overcome the impulsive behaviors. A medical clearance to ensure there are no underlying medical problems that might be driving the unwanted behaviors is also important. Consider your dog's diet, and what, if any, exercise (both mental and physical) your dog receives—these factors are also parts of the picture or puzzle. You need to examine all of these issues before you jump in and put training plans in place, since each can play a role in helping or preventing success.

To finalize your plan you will also need to understand the role your dog plays in a household: family dog, working dog, performance dog, wife's or husband's dog, and so on. Can the dog's main caretaker enlist the cooperation of other family members, or at least get a non-sabotage agreement among those in the household? If there are other people in the home, can the family maintain the management the situation requires? All of these considerations must be addressed in the quest to help a dog "chill out."

When you have looked at all the relevant issues that you can change or factor in, it's time to begin the foundation work that will direct your dog toward the "calm zone."

Mental exercise

Discovering ways to exercise your dog's mind is just as important to overall health as physical exercise. Many excitable dogs are simply bored and are looking for ways that help to stimulate their brains. Unfortunately, what they discover are often the very behaviors that drive humans crazy.

Dogs are thinkers, and it's a shame to waste their minds. Finding things for your dog to do that help to promote good brain health will not only keep your dog's mind active and healthy but will also help tire him out. Using food carrier toys, such as Kongs, to feed your dog his meals so that he has to work for his food, or puzzles where food is hidden in compartments, will result in a more emotionally satisfied dog.

Something as simple as tossing your dog's food in the yard, or putting it in a sealed cardboard box, can provide fun that will satisfy your dog's innate need to scavenge and hunt for food. After all, just because people provide pet dogs with food every day doesn't take away the dogs' natural foraging nature.

Physical exercise

The amount of physical exercise that is suggested for dogs ranges. While it's often thought that physically exhausting dogs is one way to slow them down, moderate exercise might be best. Research points to the fact that, at least in mice, too much exercise can reduce the animals' ability to learn. Since you need a thinking dog to teach calmness, this is something to consider.

It is important to find the right balance for both the mental and the physical exercise needs of dogs. If you feel as if you are wearing yourself out trying to meet your dog's exercise needs, think about slowing down. Adjusting intense physical exercise to more of a conditioning and maintenance level is a way to start finding balance. A good rule of thumb is 15–20 minutes of structured play two times per day. Be sure to choose structured play rather than mindless play, like fetching a ball over and over. Examples of structured play include earning ball-playing time, hunting for food or food-carriers in the house or yard, and a variety of K9 Nose Work games. Brisk walking/light jogging supplemented by mental exercise, such as training or the use of food carrier toys/puzzles, is another good combination.

Other thoughts about your dog's exercise needs:

- Be alert to the possibility that you might be training your dog to become more out of control if every time he acts bored and becomes annoying or destructive you try to get him more exercise. It doesn't take long for a dog to figure out that his annoying behavior results in fun activities and attention from you! With that in mind, try to stay ahead of your dog's needs by giving him physical and mental challenges before he acts out.
- Guard against the risks associated with taking a dog for infrequent runs, playing an intermittent game of fetch, visiting a dog park only occasionally, or injuring a dog that is young and still developing bone and muscle. These infrequent but high-energy activities

Chapter 7 – Solving Problems

all have the potential to stress your dog's body. Stay within a dog's normal limits or begin a more rigorous exercise program that slowly builds endurance and muscle, rather than opting for exercise that might add to the overall problem if your dog is fatigued and using muscles only occasionally. Think about how sore you would be if you tried to run a mile and had not done so for years!

- Dogs that are engaged in high-level physical activities every time they leave the house often miss just enjoying "smelling [the pee on] the roses." It's a sad waste of dogs' sensitive snouts if they never get to enjoy exploring the world with their noses because they are constantly moving.

Rest and sleep

Like kids, when dogs don't get the recovery time their bodies need, they may be more cranky, more irrational, and not as cognitively alert as they need to be for working through impulse issues. In fact, not getting enough downtime might create some of problems in the first place. According to the book *Stress in Dogs* by Martina Scholz & Clarissa von Reinhardt, the most well-behaved dogs sleep or rest 17 or more hours per day. If your dog is not getting enough of both sleep and rest, consider finding more ways to help your dog recuperate his body daily.

Giving your dog things to chew that last for a long time, such as pressed rawhides (get really big ones), raw marrow or soup bones, bully sticks, and stuffed Kongs. Be sure to supervise a dog that is chewing, at least until you know your dog's chewing style.

Diet

Excessive barking, mood swings, restless sleep, compulsive disorders, reactivity, aggression, hyperactivity, and biting can all be symptoms of a poor diet. Along with engaging in training sessions geared toward calming and relaxing your dog, consider your dog's diet. If your dog's unwanted behaviors have an underlying diet-related reason, training your dog to relax may be met with only limited success.

To avoid this type of roadblock, take time to do your homework about your dog's food. If you are feeding a commercial diet, look for a diet without grains (corn, wheat, and soy, specifically) where the first 2 to 3 ingredients are meat products. Also consider enhancing that diet with fresh food, such as meat and vegetables.

Supplements

There are several supplements that have been shown to improve brain health, but always check with your veterinarian before adding a supplement to your dog's diet. Omega 3 fatty acids, like those found in fish oil, are known to improve brain health with the side benefit of a glossy coat. When comparing supplements, look for higher concentrations of EPA and DHA to maximize the effects.

L-theanine is a supplement that increases the body's gamma amino butyric acid (GABA) levels and has been shown to have calming properties.

Using probiotics daily can also help dogs relax and calm. It takes some research to find products with several strains of active ingredients and a delivery system that can survive the stomach acids. Your veterinarian can probably recommend products that he or she is familiar with.

Finally, there are many homeopathy, herbs, and flower-essence products that people swear by. Talking with someone who is knowledgeable about herbal supplements and homeopathy is essential before changing your dog's diet, since supplements in this category can give side effects that must be fully understood.

Management

Management is simply preventing your dog from practicing unwanted behaviors as much as humanly possible. Each time your dog has the opportunity to behave (positively or negatively), he is not only getting better at that behavior, but he is being reinforced for it.

Management is about prevention, so if your dog surfs the counters, restrict access to the counter when you are unable to supervise, and keep things picked up so your dog can't self-reinforce by stealing things from the counters. Good management tools can include baby gates, crates, exercise pens, closing doors, keeping the garbage can closed, picking up laundry, and more. Managing your dog is not teaching your dog to relax, of course, but merely preventing him from getting better at the unwanted behavior.

Chapter 7 – Solving Problems

Time

Successful training plans require a commitment from you and can be approached in several ways. You can commit a concentrated effort to working with your dog, or you can drag out the training plan for much longer than is needed.

Dragging out the plan has flaws that point directly to failure for many households with dogs in need of calming. It's like potty training children. When you drag it out, that translates to more dirty diapers to take care of over that period of time. Instead, you could be done in just a few weeks and use the extra time for more pleasant activities.

Everyone has a different lifestyle and routine, of course. Finding 5–10 minutes for training once or twice a day will get you there eventually, but if you can block off 15–20 minutes two or three times a day, you will be on your way to a more relaxed dog in a much shorter time period.

Training

Teaching your dog how to self-calm and how to focus on you are two of the fastest ways to help your dog learn how to settle down. Automatic eye contact is a very rewarding behavior to teach your dog, and it can become a way for your dog to "ask permission" when he wants something. When dogs have direction and skills that help them get what they want, they are much calmer overall.

1. Set aside some training time. Each time your dog looks at your eyes, mark that behavior with a word or a clicker. Mark the second your dog looks at your eyes, even if it's just a flicker to begin with, and then give your dog a high-value food reward.

2. Turn away from your dog and wait for him to move to your front (most dogs do this pretty quickly when there are good treats involved). Wait for your dog to look up at you again; mark and reward again. Do this 15–30 times, and then say, "all done," and put the treats away.

3. Come back later and repeat the exercise until you can see that your dog is really starting to make solid eye contact, hoping you will mark him again and give him his reinforcement. Once your dog has

the hang of it, wait just a little longer before you mark so that you begin to build a little duration into the eye contact. Build duration in tiny increments, such as one second, then two. Bounce around in training duration, sometimes making it easier rather than always making it harder for your dog.

4. Once your dog is good at making eye contact, practice in different places around the home so that your dog learns that making eye contact is something he can do anywhere to get what he wants.

5. When your dog is checking in reliably, start to use eye contact for life rewards. If it's time for a Kong, wait for eye contact first. Mark the eye contact and then put down the Kong. If your dog wants to go outside, try the same thing—the door opens when you get eye contact. If your dog wants to play with a toy, wait for eye contact before engaging in play, and so on.

If your dog is really exuberant when you begin this exercise and jumps on you to get the treat, use lower-value rewards such as regular dry dog food, and/or stop training for a few minutes until he is calmer. If you keep up this training for a few weeks, your dog will have a nice skill that he can choose to use. Your dog will also be more calm and relaxed overall.

Note that food rewards should be tiny, about the size of a pea, and easy to swallow rather than something the dog has to chew a lot. Pieces of hot dogs, cheese, and chicken are at the top of the list for most dogs. Be sure to adjust your dog's daily food allotment to account for these treats to prevent extra weight gain.

Another trained other behavior that can lower your dog's arousal levels is Relax on a Mat. (For tips on starting mat training, see "Happy Together: How to Train Successfully in a Multi-Dog Household," by Irith Bloom, p. 163.) The exercise allows the dog to set criteria for each step toward the goal behavior of relaxing his body. This control helps dogs make good choices, in contrast to just being told what to do all the time. Dogs that learn they have choices are calmer, more relaxed dogs overall—just as when people have choices. When they are not sure what to do, this simple exercise helps dogs choose calmness and then, eventually, default to a relaxed down position rather than spiraling up.

Chapter 7 – Solving Problems

Ahh—relax and take a bow!

Providing your dog with skills that promote relaxation, putting in the training time, and offering your dog a balance of mental and physical exercise results in not only a more relaxed, calmer dog, but in a solid relationship with your dog. A healthier and stronger relationship with your dog is just one of many extra benefits of helping your dog discover the "calm zone."

Separation Anxiety: When Alone Time Makes Your Puppy Panic

by Terrie Hayward

Have you heard pet owners say, "my neighbors tell me that my dog barks the whole day while I'm at work," or "my dog tore up the pillows and curtains," or "my dog hates the crate and broke a tooth trying to escape?" These statements often reveal more than a "bored" or a "stubborn" dog and can provide insight into the behavior challenges of separation anxiety.

What is separation anxiety?

Canine separation anxiety is a clinical diagnosis made by a veterinarian. It is defined as the emotional challenge a dog faces when he is unable to be left alone due to an overly strong attachment to one or more individuals.

Separation anxiety can present in a variety of ways. Dogs may appear anxious or depressed prior to being left alone and/or when certain pre-departure cues signify that a departure is imminent. Common symptoms of separation anxiety may include vocalization (howling, whining, barking), self-injurious behavior (exaggerated licking, biting, or chewing of fur or other body parts), shaking or trembling, yawning, pacing, inappropriate elimination in the house, destructiveness and damage, or anorexia (when the dog is unable to eat while alone, even when presented with favorite treats).

The dog with separation anxiety is not intentionally behaving badly, nor does he understand that he has done something wrong. These dogs are in a state of panic and are not thinking rationally to consider the possibility of self-injury or potential problems with attempting an escape, and so on.

How to tell if it is separation anxiety

The first step in managing and resolving separation anxiety is to rule out any other possibilities. Make sure that the dog is not eliminating (going to the bathroom) inside due to medical reasons, other anxiety issues, or housetraining problems. (Once it has been determined that there is not a medical condition, it is still important to work together with the dog's veterinarian,

Chapter 7 – Solving Problems

since a collaborative, team approach is best.) Remove from the equation barking and other behaviors that occur while you are present, since these are not likely related to separation anxiety.

To start, observe and note when the behaviors are occurring. Does the dog exhibit them only when he is alone (even in another part of the home) and separated from his people? With separation anxiety, typically the anxious behavior starts within 30 minutes of the dog being left in the house by himself. Keeping a journal documenting when the different behaviors occur can help ascertain a pattern. Tracking the time, type, and severity of the behavior will aid in determining a starting point for the training. Also worth noting are the amount of time spent alone prior to an absence, the amount of exercise the dog receives, and the adherence to a regular routine.

Careful observation and interpretation of body language is critical. Stress in canines can manifest in a variety of ways. Dogs may present a "whale eye," where the dog looks "sideways," showing an extreme amount of the white of the eye. A dog might have a closed, pulled-back, mouth posture where lips are retracted at the corners. Lip-licking, where the dog flicks the tongue in and out outside of the context of eating, is also a stress indicator. Yawning in an exaggerated fashion that is not due to exhaustion, or excessive panting when the dog is not overheated can be indicative of stress, too.

Considering the overall body posture is important as well. A stiff, hunched, or cowed position, or one in which the dog's fur on his back or back of his neck is raised, may indicate anxiety. Dogs may also salivate excessively, escape/attempt to escape, and/or uncharacteristically urinate or defecate indoors.

Only a veterinarian can make the clinical diagnosis of separation anxiety. While there are many different labels for the behavioral problems of dogs that are unable to be left alone, separation anxiety refers specifically to the situation where the dog has become hyper-attached to one or more persons, and cannot be apart from them. Help with a behavior-based problem like separation anxiety may require referral to a veterinary behaviorist. At times, medications that lower anxiety, in combination with a behavioral-modification protocol, can yield great benefits.

What causes separation anxiety?

Family members often ask if it was something they did that caused the dog's separation anxiety. Separation anxiety does not have a definitive cause. It may be the result of environmental changes such as rehoming a dog or the family moving to a new house. It could also be due to an alteration within the home, change in daily routine (the amount of time that the primary people are absent), or a change in the family structure (new family member or a family member leaves). Sometimes it is difficult to pinpoint at which point exactly the dog began to suffer from separation anxiety.

Common misconceptions about addressing separation anxiety

Separation anxiety can be challenging from a financial, emotional, and logistical perspective. It affects every aspect of the family's lifestyle. People are desperate for solutions. Working toward resolution with separation anxiety, the goal is to look at the underlying anxiety so that the dog can eventually feel comfortable being alone. This is accomplished through a slow process of gradually desensitizing absences, until minute spans of time add up to a period where the dog is not anxious about time spent alone.

Unfortunately, there are many well-intentioned, but outdated and/or ineffective— and even harmful—"solutions" readily available. While Kongs and other food puzzles are wonderful tools, with separation anxiety you need to use a protocol of desensitization to teach the dog to be comfortable being alone, not just eating alone. Using food puzzles like Kongs teaches dogs to eat alone; it does not help them be relaxed when they are by themselves. Problems commence when the food is finished and the person is not present.

Crate training, too, is a fantastic resource in positive training. However, working on separation anxiety is frequently an exception. Dogs that suffer from separation anxiety often have accompanying confinement issues.

Other stress-relieving anecdotal suggestions include using lavender oils or playing television or music while humans are absent, or offering the dog previously worn clothing, and/or adding a second dog. While these ideas may not cause further harm, by themselves they generally do not do much to help. Again, dogs are not displaying the symptoms of separation anxiety due to boredom or lack of exercise, but because they are experiencing panic.

Another common misconception is that a dog will "just get over it." A canine panic disorder is much like a person's fear of spiders. That fearful human will not wake up one day and feel less afraid or anxious about spiders.

An equally ineffective and potentially detrimental technique is called flooding. In this scenario, the dog is exposed to the scary stimulus without the opportunity to escape. This exercise does nothing to weaken the fear component.

Action plan, part 1: The contract

Resolving separation anxiety cases can be broken down into three components. The first part of the solution involves making a "contract" with the dog. You will (metaphorically) "shake" on the deal that you will not leave your dog alone for a longer period of time than he is comfortable. The dog's part of the contract entails not barking, soiling, escaping, or destroying things.

In this figurative contract with the dog experiencing separation anxiety, you make a promise and a commitment to never leave the dog alone for longer than he can handle. This means that you commit 100% to postponing absences while working on the resolution, suspending all absences except for daily protocol practices. Even if unexpected situations or opportunities arise, you agree to figure out a way to ensure that the dog is not left alone past an interval he can handle.

While suspending absences may seem extreme or impossible, there are creative solutions that can allow you to meet this requirement successfully. Some ideas include contacting friends and family members to dog-sit, using doggy daycare, engaging in pet-care exchanges, hiring trainers, contacting veterinary offices about uncrated boarding options, hiring a dog walker, and contacting students or elderly folks who can provide some coverage.

The length of time that you have worked up to with the protocol determines the duration of appropriate alone time. This time component is critical because, along with the desensitization process, you are working to build the dog's trust.

For example, let's say you have gone to the post office and are due back in half an hour. At this point in your protocol you have reached the threshold where you can leave your dog alone for 30 minutes. What if at the post office you run into a friend who asks you to have lunch? You know that going for lunch with a friend will keep you away from home for longer than the total 30 minutes that the dog is currently comfortable with. But maybe you figure that it won't be too much of a problem. Back at home, at 30 minutes the dog is okay. At the 40-minute mark, the dog is beginning to panic a bit. At 45 minutes, the dog begins to pace, bark, and whine, and at the 1-hour mark the dog is in full-blown panic mode.

In addition to upsetting the dog, the bigger issue is that now the 30 minutes of calm that you painstakingly achieved is lost. The dog no longer believes that 30 minutes is a safe absence time because, although you had an "agreement" that he could be alone and relaxed for 30 minutes, you didn't return on time and, thus, broke the contract. In the dog's mind, your departure duration was much longer and you can no longer be trusted to leave at all. In effect, you have reverted back to the beginning and to the second-by-second absences that you need to build from the start.

Action plan, part 2: The starting point

The second part of the action plan requires you to evaluate the point where you can begin training for departure lengths. This starting point is determined by figuring out exactly how long the dog is presently comfortable being left on his own. Each dog's starting point will be different and requires an initial assessment. To figure out just where to start, watch the dog remotely using a webcam or other camera. This absence may be very brief, since you are not looking to push the dog over threshold, but only to discern exactly how quickly the dog becomes visibly uncomfortable. This measurement lets you determine where to begin. For some dogs, this may mean leaving the house for a minute. For other pups, discomfort and anxious behavior may start with the person standing up and walking to the door of the room where the dog and person have been together.

Action plan, part 3: Progress

The third part of the plan involves using a protocol of systematic desensitization to help the dog feel comfortable alone. The desensitization work is done in small, slow increments with the goal of longer relaxed absences. Create a daily plan that involves steps that increase criteria incrementally.

These tiny and varied increases allow the dog to remain below threshold. But, they slowly increase the length of alone time ever so slightly until the dog is comfortable.

The daily plan includes a number of repetitions that work toward desensitizing the dog to these gradually longer absences. Moving to the next level will be determined by the dog's body language and responses. Careful documentation of the daily plans and observable responses from the dog is important to developing systemic improvement.

In the beginning, even the person rising from a seated position may make the dog anticipate an absence and start to panic. In this situation, it might take days or weeks of slowly desensitizing to the person standing up and sitting back down, with intervals of standing or moving in place for seconds. (Yes, this approach is as exciting as watching grass grow or paint dry.)

Break down steps into tiny incremental increases; at first, you may be dealing in seconds. Possibly after days or a week, you can move to minutes. The initial steps could look something like:

- stand up
- take a step toward the door
- go back and sit down
- stand up
- take three steps toward the door
- go back and sit down
- stand up
- walk to the door
- go back and sit down

With these steps, you are helping to change the dog's response from "panic" to "calm" by repeating the same and similar low-level exercises over and over—until the dog decides that these first steps don't make him feel uncomfortable. You'll see the dog's demeanor become relaxed as he no longer needs to be on alert constantly, fearing that an absence may occur at any time.

How long does rehabilitation take?

Pet owners want to know exactly how long the rehabilitation process will take, or whether the severity of the separation anxiety correlates to the length of time until resolution. The answer to both questions is that it depends on several factors. Each dog and each situation is unique. Remember, at the start of the plan, some dogs might be able to handle the caregiver opening and/or going out the door for seconds or minutes right away. Other dogs might need to work up to that point. The individual dog will determine each starting spot. However, the severity of the symptoms (destructiveness, vocalization, and so on) does not always determine the speed of resolution.

While each case is different and individual animals react uniquely to the resolution protocols, the keys are repetition over time and a consistent, measured approach. Repetitions are a series of steps that last approximately 30 minutes and are conducted 5 to 6 days per week without exception. These steps should each have a 30-to-90-second break between them, randomly changing each break time to avoid a pattern. Adapt the steps slightly and repeat them over and over until the dog begins to feel "safe" and demonstrates that by his body language. Thus, persistence is an essential element.

Ready for departure

Helping your dog overcome separation anxiety requires patience and perseverance. The process is not difficult, but it is slow and it may be frustrating. Building trust, careful repetitions, and slow desensitization are the keys to permanent behavioral change. With a plan, over time, and working through the inevitable plateaus and regressions, your dog will begin to feel more confident for longer stretches of time until appreciable absences begin and "real-life" errands can take place.

8

Dealing with Anxious, Fearful, Reactive, or Aggressive Dogs

There is nothing more distressing for a pet parent than to deal with aggression issues in their dog. Aggression is a natural way for dogs to cope with stress, fear, nervousness, frustration, illness, or other issues. But just because it's natural doesn't mean we have to live with it. Each of the articles in this chapter explores the different causes and possible solutions to different types of aggression or fear. It is important to prevent aggressive or fearful reactions from ever occurring if possible, so many of these articles would be useful even if you have yet to experience these behaviors in your dog.

Aggressive Dogs: Nature or Nurture? 270
by Aidan Bindoff

The Four "Fs" of Fear 273
by Laura VanArendonk Baugh

Ben: An Aggressive Dog Case Study 277
by Emma Parsons

Muzzles—Not Just for Aggression Anymore! 282
by Nan Arthur

How to Help Your Fearful Dog: Become the Crazy Dog Lady 291
by Casey Lomonaco

Reducing Leash Reactivity: The Engage-Disengage Game 298
by Alice Tong

Erasing Fear: A Lesson (or Two) on Cues and Shaping 302
by Clint Matthews

How to Prevent Resource-Guarding in a Multiple-dog Household .. 311
by Hannah Branigan

The Power of Ongoing Learning 315
by Ken Ramirez

Aggressive Dogs: Nature or Nurture?
by Aidan Bindoff

"Aggressive dogs aren't born, they're raised that way."

How many times have you heard this statement? Have you ever wondered how much truth there is to it? Owners of reactive or aggressive dogs frequently say, "I've had other dogs before and none of them have been like this, so I don't know where I went wrong!"

I meet once a week with a couple of friends who have "dog-aggressive dogs." We work on behaviors like recalls and loose-leash walking with other dogs around. Each of us has two dogs and, without exception, just one of the dogs is reactive to other dogs while the other is completely sociable with other dogs. Why is this?

If owners had a deficiency in their ability to raise a pup, surely the deficiency would be manifest in other dogs that they owned? Is the aggressive behavior a problem with the reactive dog's temperament, the owner's raising and training of the dog, or a bit of both?

Aggressive behavior *is* reinforced

Let's begin by stating an important fact: aggressive behavior is operant behavior. Yes, yes, I know that aggression is usually a symptom of fear, anxiety, or stress (and, occasionally, instinct), and that most experts recommend classical conditioning to treat the cause of aggression. But the fact remains that the actual aggressive behavior is operant. It is the product of reinforcement.

An example is the dog that, uncomfortable around other dogs, barks out of fear. This may be unconditioned behavior the first time, but if it works and the other dog keeps his distance or leaves, it may serve to reinforce the behavior of barking. Barking then becomes operant behavior. The next time the fearful dog sees another dog, he has a behavior that has worked in the past to keep the other dog away. So, he repeats it.

The dog's owner is likely to be lambasted by well-meaning folk for not socializing a dog adequately, or for not being "alpha," or for not earning the

Chapter 8 – Anxious, Fearful, Reactive, or Aggressive Dogs

dog's trust—or it may even be implied that the owner leads by a fearful or aggressive example.

Having followed the socialization prescription to the letter with one of my own dogs—a reactive dog—I would bet money that it is the *quality* of adequate socialization that inoculates the young dog against developing fear-based aggression, not the *quantity* of socialization. Socialization experiences that are not beneficial are just as likely to cause fear-based aggression as too few socialization experiences.

So, aggression is operant behavior, since every socialization experience that reinforces aggression maintains or increases it. That said, dog owners must provide frequent and varied socialization experiences so that the dog learns that other dogs and other people, new places, new sounds, and new objects are not something to be feared. This level of exposure is what I mean by "adequate"—enough to reinforce appropriate behaviors and have those behaviors generalize to new and varied experiences.

Certainly it is possible for a dog's owner to reinforce fearful or aggressive behaviors in a dog. This reinforcement can come from attempts at soothing, from removing the dog from stressful situations immediately after he has displayed aggressive behavior, from putting the dog into situations where the dog is likely to display reactive behavior in order to cope, or from botched attempts to reprimand aggressive behavior.

Set up for success—and get help when needed

The Golden Rule in dog training is to set the dog up for success, then reinforce that success. Experienced dog owners may pick up the signs of fear or anxiety early enough to take decisive and beneficial action and then reinforce appropriate behaviors. Less experienced dog owners should seek help from a competent instructor as soon as they get a pup, or, if not then, at the first sign of trouble—before accidentally worsening the aggressive or fearful behavior.

Genetics matter

A genetic predisposition toward fearful or aggressive behavior can make it difficult for even experienced dog owners to avoid having fearful or aggressive behaviors reinforced in a dog. Some dogs will never be completely comfortable around whatever their aggression target is, even after being trained so that they don't display aggressive behavior any more. The safety of the aggression target is never assured. I trained one of my dogs not to attack people on bikes under virtually any circumstance, at any speed, even off leash. Yet one day, while I was tying my shoelace, she lunged at a rider as he passed. I hadn't trained for that! Hope that the training will generalize, but even if it does, do not expect 100% reliability.

Some dogs, and some breeds in particular, are more likely to fight than flee when faced with a stressful situation. It is no coincidence that my golden retriever runs from a stressful situation while my German shepherd will stay and face the threat head-on. Both responses are entirely normal for the breeds (to a degree). It would be difficult to train a police dog who ran away when faced with threat. That doesn't mean that all phenotypically ideal German shepherds will be aggressive, but it may mean that extra care is required to ensure that behaviors appropriate to the situation are reinforced and trained to fluency.

Separating interconnections is difficult

Dog owners certainly can and do make mistakes that contribute to a dog's aggression or reactivity, but it wouldn't be fair to place the blame solely on a dog's owner. There are many factors and events in a dog's life that contribute to aggressive or reactive behavior. If we could go back in time and erase all the owner's mistakes, in many cases the dog would still learn to use aggressive or reactive behaviors. The good news is that behavior is changeable. We can shape it one click at a time.

Chapter 8 – Anxious, Fearful, Reactive, or Aggressive Dogs

The Four "Fs" of Fear
by Laura VanArendonk Baugh

It's autumn—the season of shorter nights, crackling leaves, the hunter's moon, and, of course, Halloween. Costumed creatures come to your door and scary monsters parade across your television screen. Maybe your pulse will quicken as you get reacquainted with Vincent Price, Christopher Lee, and Boris Karloff, and maybe your hands will get sweaty. *And maybe you'll see behavior in action.*

Yes, a room full of people watching a horror film can be a great example of an important behavioral concept. Let's talk about the Four Fs, specifically about the third F.

The four Fs

Ted Turner (the behavior expert, not the film mogul) created a series of videos that I stumbled upon early in my clicker training education. In one, he talked about the possible responses to stress or threat, responses that he summarized as the Four Fs:

1. fight
2. flight
3. fool around
4. …fornicate (my own paraphrase)

When considering stress behaviors, we often think of the first two, but not of the latter two (although #4 seems fairly *de rigueur* in bad romance novels and many film genres). But, fight and flight are probably the final stages in stress reaction, chosen when other coping mechanisms are not perceived to be working. (There's a potential fifth F, too—"freeze," or do nothing and just hope for the best. But we're talking here about *active* responses.)

We'll leave #4 for another time. But #3 happens far more often than many realize. If stress is addressed at that stage, it can prevent an escalation to #1 or #2.

Fooling around

"Fooling around" can appear frequently as a displacement behavior, out of place and sometimes inappropriate. Have you ever been at a funeral or visitation when someone made a joke and everyone laughed too quickly, or more than the joke seemed to deserve? That is classic stress relief by "fooling around." A bit of humor, appropriate or not, can be a coping mechanism to relieve stress. Storytellers know this, which is why many dramatic films also include "comic relief."

With dogs, fooling around often presents as intense play, such as jumping up on a person, play bows, very pushy greetings, or any over-the-top behavior. Some dogs that can't stop bothering visitors with a ball or tug toy really just want to play, but some are engaging in a coping mechanism.

Is the third F still unclear? Like many concepts, this is one that can be easier to perceive first in the human species and then look for corollary behavior in another species. Here are some examples of people feeling fear but reacting in a way that looks quite different.

Example: Trapped

During my college years, a friend and I were once in a smallish room on an upper dorm floor. A guy we didn't know came in, looking for someone. He didn't leave, and while he kept his eyes on us he positioned himself firmly and deliberately in the room's single narrow entry. He wasn't a threat when he entered and asked after his friend, but when he blocked the exit and fixated, he became a threat. When he began to flex and posture over our couch, he started to scare us. It's possible this guy was simply showing off his musculature to impress the girls, but he had quite the opposite effect. We knew we didn't stand a chance if he decided to stop us from getting out; we were afraid, not attracted. In matters of fear, perception always matters more than intent.

I was afraid, and so I got angry. I didn't do much to act on the anger though, because I was afraid of triggering a response in our visitor. But I was ready to move to fear-aggression, or fight, when my freeze was no longer working.

Chapter 8 – Anxious, Fearful, Reactive, or Aggressive Dogs

My friend was equally afraid. I remember being angry with her as well because she kept giggling. When I look back, I think the guy might have interpreted the giggling as some sort of flirting, and so he kept escalating his flexing and posturing and eye contact. But it wasn't flirting, it was her fear.

Eventually the guy got frustrated, snapped some insults at us, and left. Today I see this episode as not just a creepy incident from my past, but a set of clear behavior cases:

- lack of predictability and control resulted in a perception of threat (for my friend and me)
- frustration produced aggression (in the guy, when we didn't rise to the flirtation level he wanted)
- fear was expressed in aggression (by me)
- fear was expressed in humorous displacement behavior (by my friend)

Afterward, my friend and I never spoke of the incident, and I never told her I was mad at her for laughing in what felt like a serious situation. I shouldn't have been angry with her, though, because it wasn't really a choice for her. She was having a perfectly normal stress reaction. There's a reason we call it nervous laughter.

Example: Horror film behavior lab

A group of us were invited to watch what we were warned was a suspenseful horror film. A good story doesn't need gore, which, in my opinion, just detracts. I will confess to being a total wimp before a good suspenseful horror flick, though. The title of this particular movie isn't important; if you would not find it particularly scary, that does not discount the effect on those who did.

We were perhaps 20 people in a little theater space, and for the first third of the film we were quiet—mostly. There were some jumps and screams at the first big scare. As the movie's tension rose, though, the room became less quiet. People began to shuffle in their seats (physical displacement behaviors) and comment aloud on the film. As the plot entered the third act and the stakes were highest for our imperiled protagonist, people began to make jokes and laugh at film events that weren't funny. Generally, those who made the most jokes were those who jumped the highest and screamed the loudest. They were fooling around. The third F.

Dogs don't tend to watch many horror films, or mine at least seem unimpressed by them, so the movie "fear-fun" might be harder to picture with dogs. But you've probably already seen it. How about when a conflicted dog moves forward toward and backward from a stranger, alternately barking and play-bowing? That's fear-fun. Puppies, especially, rely on this kind of response to stress, because they know inherently that flight and fight are not valid options for them yet. Puppies are slow and weak, so they need to appease a threat or wiggle out: "I'm just a cute li'l puppy that wants to play!"

In my own home, I see fear-fun when a particularly big storm is rolling in and Laev begins to jump up on me and throw bows in my direction. It's an early expression of what might become more serious fear if I do not intervene with melatonin or a chew to help her relax.

Fear-fun can also be frantic or desperate play behavior, when a dog engages in manic play or invitations. That over-the-top dog that seems basically friendly under all the ridiculously pushy behavior? He might be merely untrained, or he might be coping with stress in the only way he knows how. It's easy to assume a dog is just being rude or is over-excited (and that might be the case), but sometimes it can be a desperate-to-fool-around response to fear or stress.

Fear responses vary in both humans and dogs. The "fooling around" response is common to both and, when acknowledged and addressed responsibly, can eliminate the need for more intense reactions. With dogs, be aware of *any* reaction to stress, expected or not, so that the source of the stress can be eliminated for your pet. In other words, keep an eye out for all of the possible Fs!

Chapter 8 – Anxious, Fearful, Reactive, or Aggressive Dogs

Ben: An Aggressive Dog Case Study
by Emma Parsons

What I am going to present to you is my own case study about my golden retriever, Benjamin. It was through Ben that I met Karen Pryor and, thus, found some of the most effective ways to deal with aggression and fear-based behavior in dogs.

I purchased Ben from a breeder at seven weeks of age with the intent of showing him in competition obedience. At the age of five months, we started working with a wonderful obedience competition coach by the name of Patty Ruzzo, who employed purely operant conditioning training techniques. Ben blossomed under her tutelage.

At the age of 7 months, I started to notice that Ben occasionally growled at other dogs. He barked at them and hastily pulled me toward them. I was not sure of his intent. Frightened by this behavior, I sought help from an aggression expert in my area. I knew that physical corrections might be used to deal with Ben's reactivity, however, I had no idea of the trauma that Ben and I were about to experience.

As Ben and I walked toward the trainer, Ben barked and started pulling me toward the instructor's dog. The instructor proceeded to put his dog into the down position, walked over to Ben as he quieted, and hung him severely on his prong collar. The first time he lifted Ben off of the ground, Ben bared his teeth at him. This was met with an even harder correction. The second time Ben was hung, he finally submitted. The instructor lowered Ben to the ground, at which point, Ben urinated and defecated all over himself. At the end of the session, the instructor handed me back my leash and said, "This is what you need to do the next time Ben shows any aggressive cues to another dog." I knew this was not going to be possible. Not only was I physically unable to lift Ben as this man had done, but I was horrified by the severity of the corrections given. I would rather euthanize Ben than treat him in such an abusive manner.

I didn't realize how much damage the instructor had done until about a week later, when I took Ben to an obedience club. In the parking lot, at the mere sight of another dog, Ben flew into a rage. He lunged, bared his teeth, and screamed, as globs and globs of saliva started dripping from both sides of his mouth. Again, I was horrified. I tried to keep him in the environment to see how long the reaction would last, but once he started vomiting, I knew we had to leave. Now what could I do? The side effects from Ben's punishment were much more traumatic than the original behavior we started with. Though I contemplated whether or not this trainer could help us, in my ignorance, I never suspected that he could cause the behavior to worsen.

Ben had no threshold level. He would aggress at a dog two feet away as well as twenty feet away. He would react not only to the physical presence of dogs in the environment but also to things like dogs on TV, car doors opening, or the jingle of car keys. Desperately, I began to search for seminars or conferences that were offered on helping to curb aggression in dogs. This is how I met Karen Pryor.

I met Karen in Hawaii while she was giving a talk for the National Association of Dog Obedience Instructors, of which I had just become a member. During lunch, I sheepishly went up to her and asked her how to treat my dog-aggressive golden retriever. Her answer, "Start clicking somewhere in the middle of the aggressive cues. Spaces will open up." When I asked where I should click, since these cues come fast and furious, she asked, *"He does breathe doesn't he?* Watch his breath. Click as he's taking a breath."

To work on this problem, Ben and I were invited to attend a class that Karen was teaching in our area. Participation was by closed invitation only. Each student had a particular project that they were working on: some worked with autistic children (learning techniques through their dogs), some worked with obedience and agility, Ben and I worked on aggression. This class originally was going to stay together for 9 weeks; however, we enjoyed the class so much that we decided to stay together for nine months! Karen has written extensively about this class in the American Kennel Club's magazine *The Gazette*.

Chapter 8 – Anxious, Fearful, Reactive, or Aggressive Dogs

The rehabilitation process

These were the four steps of Ben's rehabilitation process. I also use these steps when I am treating a client's dog, depending on where he might fall on the "reactive" continuum.

1. **Effective home management:** Teach the dog to allow the humans in the household to make the right decisions for him. If it is not happening in the home, it certainly is not going to happen in the real world, especially if the dog considers it a "dangerous" environment. Foundation behaviors are taught via clicker training, so that after the dog learns to think in the environment, he might perform the desired behaviors. Foundation behaviors include: sit, down, heel, stay, targeting, holding an object, kennel up on audible cue, come and sit front, leave it, come when called, and get behind.

2. **Create a "thinking" dog:** I am convinced that when Ben saw another dog, he reacted involuntarily. Once in this cycle, he could not stop, even when my husband picked him up off of a dog and brought him into another room. Ben still kept reacting as if nothing had changed. In order for a dog to look at his owner for direction, he needs to be able to make that deliberate decision to do so. He needs to be able to think in that environment.

3. **Insert incompatible behaviors:** Use differential reinforcement of incompatible behaviors. What do you want your dog to do instead of aggressing at other dogs? Teach him what to do rather than teach him what not to do. It is only when the dog is a "thinking" dog that he is capable of making deliberate decisions. He can then perform single-cued behaviors that are incompatible with performing the aggressive behavior. "A busy dog has no time to be fearful," Karen says.

4. **Teach more advanced skills:** What are your final goals? With Ben, I just wanted a dog that looked "normal" when I walked him down the street. Some of my clients want their dogs to have "friends." Whatever the case, decide how to take the behavior to the next level via the principles of learning theory.

The process of extinguishing aggressive cues

First, I needed to take the "lunging" behavior out of the aggressive display, so I put Ben on a Gentle Leader head collar. This served the purpose well. Even though Ben did not like the collar, despite many attempts at desensitizing him to it beforehand, it served beautifully as a deterrent when I needed to simply get him into an environment, with even just one other dog.

I began to click and treat Ben at the lowest points of the intensity of the aggressive behavior. This is the differential reinforcement of lower intensity behavior, or DRL. I knew that if I could catch these quieter pieces, it would help to lower the frequency and intensity of the aggressive cues across the board. I tried to shut off the "noise" and focus on his breathing. (Please note that it took Ben about two months to begin eating the treats during these sessions. I clicked, attempted to feed him, and he just let the treats fall to the ground. After the session, I sadly swept them up. Karen had mentioned that Ben would eat when he was ready, but in the meantime, keep clicking. The sound of the click is thought to be calming to the amygdala of the brain.)

As we continued working in this manner, I started to notice that tiny windows of silence started to open up. As these windows became more plentiful, I now had more of a chance to click in the appropriate spots.

After successfully lessening the reactivity, now I could establish a threshold. How far away would Ben have to be to not react to another dog? Determining this distance was my next step.

After establishing the right distance, I could click and feed Ben for the absence of the aggressive cues. I worked in small, successful approximations. Initially, sessions ranged anywhere from 30 seconds to 2 minutes. With success, I worked in three-to-five minute increments and increased exposure from there.

It is here that I started clicking and feeding Ben for looking at and hearing other dogs in the environment. I also clicked and fed him if another dog acted aggressively toward him. The payoff was big if another dog threatened Ben! I wanted Ben to learn how to look at other dogs without provoking an aggressive display.

Chapter 8 – Anxious, Fearful, Reactive, or Aggressive Dogs

The end result is that the presence of the other dog(s) in the environment became the cue, in itself, to look at you. Think about what this means! You no longer need to compete with the heavy distractions in the environment, physically struggling to get your dog's attention. Instead, the distraction of the other dogs in the environment becomes the cue, in itself, to look at you! Now that you have eye contact, you can cue the appropriate incompatible behaviors. Foundation behaviors work beautifully here.

Teaching dog-to-dog interaction

As Ben progressed in his training program, I taught him how to interact with dogs more successfully. For example, I taught him how to target another dog's body on cue. This made every dog he met a "clickable" encounter. It totally changed his attitude about getting close to other dogs.

I also taught him that it was a great thing for other dogs to touch him. He would get clicked and fed for other dogs touching or sniffing him. This was to prepare him for the real world when other owners would allow their dogs to go up to him despite my previous protests.

In summary, clicker training is so effective in treating aggressive cues because it is able to mark the correct behavior so precisely. Sometimes one can't click fast enough! The clicker means the same thing, all the time, no matter who is holding the clicker. It conveys confidence, even if one's hand is sweating in apprehension. Also, as mentioned above, the sound of the click is thought to be calming to the amygdala of the brain. The brain interprets it faster than a spoken word. Lastly, learning is enhanced because you are using classical and operant conditioning principles simultaneously.

Muzzles—Not Just for Aggression Anymore!

by Nan Arthur

For many people, the idea of a muzzle evokes a long-standing association with aggressive dogs. That impression can create feelings of fear and worry when people hear about or witness a dog in a muzzle. There is no denying that when many people see a muzzled dog, they envision the likes of a Hannibal Lecter character (a monster, but in fur)!

But muzzles are not just for aggression anymore. It's high time to dispel those negative mental images. Rather than vilifying muzzles, it's time to appreciate muzzles for all the good things they can do for dogs.

The vet view

One place to begin is with some insight from the veterinary community. Jeannie Brousseau, RVT (Registered Vet Tech) with the Pasadena Humane Society and SPCA, once said, "Muzzles keep a good dog good."

Think about a typical vet visit with your own dog. Is she nervous, worried, anxious, or fearful? Many times dogs displaying those emotions are taken "to the back," where they receive routine care such as vaccines. This is usually done to save you anxiety, in case your dog panics when handled for these procedures, and also to avoid bites. If a dog taken away from the owner shows any signs of biting, the dog is often muzzled—usually on the spot, and sometimes with a quick, but invasive, gauze wrapped around the snout.

If your dog has never worn a muzzle or been made to feel comfortable with one, there is a good chance that having one placed on her face abruptly could cause future handling issues, and more terror, the next time she has to visit the vet. This experience and reaction could easily generalize to not only the vet staff, but to other situations that might feel threatening to your dog when people approach your dog's head or face.

Chapter 8 – Anxious, Fearful, Reactive, or Aggressive Dogs

Start early and reap benefits for routine and emergency care

Being proactive and teaching your dog to love her muzzle before your next vet visit will minimize the handling, and/or the restraint by the vet staff. When you teach your dog to love wearing a muzzle, you can bring your dog's muzzle with you to the vet. Play fun muzzle games with the muzzle, and the end result will be that your dog will not have to be manhandled to get a muzzle on her when she needs to be examined or taken to "the back" for treatments.

If your dog is ever injured or hurt, having her comfortable with a muzzle can prevent a bite to the veterinary staff members trying to help your dog. If your dog bites someone at the vet, even if your dog is in pain, that bite is usually reported to the local Animal Control agency. As a result, in most states your dog will have to be placed in quarantine for approximately 10 days, adding insult to injury.

Keep in mind that if your dog is injured or in pain, placing a muzzle on her before you try to move her or transport her may also prevent a bite to you or to anyone else trying to help your dog get safely to a vet.

Touch can mean treats and trust

Teaching puppies to accept a muzzle is a wonderful way to work on general touching and handling. This training also teaches puppies to keep their mouths, and those sharp little teeth, away from you. Working on muzzle training produces the wonderful association between human hands and treats: "When hands come near my face, good things happen." With this motivation, puppies are quick to focus and learn to get their faces in the muzzle, and not to use your hands for teething.

The more puppies associate wearing a muzzle with a fun game, the quicker handling and touching exercises go overall, making it easy to make contact and reinforce touching other parts of the dogs' faces and bodies. If you have any remedial work to do with your dog in the area of handling, husbandry, or grooming, teaching your dog to wear a muzzle is a terrific way to desensitize common handling around the face and ears before moving on to additional behavior modification for those sensitivities.

It is important to realize that desensitizing to handling and similar experiences takes more time than just teaching your dog to be comfortable wearing a muzzle. The time will be worth it in the long run, since your dog will feel safer. So will you, and others who might need to handle your dog. Take the time to associate the muzzle, and all the handling components necessary to fasten it, with pleasurable experiences. When you reward and reinforce with amazing food, you make the process even more agreeable for your dog.

The positive associations that go along with muzzle training will lead your dog to trust you. When you are more relaxed, your dog will be as well, making any process much easier.

Muzzles for new situations, new friends, and new challenges

The use of a muzzle can be an important tool in behavior modification if a dog is reactive. The muzzle allows you to be safe as you work around other dogs, or around people. Work with an experienced trainer, of course. If something goes wrong or if a boundary is crossed unknowingly, the muzzle will prevent your dog from biting, giving you peace of mind in a training class or similar situation.

Muzzles are also a valuable safety tool to employ when introducing another species to your dog during a desensitization program.

Traveling abroad with your dog is still another reason for teaching your dog to love a muzzle. More and more countries now require dogs of certain types and/or weights to wear muzzles. A ruined vacation might be in your future if you travel with your dog and have not taught her to enjoy wearing a muzzle. France, for instance, requires muzzles for larger dogs.

There are places right here in the United States where muzzles are now required. More and more cities are requiring breeds like pit bulls to wear a muzzle in public. Malden, Massachusetts, and Jefferson City, Missouri, have joined the ranks of cities that require pit bulls to wear muzzles, for example. These rules may not seem fair, but they are better than an outright ban on a breed as in Denver, Colorado, where pit bull and pit-bull-types are outlawed in the city.

Chapter 8 – Anxious, Fearful, Reactive, or Aggressive Dogs

Sports and games

Gaining in popularity is the dog sport of dog racing. Traditionally, this has been a sport for sight hounds, but now it's open to all breeds that love to run. Muzzles are required!

Muzzles can be used as a fun food toy. Use a basket muzzle as a puzzle by letting your dog figure out how to get treats from inside the muzzle, or ask your dog to use her tongue to lick up treats from the hole in the front of a soft, mesh muzzle!

Fitting a muzzle

Before discussing or describing the different types of muzzles, it's important to understand what a well-fitted muzzle looks like. The final fit for your dog should come after you have done basic training. It's not important in the early stages of training that the muzzle fit perfectly, only that your dog learns to love to put her face into it willingly.

When you are ready to size the muzzle, the first rule for a good fit is that the muzzle be snug, but not tight. The muzzle should also allow your dog to open her mouth, but it should prevent her from opening it all the way.

Having several adjustments from which to choose is important. Muzzles for larger dogs may have a strap that travels from the top of the head to the top of the basket to hold it in place; the strap should have its own adjustment.

Most muzzle companies will have guidelines for sizing the correct fit. However, if there is a store or outlet where you can take your friendly dog or puppy to be sized for the best fit, that is even better.

Muzzle choices

The most common muzzles are the basket-types (often known as a Greyhound muzzle) and the soft-mesh muzzles.

Basket muzzles are bulkier, but have advantages over most other muzzles. It's easy to feed dogs through the slots of a basket muzzle, and basket muzzles allow dogs to pant (sweat) and drink. Basket muzzles are made from plastic or metal, and sometimes a combination of both. There are also basket muzzles with combinations of wire and leather, as well as leather-only versions. For general long-term wear, this type of muzzle is the safest, allowing dogs to pant and preventing bites.

Mesh-type muzzles are ideal for quick use, such as at the vet, and are easier to transport due to their lightweight design. They can be folded easily and tossed into a bag or pocket. Since soft mesh muzzles don't allow panting, and because they keep a dog's mouth closed more (making treat delivery more difficult), these muzzles should be considered for short-term use only.

A *softie muzzle* is another option preferred by some trainers. These muzzles offer a comfortable fit, one that also allows dogs to pant. However, some reports have warned about the possibility of dogs being able to bite through the soft sides. In the case of severe aggression, the softie muzzle could defeat the original purpose in using a muzzle.

Another option, while not very effective, is certainly cute. The *quack-duck-billed muzzle* does a wonderful job removing some of the negative associations with muzzles, but has a wide enough opening that a dog could still bite. It might be fun for training a dog to wear a muzzle, though, and it would keep dog owners laughing! Consider the duck-billed muzzle as a transition muzzle while you work toward the real thing.

Avoid using Gentle Leaders or other head halters as substitutes for a muzzle, since they are not muzzles and should not be used in place of one. Head halters may partially close a dog's mouth, but will not prevent bites. Head halters are also reliant on the handler being able to hold the dog's head up with the leash—something that is not always practical with a large or powerful dog or for a person of small stature. Overall, head halters do not provide the same level of control or safety as a muzzle.

Two-step training

Think about muzzle training as a two-step process. The first step is getting your dog comfortable placing her face in the muzzle. The second step is working your dog toward the goal of having the buckle or Velcro fastened.

Step 1: Teach your dog to place face in muzzle
1. Hold the muzzle with the large opening facing your dog and any straps folded back and out of the way.
2. Show your dog the muzzle, and click or mark with a word such as "Yip," or "click." Follow up with a food treat that your dog loves.

Chapter 8 – Anxious, Fearful, Reactive, or Aggressive Dogs

3. Your dog needs only to look at the muzzle to earn the click and reward. However, if your dog is comfortable with new and novel things, you may be able to move closer to your dog as you start. Test it out by clicking quickly a few times and rewarding with treats for just looking at the muzzle. Proceed if you see that it's no big deal for your dog.

4. Move the muzzle slightly closer after you have established that your dog is comfortable viewing the muzzle and then click and treat several times.

5. You are shaping your dog to interact with, and eventually place her nose into, the muzzle, so keep the steps small. Click and reinforce with the treat close to the muzzle to emphasize the association of treats around the muzzle. Ultimately, the treats will be in the muzzle.

6. Dogs that are uncomfortable touching the muzzle on the outside might be more hesitant putting their faces into the muzzle. For a hesitant dog, switch to treats that the dog might lick (squeeze cheese, cream cheese, peanut butter, and so on) and that you can place on the edge of the inside of the muzzle. Allow the dog to lick from the edge. After a few times, begin to place the reinforcement deeper into the muzzle. Progress slowly!

7. Move the muzzle away between each of the up-close trials so that your dog is a little disappointed. Your dog will be excited when you present it again.

8. If you move slowly, take lots of breaks, and use high-value treats that help your dog linger with her nose in the muzzle, you should be able to move to the fastening stage of training pretty quickly.

9. Before you proceed to the fastening component, give the behavior a cue, like "muzzle," or "face."

10. Once the behavior is on cue, practice holding the muzzle at different heights, as well in different areas around the house. Your dog will learn to move to the muzzle from different distances and in different places when asked.

Step 2: Fastening the muzzle
This can be a more difficult process since it requires more invasive handling. The fastening also creates sounds that your dog might not be familiar with near her ears. Again, go slowly. If you think you are going slowly, go even more slowly, especially if your dog has any sound sensitivities!

1. Start with clicking and reinforcing your dog for hearing the sound of the fastener. If you think your dog will be sensitive about the sound, start at a good distance away, fasten the muzzle and then mark and treat just for hearing the sound.
2. Continue to reinforce after the click by placing a treat in the muzzle. Remove the muzzle after the reinforcement is consumed.
3. Be sure to lower the criteria for your dog at this point. She doesn't need to place her face in the muzzle for now (other than to get the treat). Work only on the sound of the fastener.
4. Stay at this level until your dog is comfortable with the sound coming closer and closer to the top of her head. It's not important to fasten the muzzle yet, just work toward having the sound be acceptable near your dog's head. The sound of the fastener can act as the click or marker, leaving you with both hands free to handle the clasp.
5. When you feel that your dog is comfortable with the sound of the fastener at a distance, slowly work toward creating the sound near your dog's ears.
6. Next, run the straps around your dog's head. Keep in mind that at this point it doesn't have to fit correctly. You will be working on the straps coming around and clipping the fastener.
7. Cue your dog with the muzzle cue you have chosen. When she has placed her nose into the muzzle, clip the strap and reinforce your dog through the front of the muzzle.
8. Once you can clip the straps around your dog's head successfully, then progress to the tighter-fitting straps.
9. Well-fitting muzzles will be snug thanks to the straps that go around the top of the head and just behind the ears. When you have

Chapter 8 – Anxious, Fearful, Reactive, or Aggressive Dogs

progressed to having the straps fitted, you are ready to put the pieces together.

10. When you have combined the pieces, the next goal is for your dog to be comfortable wearing the muzzle for longer periods. Offer multiple treats through the front of the muzzle to cement your dog's comfort with the muzzle. When you remove the muzzle, the treats should stop until your dog is wearing it again.

11. Build more duration by bouncing around with your training rather than just making it harder each time. Sometimes give the muzzle cue and mark when your dog puts her face in the muzzle—but don't clip the fastener. Other times, only do the fastener. Other times, put it all together but delay the click for a few seconds.

Continue to build duration by adding just a few seconds at a time before your click, but always add in some fast and easy requests and reinforcement as well.

Muzzles make a difference

It won't be long before your dog will scamper to you to wear her muzzle! Remember that muzzles shouldn't be used only when scary things are about to take place. Use the muzzle as a training tool that is sometimes employed in uncomfortable situations for your dog.

Muzzles are like any other training tool in that they provide opportunities to do fun training with your dog. They can also be considered part of your emergency kit, something that may come in really handy to relax your dog and, possibly, even prevent your dog from biting in stressful situations.

When more muzzles are used as routine training and traveling tools, their appearance will not be as startling. The impressions associated with muzzles will improve and the automatic label or stigma of "aggressive" will fade.

Important reminders:

- Proceed at your dog's pace. In other words, take your time. Rushing past important steps can set you back, and training will then take even more time.
- Use really good, high-value food treats. You want your dog to believe the muzzle is really fun and reinforcing.
- Stay at each step until your dog is successful (5–20 trials) and then move on to the next step. Your dog should look comfortable and ready for another repetition at each level before moving to the next level.
- Working with a basket muzzle allows you to feed your dog through the front easily or to place larger treats into the muzzle for your dog.
- Many people find using a marker word or using the i-Click with a foot easier than trying to manage a clicker, treats, and the muzzle. If you choose to use a clicker, don't click near your dog's face or ears, as that can be an aversive experience. Choose what works best for you and what's comfortable for your dog.
- If your dog has a strong nose targeting behavior to a hand or other object, use that behavior to encourage her to touch the muzzle using your established cue. You might choose to teach the nose target before introducing the muzzle.
- Keep your sessions short and take many breaks. A good rule of thumb is 5–15 minutes, with breaks after 10–15 treats for play, a drink, or to allow your dog to process the lesson.
- The end goal is to have your dog push her face into the muzzle and steady her head as you buckle or fasten the muzzle.

Chapter 8 – Anxious, Fearful, Reactive, or Aggressive Dogs

How to Help Your Fearful Dog: Become the Crazy Dog Lady

by Casey Lomonaco

My two dogs and I were out for a walk one morning, enjoying the fresh air and the exercise. Mokie and Monte walked next to me with their tails wagging happily. They were probably laughing at me as I hummed along with my iPod.

About three blocks away, a dog rounded the corner and began walking toward us. Despite Monte's full-body hackling, despite his rigid and tense body posture, and a deep, low, rumbling growl, I quietly told him what a good boy he was. I began shoving meatballs, liverwurst, and smoked Gouda into his large jaws at a rapid pace, creating as much distance as possible between the approaching dog and the three of us. I continued to feed Monte until the dog was out of sight, at which time the tasty treats disappeared back into the abyss of my faithful treat bag.

I've often thought about having shirts printed with our company logo on the front and the phrase *"I'm not crazy—I'm just training my dog"* on the back.

I bet that many of my neighbors think I'm quite insane. Frequently, I can be seen chasing squirrels with my dogs, yelling "Let's get 'em!" or walking around the neighborhood putting hot dogs in my footprints to set up scent games for the dogs. I pick up every pile of dog poop I see along the way, and practice heeling while skipping, jogging, running, and spinning in circles. Balls and tug toys drip from every pocket, and I can pull a mashed-potatoes-and-gravy-filled food tube, or can of EZCheese, out of thin air!

To any observer, it appears as though most of the things I do are strange, and the rest of the things I do are totally wrong. For example, the instant Monte noticed that other dog on our walk, he began growling. At the very same instant, he had liverwurst shoved into his face.

Positive trainers often say "you get the behaviors you reinforce." So wasn't I reinforcing growling by providing "reinforcers" as that behavior occurred?

Really, why does that crazy woman shove treats into the mouth of, or encourage a tug game with, that "aggressive" Saint Bernard of hers?

There are good answers to these questions!

What scares you the most?

What are you afraid of? Snakes? Spiders? Being approached from behind in a dark alley? Let's assume you're afraid of snakes.

You're reading in the backyard, soaking up some sun. Over the top of your favorite book, you notice a snake slithering through the grass, approaching you. You're terrified. Your heart races, you scream (something that can be perceived as an act of aggression in humans), you grab the nearest weapon, and you frantically attempt to ward off the harmless garter snake (also an action that could be perceived as aggressive).

I approach you, pat your back and say "Hey, let's get out of here," and lead you inside, away from the snake. Inside I give you a hug and some iced tea. Did I make your fear of snakes worse? Better? Chances are, no. You're probably just as afraid of snakes as you were. The only change may be how you feel about me. The next time you see a snake, your heart may still race, you may still break out into a cold sweat and grab the nearest shovel—and you may also wish for a friend to help you cope with the stressful situation.

Now, let's say you saw a snake, and, as soon as you grabbed a shovel as a weapon, I smacked you. Would you feel less afraid of the snake? Can you have the fear of snakes "slapped out of you?" If I slapped you when you reacted to a snake, how would you feel about me being near you next time you ran into one—more or less anxious? Your fear of snakes would likely be as intense as it ever was. The only difference would be how you felt about me when a snake was around—and at any other time!

Deep breathing versus snake

Deep breathing helps people relax. But when the snake approaches you in the backyard, do you think about your reaction to the snake, the dilation of your pupils? Is screaming a conscious decision? Is grabbing the shovel a reflex or a conscious thought? Do you consider the calming effect of deep breathing and how it might help you relax?

Chapter 8 – Anxious, Fearful, Reactive, or Aggressive Dogs

I'd guess that you don't think of deep breathing (an alternative, incompatible behavior to screaming, and also an operant response) when you see that snake. You're in survival mode; you are reacting rather than acting in an operant manner.

Similarly for dogs, growling, hackling, lunging, and snapping may be symptoms of an innate desire for self-preservation when they are confronted with stimuli that make them fearful.

Symptoms of fear are not conscious reactions. Just as you don't choose to make the hairs on the back of your neck stand up when you see a snake or spider, your dog doesn't decide, "That dog makes me nervous. I should raise my hackles and growl!"

Even if you know deep breathing may help alleviate your fear, chances are that the thought doesn't pop into your mind when you most need it—in the face of extreme anxiety or fear. Likewise, your lunging dog's mind may be more focused on surviving than on performing even well-proofed cues for behaviors that are incompatible with the aggressive display.

Giving treats to a growling dog

Operant conditioning is a way all animals learn; it's based on the theory that the relative frequency or infrequency of a behavior is controlled by the behavior's consequences. In operant conditioning, the dog learns that his behavior can result in one of four possible consequences: positive reinforcement (good stuff happens), negative reinforcement (bad stuff stops happening), positive punishment (bad stuff starts happening), or negative punishment (good stuff stops happening). If behaviors are reinforced, they are more likely to occur in the future. If behaviors are punished, they are less likely to be offered in the future.

Remember Pavlov's dogs? Dogs salivate when presented with food. This is not an operant behavior but a physiological response—classical conditioning. Pavlov learned that after repeated pairings (lab coat or bell reliably predicts the arrival of food) previously neutral stimuli were able to elicit the same salivary response that the presentation of food would elicit.

Think of Pavlov's dogs when using classical conditioning to modify aggressive or reactive behavior. The stimulus (trigger) should predict the arrival of food—just as a bell or lab coat would for Pavlov's dogs. The reinforcement is contingent not on the dog's behavior, but on the presentation of the stimulus. The dogs got fed no matter what they were doing.

Just as in Pavlov's experiment where the lab coat, rather than the dogs' behavior, predicted the delivery of the primary reinforcer (the food), the appearance of the other dog on our walk predicted the delivery of my treats.

Desensitization and counter conditioning

When you are working with aggression and reactivity, the trigger (generally other dogs and/or people) is no longer a neutral stimulus to the dog. Using desensitization, it's possible to "neutralize" or "shrink" the stimulus by manipulating distance. Counter conditioning uses a primary reinforcer to classically condition a positive emotional response.

To begin desensitizing the dog, accurately identify the triggers—what is the dog reacting to? Once you've identified the triggers, decide what the dog's threshold is for each trigger—how far away does the dog need to be from another dog without reacting? In other words, to desensitize, manage the environment to avoid provoking a full-blown reaction; remove the opportunity for the dog to exhibit reactive behavior.

The dog should notice, and even feel mildly anxious about, the stimulus at the threshold distance. To determine the threshold distance, watch the dog's body language—what are the first steps of the reaction? If your dog is happily taking treats at a distance, but gets mouthy and starts chomping on your fingers to get the treats as you move closer, you are nearing his threshold. Dogs cannot eat when they are extremely stressed, so if your hungry dog will not eat even the best of treats, he is over his threshold. The best thing to do at that point is to create distance using a previously taught "Let's go!" cue.

When the dog's triggers and the threshold distances are known, it's time to begin counter conditioning. Counter conditioning conditions an emotional response that is incompatible with the aggressive behavior; the goal is called a positive conditioned emotional response (CER). For counter conditioning, you will need some great treats and could also benefit from the help of one or more stimulus dog/handler teams. This training works best if your dog is somewhat hungry (has not just finished a meal).

Chapter 8 – Anxious, Fearful, Reactive, or Aggressive Dogs

You achieve the CER using what Jean Donaldson has called the "open bar, closed bar" technique. When your dog sees another dog, the bar opens immediately. When the dog is no longer in sight, the bar closes. These are the rules—regardless of how your dog is behaving. The appearance of the other dog, not your dog's behavior, predicts the delivery of the reinforcer, a reinforcer that is only provided in this context. What should you serve at "the bar?" Really good stuff! Find out what your dog loves best, and only give it to him when the counter-conditioning bar is open.

Over time a dog's threshold will decrease. Only move closer when your dog is able to see another dog and look back at you happily, tail wagging, expecting delivery of the ultimate treat—that is the CER you seek. End each session with success, and always leave your dog wanting more.

Remember also to reflect the behavior you want your dog to display. If you tense up when you see another dog, that tension will travel down the leash to your dog. Go for practice walks without your dog and rehearse deep breathing when you see another dog, so that you can display the same relaxed confidence you'd like to see in your dog.

Being the crazy dog lady is a good thing

Be prepared for the likelihood that your neighbors will not understand the training you are doing. Remember that it's your job to be your dog's guardian—gaining his trust by not allowing bad things to happen to him.

If your dog is aggressive toward other dogs and a neighbor walking her dog says, "My dog is friendly!" as she approaches, be prepared to intervene on behalf of your dog. Create distance, move in another direction. If your dog is afraid of children, use your body to block a child from running up to your dog. You may need to be the "crazy dog lady" in the neighborhood to rehabilitate your dog successfully.

Sometimes doing what is right for a dog is not easy. There is a stigma associated with owning an "aggressive" dog. There is also great responsibility, and great liability.

A supportive network can boost your morale and commitment if you get frustrated. It's important to establish a support network that includes, at minimum, a behavior-savvy veterinarian and a behaviorist with experience using desensitization and counter conditioning (D/CC) techniques to modify aggression and reactive behavior in dogs.

Ideally, your network should also include some supportive family and friends, and, whenever possible, other pet owners who have been through similar experiences with their own dogs.

Other considerations for aggressive and reactive dogs

Working closely with your veterinarian and behaviorist, you may find that you require additional tools beyond D/CC and more elaborate management techniques. You may also need to desensitize your dog to wearing a muzzle if he has a well-established biting history or if you are doubtful of your ability to manipulate the environment so that your dog can remain below his threshold consistently. For information on muzzle training, see Nan Arthur's "Muzzles—Not Just for Aggression Anymore," p. 282.

Some fearful and aggressive dogs benefit greatly from medication. These medications are not tranquilizers, but are medications given to correct chemical imbalances in the brain. Providing a fluoxetine prescription for a dog or human is just like providing insulin to a diabetic patient—both are medications intended to correct hormonal and chemical imbalances within the body. Unfortunately, I've seen a cultural bias against pharmaceutical treatment of mental illness extend to four-legged creatures, too.

All the training in the world cannot correct a behavior problem that is caused by pain or faulty brain functioning, but medications are not a cure-all either. Just as humans taking anti-depressants see the most rehabilitative results when they attend therapy sessions, medication for reactivity must be accompanied by appropriate and thorough dog training. A full medical evaluation is required for all dogs displaying aggression problems, and a complete thyroid panel is strongly advised.

A number of holistic treatments may also be helpful in managing reactivity and aggression. It never hurts to bring a holistic veterinarian to the consultation team. A good holistic vet should be able to talk to you about how diet and dietary changes can contribute to or improve your dog's behavior. He or she may be able to suggest herbs, supplements, flower

Chapter 8 – Anxious, Fearful, Reactive, or Aggressive Dogs

essences, homeopathic treatments, or massage techniques to set your dog up for rehabilitative success.

Rehabilitating an aggressive dog is not easy. It can be a frustrating process, and it can seem as if you are taking one step forward and two steps back. However, for a dog owner there is no reinforcement greater than seeing a rehabilitated dog greet life without fear. So, be crazy if necessary—the results are well worth it!

Reducing Leash Reactivity: The Engage-Disengage Game
by Alice Tong

Many dogs struggle to stay relaxed when they see another dog, a person, or a specific environmental stimulus and end up reacting with an intense stress response. Stress responses can be categorized into fight (such as barking, lunging), flight (such as avoiding, hiding), freeze (such as cowering, shutting down), or fool around (such as jumping, mouthing) behaviors.

The Engage–Disengage Game is helpful for dogs that respond with a "fight" or "fool around" response. These dogs often become over-aroused quickly and end up hurling themselves toward the trigger out of fear, anxiety, or frustration. Unlike socially savvy dogs that self-interrupt frequently in order to keep interactions fun and safe, these "fight" or "fool around" dogs have immense difficulty disengaging from the trigger in order to self-interrupt.

The Engage–Disengage Game decreases a dog's stress around the trigger and teaches the dog the peaceful coping skill of self-interruption. This ability to disengage and self-interrupt is similar to the practice of mindfulness, if you are at all familiar with Buddhism, yoga, or elements of the field of psychotherapy.

Manage exposures, decrease reactions

Before diving into a training plan to treat the issue of stress response, first learn about and try some positive management methods to decrease how often your dog is reacting to the trigger. Every time your dog practices an undesired behavior outside of training time, he is regressing in training and will continue to feel stressed or anxious around the trigger. Try to decrease the number of undesired reactions he is having each day.

If your dog has bitten or caused injury to a person or another animal, first consult with a certified positive reinforcement trainer or board-certified veterinary behaviorist to make sure you are implementing the necessary safety precautions.

Chapter 8 – Anxious, Fearful, Reactive, or Aggressive Dogs

The Engage–Disengage Game: Reinforcing new feelings and desired behaviors

Reducing aggression, reactivity, or fear means gradually desensitizing and counter-conditioning your dog to like the trigger, and teaching an alternate response behavior. The Engage–Disengage Game uses positive reinforcement methods, and provides a structured way to reduce a stress response and train a safe and appropriate behavior instead.

There are two levels to the game. The first level rewards the dog for engaging with the trigger when he is not showing the stress response, which builds positive feelings toward the trigger. The second level rewards the dog for offering the alternative behavior of turning away from the trigger, which is a behavior incompatible with barking at, pulling toward, or biting the trigger.

Game prep

Before beginning the Engage–Disengage Game, gather the following supplies that you will need:

- High-value treats
- Clicker
- Humane harness or collar

Practice fast U-turns by luring your dog, placing a treat near or on his nose, or tossing "find-it" treats on the ground as you both change direction quickly (walking toward the treat). Take a break if you notice even subtle stress signals (displacement behaviors) such as excessive lip-licking, yawning, or scratching.

Level 1: Engage

1. Start at a safe distance away from the trigger, a place where your dog is not reacting. Be quiet and still so that your dog notices the trigger on his own.
2. At the precise moment your dog *engages* by looking at the trigger, *click*.
3. When your dog turns his head toward you after hearing the click, feed him a treat. If your dog reacts or does not turn back to you after the click, move farther away from the trigger to reset at an easier distance.

The goal of Level 1 is to succeed with at least 3–5 repetitions in a row at the same distance before moving on to Level 2. A successful repetition is when your dog turns back to you immediately after the click.

If the trigger is moving or changing in intensity, keep playing Level 1 until your dog has calmly looked at or engaged with the trigger from every direction. *Then* move on to Level 2.

Level 2: Disengage

1. Again, let your dog notice the trigger, but this time wait 1–5 seconds to see if your dog will offer to look away from the trigger on his own. If your dog is fixating on the trigger for longer than 5 seconds, go back to Level 1.

2. At the precise moment your dog *disengages* by looking away from the trigger, *click*.

3. After the click, feed a treat. If your dog reacts or is not turning back to you after the click, move farther away from the trigger to reset at an easier distance.

The goal of Level 2 is to succeed with at least 3–5 repetitions in a row before moving 1–5 steps closer to the trigger. A successful repetition is when your dog disengages with the trigger comfortably on his own.

As you move closer, keep playing Level 2 if the trigger is not moving or changing in intensity. If the trigger is moving or changing in intensity, go back to Level 1 at the new distance.

Each time you play the Engage–Disengage Game, play for 1–5 minutes, and then take a break. If your dog is ready and eager, you can repeat this pattern.

How close?

Remember to keep your goals realistic. For example, if your dog is triggered by other dogs, it is important to acknowledge that he may not be destined to be a "dog-park dog." Some dogs may simply prefer the company of humans more than other dogs, or may not enjoy physically interacting with dogs that have different play styles. Some dogs may have more introverted social personalities. Going to the dog park or walking through a busy crowd

Chapter 8 – Anxious, Fearful, Reactive, or Aggressive Dogs

of people can be like a rave or punk concert that your dog is just not interested in attending. Instead he may prefer to snuggle down next to you on the couch—just as when you settle down to read a good book or watch a movie.

In many cases, working your dog up to walking by another dog or person calmly on leash is a perfectly acceptable goal for both of you. As a responsible dog parent, it is important to have expectations that respect your dog's capability and personality. Remember to take training at your dog's pace and to make things easier if he is showing stress signals. Keeping your dog under threshold will actually help him learn faster and give you longer-term results.

If it is appropriate for your dog to engage in polite greetings and physical interactions with the trigger, you can still play the Engage–Disengage Game by clicking for more interactive "engage" behaviors, such as sniffing the trigger or targeting a safe area of the trigger with nose or paw. A certified positive reinforcement trainer or board-certified veterinary behaviorist can help you determine if greetings and physical interactions are appropriate for your dog and can also assist in creating an individualized greeting plan that prioritizes safety and success.

Proof positive

The Engage–Disengage Game can come in handy for many situations. I have used it to teach dogs how to remain calm and happy around a new baby in the home; around other dogs or people they are scared of; around other dogs or people they love so much that they want to jump on and mouth them; around bikes, skateboards, doorbells—and the list continues.

Science and research in dog training have revealed that intimidation, pain, or the threat of pain are simply not necessary and cause more problems training an aggressive, reactive, or fearful dog. Instead, using positive reinforcement methods like the Engage–Disengage Game, help your dog become less anxious and fearful of the world, and teach him that he has the ability to choose another behavior that is both fun and safe instead.

Better Together

Erasing Fear: A Lesson (or Two) on Cues and Shaping
by Clint Matthews

Here is a fascinating account from a gun-dog owner, Clint Matthews, of using the clicker to help his three-year-old dog overcome a traumatic experience from puppyhood. The experience had created a pattern of fear—of the owner's truck, of being in the truck, even of stepping into the back hall leading to the truck. The fear was getting in the way of taking the dog hunting, the work he was bred to do.

Clint had already done a lot of fun-type clicker training around the house with his dog. Removing the fear was much more of a challenge. This project took the owner 15 clicker training sessions, of a few minutes each, over a period of weeks. At each step, Clint's main criteria were that the dog's tail should be up and the dog relaxed and happy. At each step, Clint assessed the animal's emotional response. If the dog showed reluctance or fear, Clint shifted some aspect of the training.

This ingenious trainer sometimes modified his criterion, settling for going halfway down the scary hall, not all the way. Or he changed the behavior that was being clicked, switching from going to a goal area to retrieving a toy in the goal area. He added distractions—turning the truck engine on and off remotely. He changed reinforcers, from food to better food to the JACKPOT where the dog was invited to go for a run with Clint's wife.

Brilliant success! Just read Clint's story and look at what you can do with a few principles, good timing, and creativity! I'm especially stoked to learn that Clint picked up his strategies from reading one book, my Reaching the Animal Mind. *It's all stories, not that much instruction. That worked for Clint Matthews—did it ever!*

—Karen Pryor

Problem: truck terror

Gus, a three-year-old German shorthaired pointer (GSP), is fearful of our truck. Gus shows undesirable body language (tucked tail, head lowered, and slinking movement) in the general vicinity of the truck and in the garage. He

Chapter 8 – Anxious, Fearful, Reactive, or Aggressive Dogs

knows when it is time to go to the truck—when I go out into the backyard on Saturday mornings to take him to the truck, he shows the same body language. Gus especially dislikes the long hallway that leads from the kitchen to the garage because he knows the truck is right behind the door!

Until now I have had to use strong and forceful voice commands to get Gus to go to the truck and load. I was getting it done, but he wasn't happy about it. I tried many things to change his body language, such as not bringing him through the house to the truck. It was all trickery. But, there was no fooling him—as soon as he saw the truck and knew my intentions, Gus began to slink.

Desired outcome: fear-free truck travel

The goal was for Gus to lose his fear of the truck, loading into the truck with good body language (wagging tail, head and ears up) and without any coercion.

Techniques used: positive reinforcement-based clicker training

I chose to use the click and treat methods described in Karen Pryor's book *Reaching the Animal Mind*.

1. Targeting
2. Shaping
3. Cueing
4. Shaping an absence

Tools used

Clicker, jerky treats, bowl of food (daily meal), remote starting key fob, rug, morning run, vehicle, packrat in a trap, favorite retrieving toy.

Background information

I think Gus began this behavior the day I brought him home as a puppy. He didn't like being taken from his family and he moaned all the way to my house traveling in his kennel. Two days later I loaded him up and took him on a long drive to Sonoita for training. The upsets from these trips could have been avoided or managed better with a little help from the breeder, or if I had more knowledge, or if I had taken a slower approach. Gotta walk before you run!

Gus is no stranger to the click-and-treat method. We began using clicker training when he was 10 weeks old. Over the last three years he has developed a skill set that includes:

"Whoa," "Heel," "Come," "Leave it," "Find it" (find something in the general vicinity), "Outside" (go outside), "On top" (jump up onto anything I point to that is elevated), "Retrieve," "Settle" (lay down), "Room" (go to Clay's room), "Pool" (go jump in the pool), "Kennel," "Hold" (hold in his mouth anything I put in his mouth), "Toy" (go find your toy and bring it to me), "Over" (move over on to the shoulder and away from the road because there is a car approaching while running with Alison against the traffic).

Training plan

It is extremely important to note that the following training steps were completed with very few verbal cues. Most of the time, the only noise would be the click. I only clicked when Gus offered me the desired behavior with good to neutral body language. He was fed only once per day, after the training session was completed in the evening.

> **Session 1: Teach Gus to target my hand.** Put piece of jerky treat in my hand, made a fist, and clicked for touching my hand with his nose. This step went extremely quickly. One five-minute session and Gus had it mastered.
>
> **Session 2: Move Gus around the house using my fist as a target.** Using the same technique as in Session 1, I moved away from Gus and made him come to me and touch his nose to my fist. I went all over the house and he followed me anywhere. I stayed away from the "dreaded hallway to the garage," since I wanted him to master the cue without bringing him to the aversive location.
>
> **Session 3: Move Gus down the dreaded hallway using the target.** Using the same technique as previous sessions, I started in neutral locations in the house and slowly progressed to the dreaded hall entrance. Next came one step into the hallway, then a couple of steps. I could get Gus to go halfway down the hall, but not to the end. I finished the session there, successful in moving halfway down the hallway. I made sure that we finished on a successful attempt.

Chapter 8 – Anxious, Fearful, Reactive, or Aggressive Dogs

Session 4: Get Gus to go to the end of the hallway using the target. Using the same techniques as the previous sessions, I started at the entrance to the hallway, and slowly progressed to the end of the hallway. This process took about five clicks. There was some hesitation. Gus paused and yawned a few times.

Session 5: Get Gus to go into the garage using the target. Using the same techniques as the previous sessions, I started at the entrance to the hallway and quickly progressed to the end of the hallway. As soon as I opened the door to the garage, Gus went through the door on his own, but his tail was tucked. He would not give me good body language no matter how patient I was, so he was not rewarded. I backed up the training steps and ended the session (successfully) with the door to the garage closed, just as in the previous session.

New approach, new team member

It was clear to me that I needed a new approach. I had just read about "using cues when clicks won't work" in Karen's book, and that sounded helpful. I also felt that it might be necessary to take myself out of the equation.

The next morning I witnessed a behavior I had never seen from Gus. I was home on a holiday and my wife, Alison, was getting ready for her morning run. She has an elaborate process of getting ready—putting on her running shoes, strapping her iPhone to her arm, and getting the leash for Gus. Gus watches Alison get ready by looking through the glass doors from outside. He whines as if to say, "Don't forget about me!" He loves his morning runs.

When Alison opens the back door, Gus, tail wagging, runs down the dreaded hallway and prances impatiently waiting for her to open the door to the garage. He has no fear! In fact, Gus is really excited. When Alison opens the door, he runs into the garage, past the truck, with his tail wagging. Ah hah! A light-bulb moment!

I decided to try a two-pronged approach. First, I'd have Alison ask Gus to get into a vehicle in the garage before they go on the morning run. If Gus loads with a neutral or positive body language, then he gets to take his morning run. The second approach was to teach Gus a new target that was independent from me.

Alison accepted this new challenge and, of course, Gus loaded with no problems. Over the next few days, she lengthened the time he had to stay in the truck. This process helped me, as Gus learned that the truck is not a bad place—just a stopping point before the morning run. Gus was associating a good experience with the truck!

Alison followed this routine every time she took Gus on a run, three to four mornings per week. She moved on to asking him to get into the kennel while he was in the back of the truck. It became a habit after several weeks.

A real throw rug

I decided that the new target would be a small throw rug. The goal was to teach Gus to lie on the throw rug, and then I would slowly move the rug from a comfortable place in the house to the back of the truck. Using the rug gave us a place for Gus to hang out in the house (off the furniture and the carpeting), and it provided a bridge from the house to the truck.

> **Session 6: Teach Gus to stand on the rug.** I placed a small rug on the floor in the kitchen and brought Gus in to let him wander around the kitchen. I clicked and treated with jerky when Gus looked at the rug. Clicked when Gus moved toward the rug. Clicked when Gus sniffed the rug. Clicked when Gus stepped on the rug. Clicked when Gus put all four feet on the rug. After every click, Gus came to me for his treat.
>
> **Session 7: Teach Gus to lie on the rug.** Using the same technique/location/props as the previous session, I clicked when Gus stood on the rug with all four feet. He came to me for a treat, and then he ran over to the rug again. I didn't click.
>
> This was the first time I used my voice. I used the cue "Settle" while Gus was standing on the rug. I clicked as he settled. I used this cue only once to show him what I wanted. He came to collect his treat, and then he ran back over to the rug and stood.
>
> I didn't click and I didn't speak. Gus yawned. Then he sat down. I clicked. He came for his treat, and then he ran over to the rug and sat. Again, I didn't click. Gus lay down halfway and tentatively. I clicked. He came to collect his treat, and then he ran over and lay down with confidence. I clicked. We did this three more times with success.

Chapter 8 – Anxious, Fearful, Reactive, or Aggressive Dogs

Session 8: Teach Gus a visual cue for lying on the rug. I set up the same environment and brought Gus into the house. He was focused on me. I pointed to the rug. He saw it and immediately ran to the rug to lie down! I clicked and he came to collect his treat. Gus made a move toward the rug and went back to lie down. I didn't click, but turned my back and walked away.

Gus followed me. I turned around and pointed to the rug. He made a move to the rug and lay down. I clicked. He came over to me to collect his treat. And he stared at me! I said "Rug" and pointed to the rug. Gus ran and lay down on the rug. Click!

He had it! We did this three or four more times. I had progressed further than I thought I could. We were successful in associating a verbal cue as well as a visual cue.

Session 9: Use the new target to move Gus down the hall. In this session I moved the rug to the entrance of the hallway. I gave Gus the verbal and visual cue for the rug and he performed the behavior flawlessly. Click and treat. I moved the rug down the hall and closer to the door in 3-foot increments with a series of clicks and treats and finished up with Gus performing the behavior at the end of the hall.

Session 10: Using the target, have Gus lie on his rug near the truck. This time we moved to the driveway behind the truck with the garage door open so Gus could see the truck. We started 20 feet from the truck and I asked him to lie on his rug. In a succession of 3-foot increments, I moved Gus from 20 feet away to a place just behind the truck. It took about 6 click-and-treat combinations to achieve this.

I got greedy. I opened the tailgate and placed the rug on the back of the tailgate. Gus put his front feet up on the tailgate! I clicked and treated. His body language was neutral. We ended the session right there!

Session 11: Using the target rug, have Gus lie on the rug on the tailgate. We began the session with the rug on the ground behind the truck. Gus performed the behavior with neutral body language. Click and treat. I then moved the rug to the tailgate. Gus put his front paws on the tailgate. I clicked and treated. I gave him the cue again. He put his front paws up again. I didn't click. Gus put his feet back on the ground and just stood there. I decided to help him. I gave him the "On top" cue. He jumped up onto the tailgate. I clicked and offered the treat. Right now, I didn't care about his body language. He made progress.

Gus didn't take the treat and wanted to get down. I let him. (Pressure on, pressure off.) I walked him away from the truck for a few moments. We then moved back toward the truck and, without a cue, Gus jumped onto the tailgate with neutral body language. I was ready and clicked as he left the ground. I offered the treat; Gus didn't take it.

This was a breakthrough moment! Gus offered behavior that I wanted without coercion or even a cue.

Gus wanted to get down and I let him. We walked away again. We turned back toward the truck and I gave him the cue. Gus jumped onto the tailgate with neutral body language again. I clicked just as he picked his front feet off the ground to jump up. I offered his entire food bowl as a jackpot while he was on the tailgate. This time, he ate!

Session 12: A training day in Sonoita. The goal was to get Gus loaded with neutral body language. In the morning I noticed that I had trapped a packrat in a live animal trap the night before. I let Gus smell the rat in the trap and let him follow me over to the truck. His attention was solely on the rat. I put the trap in the back of the truck and Gus jumped into the truck to get at the rat. He even walked around the bed trying to get a better look at the rat. He had positive body language. I asked him to get into the kennel and he did, willingly.

Session 13: Have Gus in the bed of the truck while the engine is running. This session began the same way as Session 11. This time, instead of putting the rug on the ground, I opened the tailgate to put the rug down. Gus jumped into the truck bed on his own! Of course, I wasn't ready for this, so I let him just stay there. Gus got down within a few seconds.

When I was ready, I gave him the cue. I clicked as he left the ground. Gus still didn't take the treat. He performed this several times—each time receiving clicks but not accepting the treat. But Gus wanted to eat his food, so I gave him his jackpot. While he was eating his food in the

Chapter 8 – Anxious, Fearful, Reactive, or Aggressive Dogs

back of the truck, I used my remote key fob to make the truck lights flash—standing behind him and a good distance away. The lights alerted Gus for a second and he jumped down. Immediately he got back up and continued to eat. I again flashed the lights, and Gus gave no response but continued to eat. Next I started the truck with my remote key fob. He was again alerted and stopped eating, but didn't jump down. I turned off the truck immediately (again, pressure on, pressure off), and let him finish his meal.

Session 14: Same scenario as Session 13, but the truck running longer. The setup was exactly the same for this session, except that I didn't use the rug. As I dropped the tailgate Gus jumped up without me asking him. I walked away and he got down. I gave him the cue, and he jumped up. I clicked and treated. Gus still didn't want his treat, but his body language was neutral. I gave him his bowl of food to eat. While he was eating, I flashed the lights again. He was not alerted. I started the truck. Gus looked up and then went back to eating while the truck was still running. I let the truck run for 10 seconds before I turned it off. I waited another minute and started the truck again. This time Gus kept eating without looking up. I let the truck run even longer, maybe 30 seconds, before I turned it off and ended the session.

Session 15: Retrieving Gus's toy from the bed of the truck. We began the same way as Session 14. Gus offered to jump in the back of the truck, this time with positive body language. I got him down, and put his favorite toy on the tailgate. I asked Gus to retrieve the toy. He did and got rewarded. I placed the toy further into the truck and asked Gus to retrieve it. He did, and received his reward. The next time, Gus was 20 feet away from the truck when I threw the toy deep into the bed. He retrieved the toy perfectly!

I jackpotted him again and had him eat on the tailgate. While Gus was eating, I started the truck three times and turned it off, letting it run longer and longer each time. When Gus finished eating, he stayed on the tailgate wagging his tail and surveying the area.

Mission accomplished!

Slow, steady, successful

In 15 short (5–10 minute) sessions I was able to teach Gus how to load into the truck with positive body language. Because he was challenged on a daily basis and was successful each day, his overall demeanor became bolder and more confident.

Gus learned a new cue (Rug) that can be used in a practical way around the house. I learned that there are many different techniques for accomplishing a goal. Sometimes using all the techniques together is required to reach the goal! Evaluating training results as you work allows you to make adjustments in your training techniques and plans.

I don't think I want Gus to lose his fear of trucks completely; maybe it will keep him safe if he stays away from moving cars. I will continue to work on this new behavior with Gus to build confidence and to make the behavior a comfortable habit.

How to Prevent Resource Guarding in a Multiple-dog Household
by Hannah Branigan

Resource guarding among dogs is an extremely common and normal behavior. Dogs are pre-programmed not to want to share valued resources with others. For pet dogs, resources may include food, toys, or even the owner's attention. In most households, resource guarding is limited to simple communication, but sometimes the behavior can escalate in frequency or intensity and injuries can occur. If you are ever concerned about aggressive behavior in your dog, related to resource guarding or not, it is best to contact your vet or other qualified professional for help before proceeding on your own.

While there are many protocols to reduce conflict in dogs that guard resources from their humans, guarding from other dogs presents a unique set of challenges. However, the principles for working with a dog that guards resources from humans and a dog that guards resources from dogs are basically the same. The emotion underlying the behavior is usually fear.

For animals in the wild, keeping or losing a meal can be the difference between life and death. So even though beloved pets are never in danger of starving (far from it!), the instinct to protect valuable resources is still intact. The goal of any training method is to reduce or eliminate the fear and conflict so that the dog feels more relaxed with a resource. Using positive reinforcement and counter-conditioning it is possible to change a dog's emotional response and motivation. As a result, the behavior itself goes away.

Steps to success
The main difference between a dog guarding from people and a dog guarding from dogs is that most of the time the human doesn't actually want the slimy, old, rawhide resource, but most of the time the other dog does want it. Working with two dogs in a household, there are two training tasks to address.

The first is to teach the guarding dog to feel more relaxed when approached, and the second is to teach the approaching dog not to steal other dog's belongings.

The first step in modifying resource-guarding behavior is to use good management strategies to prevent the undesired behavior. Practice makes perfect! Make a list of items, spaces, or situations that are likely to provoke the dog's guarding behavior. Then, either change the environment to eliminate the opportunities, or eliminate the dog's access. This may mean removing treasured toys, restricting access to certain rooms or furniture, confining the dogs separately during feeding times, and other management strategies. Crates, baby gates, and pens are great tools that help control your dog's space and prevent undesirable behaviors. Note that in some cases dogs may have to be completely separated except during training times.

After setting up a dog up for success with good management, it is time for the business of training. Before working with two dogs together, it is extremely helpful to teach some solid, positively trained foundation skills individually. Introduce the dogs to clicker training, if they haven't been introduced already. Practice a strong "leave it" behavior and a solid "stay" behavior. It is also helpful to practice relaxation and self-control behaviors like mat work and Doggie Zen.

Train and treat the two

Next start working with the dogs together. You will need two handlers, one for Dog A and one for Dog B. Start by working with a fairly low-value item, something your dog likes, but isn't that crazy about. A typical resource value hierarchy for many dogs might be: stuffed toys (low value), chewies (medium value), food (high value).

The goal is for all interactions to be positive and educational. Keep the dogs "under threshold" at all times. This means that if everything goes as it should, you'll never see any aggressive behavior.

To begin, both dogs should be leashed for safety; the guarding dog (Dog A) could even be tethered for extra security. The goal is error-free learning, but it's better to be safe than sorry!

Place the resource near Dog A. Next bring in Dog B, stopping far away from Dog A and well outside the point where Dog A might be concerned.

Chapter 8 – Anxious, Fearful, Reactive, or Aggressive Dogs

This distance is going to depend on the dog, so err on the side of caution. Click and treat Dog A for remaining calm, lead Dog B away, and click and treat Dog B for not going for the resource.

Repeat, decreasing the distance between dogs slightly, again clicking and treating Dogs A and B for appropriate behavior. If at any point either dog shows behavior that is not calm and relaxed, go back to the last distance where they were both successful and repeat. Gradually decrease the distance in small increments until Dog B can walk right past Dog A and neither dog reacts.

At this point, go back to the beginning distance, but use a more valuable resource. Go through the same steps, always keeping both dogs under threshold until Dog B can walk right past Dog A and both dogs are comfortable. Repeat the process with resources that are more and more valuable until you are working with the best stuff. You can also practice this exercise in different locations, especially any location where Dog A has a tendency to guard, like the couch.

One for you, then one for you

Try another fun exercise. Sit the dogs far apart, one on either side of you, tethering if necessary. Say Dog B's name and give him a medium-value treat. Immediately say Dog A's name and give him an even better treat. If either dog appears uncomfortable at all, move them farther apart and start again. Repeat until both dogs are holding their sits patiently while the other gets a treat. Gradually reduce the distance between the dogs until they are comfortable sitting as little as a body length apart.

Remember, safety first! Both dogs need to feel completely comfortable at all times. The goal of this exercise is to teach Dog A that when Dog B gets a treat, it predicts him getting an even better treat! Dog A will start anticipating Dog B's treat because it means his own goodie is imminent.

Unexpected trouble

What should you do if, between exercises, your dog guards something unexpectedly? First and most importantly, stay calm! Getting upset will only exacerbate the situation. That is easier to say than to do. There's nothing like a growl and a set of flashing teeth to set off an emotional response in a human, but do the best you can. Resist the urge to punish the guarding dog, because that would be unproductive. Calmly remove the dogs from the situation, preferably without touching either one. Sending them to their mats is a good way to diffuse the tension. Separate the dogs for a short time to let everyone calm down.

Meanwhile, try to examine what happened. What resource was the catalyst? If possible, remove the resource or otherwise restrict access to it before letting the dogs back together. Later, add that particular resource, location, or context to your training plan. Eventually you will have the opportunity to reward the dogs for calm behavior in the same situation.

Sharing nicely

Modifying resource-guarding behavior is not fast or easy! Don't hesitate to ask for help from a qualified professional trainer or veterinary behaviorist. It will take time and attention, and many dogs will always require some level of management for safety and sanity. But, resource guarding is a behavior, and all behavior is modifiable!

Chapter 8 – Anxious, Fearful, Reactive, or Aggressive Dogs

The Power of Ongoing Learning
by Ken Ramirez

I'd like to share a few amazing behavioral transformations I've seen in my work with rescued dogs. I believe that exposure to complex training tasks helps resolve many behavioral challenges that animals face. The exposure may prepare dogs to cope with the world a bit better. The more training animals receive, the more resilient they become, the more confidence they gain, and the more innovative behavior they demonstrate.

I have worked with many dogs that had severe aggression problems. Most were destined to be euthanized because shelter personnel deemed them too difficult to rehabilitate. I am often brought into these cases as an advisor.

Advanced training and long-term success

Given the proper tools, training, and environment, animals can learn solid skills that help their behavior evolve in a desirable direction naturally. I have observed that once a solid foundation for learning and behavior is put in place using positive reinforcement and is combined with complex learning taught by a skilled trainer, animals will develop desired behavior even when the main focus of later training is not directed toward the original problem behavior.

Here is the successful model I have seen repeated many times:

1. Animal is in a shelter due to various types of severe aggression.
2. Some type of context-specific, aggression-reduction training protocol is implemented successfully.
3. Animal is adopted into a stable, loving home where exposure to triggers is minimized.
4. Ongoing training and maintenance of behavior using positive reinforcement is practiced.
5. High-level advanced training is implemented with dog for at least one year while avoiding exposure to aggression triggers.

6. After several years, aggressive behavior is gone or greatly reduced in non-trained contexts.

Conversely, I have seen that when step number 5 is missing—there is no advanced, complex, or specialized training that stretches the animal's thinking—the animal's aggression in new contexts usually does not improve. I have witnessed this difference so many times that I believe there must be a correlation between the advanced training during a period of no exposure to triggers and the reduction in an animal's aggressive repertoire.

All of these cases began with well-designed, aggression-treatment protocols, giving the animals a solid foundation. Once in a stable home, the trainers were careful not to give the animals an opportunity to rehearse aggressive behavior; other than wise management, no aggression-specific protocols were implemented. Yet, over time, the undesirable aggression fades away.

I present these case studies simply as food for thought.

Mickey

Mickey is a pit-bull terrier and former fighting dog that exhibited severe aggression easily triggered by other dogs and by most men. His aggression was managed through the application of counter-conditioning and desensitization techniques. He was adopted by a professional search-and-rescue dog trainer named Jim. Jim focused Mickey's aggression treatment on becoming comfortable in his new home and living with the dogs already in that household. Mickey settled into that environment well, and Jim was able to make sure that Mickey did not encounter strange dogs or men. Mickey's aggression was under control and well managed.

Jim began training Mickey basic search–and-rescue skills, not to introduce him to rescue work but to keep him active and allow him to participate in social activity with Jim's other dogs. Mickey was a fast learner. Later on, Jim offered to let me use Mickey as part of an imitation project that I had initiated. Mickey became quite proficient at copying the behavior of other dogs, and the project really stretched his cognitive abilities.

After 18 months in his new home, Mickey was out in the field with Jim's other dogs when they had an unexpected encounter with three unknown dogs and two men. Jim was surprised that Mickey exhibited no aggressive

Chapter 8 – Anxious, Fearful, Reactive, or Aggressive Dogs

behavior; Mickey simply ran to Jim looking confused. Jim reinforced Mickey and moved him away from the strangers. A few months later, they had another surprise encounter with similar results, something that would not have been possible when Mickey first moved to his new home.

Because of those good reactions, Jim began to introduce Mickey to new dogs and men carefully and deliberately. I suggested that Jim keep track of these interactions and document Mickey's responses. Over the next several years, Mickey had more than 50 encounters with men or dogs that previously would have sparked severe reactivity. In all of those encounters, there were only four instances of mild barking, which subsided quickly and did not manifest in any aggressive behavior.

Mellie

Mellie, a bouncy Rottweiler mix that had been confiscated from a fighting-dog ring, was distrustful and aggressive toward all dogs. Leanne, a professional trainer who assisted the local shelter with severe aggression cases, treated Mellie for her reactivity issues using the Click to Calm approach. (Emma Parsons worked out the nuts and bolts of her Click to Calm approach in dealing with her reactive Golden retriever, Ben. See "Ben: An Aggressive Dog Case Study," p. 277.) Gradually, Mellie was exposed to new dogs below threshold and reinforced for accepting those dogs. This introduction procedure used a combination of counter-conditioning and redirection strategies.

Leanne fell in love with Mellie and decided to adopt her. Leanne was also an agility competitor, with three dogs at home. Although Mellie was still reactive to many dogs, she had progressed far enough that her training was focused on simply getting to know Leanne's other dogs. Leanne lived on a farm and could control Mellie's exposure to triggers easily.

Leanne introduced Mellie to agility training, which gave Mellie an outlet for her unbounded energy. Leanne also started using Mellie as a demo dog for her students. Mellie became one of the dogs the students could use to practice their skills. Mellie seemed to love the challenge of working with new people. Being a trainer-dog required patience and taught Mellie to generalize to constantly changing styles.

Due to several personal changes in Leanne's life, she had to relocate to the city. Mellie had lived on the farm for three years and had not been exposed to strange dogs in all that time. But in her new living environment, she was suddenly and regularly exposed to new dogs. Much to Leanne's surprise, Mellie did not react with the severe barking that had been normal for her. She seemed anxious and nervous, but Leanne was able to use redirection and high rates of reinforcement immediately to get through those situations. During their first nine months in the city, Mellie had hundreds of encounters that previously would have triggered aggression. In all of those encounters, Mellie had a mild growling reaction on just three occasions, but was easily redirected.

Coral

Coral is a high-energy Airedale mix that had been given up to shelters by two different families due to severe reactivity to people, dogs, vehicles, wind-blown leaves, and almost anything that moved. She had bitten several people and was considered a high-risk dog. I decided to bring her into a formal training program, and she was treated for dog-reactivity through a cooperative training protocol that focused on desensitization to context-specific situations. Coral lived in a stable environment with three other dogs. She was cared for by a group of professional trainers, and she participated in educational programs and shows that were designed to teach people about pet adoption and the importance of training. Although reactivity was still an issue, it was managed by being careful not to expose Coral to things that were known to be triggers. She became stable as long as the environment remained stable.

In addition to daily show-training, I included Coral in a two-year quantity-recognition project that tested her cognitive skills significantly. During that project, she was adopted to a home environment where she was exposed to fewer triggers. Michele, one of her trainers on the project, adopted her, and Coral moved into a household with two other dogs. Michele continued Coral's training and began taking her to agility classes.

Coral had been through a lot in her life, but, as we assess her today, her reactivity issues have decreased in all but one context: exposure to rowdy kids. Coral is exposed to many other of her previous triggers, such as men, dogs, and bikes, several times daily, with no reactivity.

Chapter 8 – Anxious, Fearful, Reactive, or Aggressive Dogs

Bud

Bud is a nervous boxer highly reactive to loud noises and nervous in the presence of other dogs. He was treated for reactivity to other dogs with a cooperative training protocol, working with other dogs on opposite sides of a fence or gate. Bud became quite comfortable around other dogs but remained quite reactive to loud noises.

A social worker and child therapist named Theresa adopted Bud. Theresa lived alone, but worked from her home, meeting troubled kids and their parents in her home for consults. Theresa spent a great deal of time training Bud on basic behaviors, and they did training sessions every day. When they encountered other dogs on walks, although nervous, Bud was well-behaved. Theresa worked hard to prevent Bud from experiencing loud noises, but he would occasionally hear something and react adversely, growling, barking ferociously, and lunging toward the sound. While Theresa was seeing her clients, Bud was in other parts of the house, since many of her child clients could be rather unpredictable and noisy.

Nine months after adopting Bud, Theresa was hospitalized and was bedridden for nearly six months. A trainer friend of hers, Safia, came into Theresa's home to care for Theresa and Bud. Safia was a graduate student working on her master's thesis on dog behavior. She asked Theresa if she could use Bud for a series of matching-to-sample studies. These studies continued for more than a year, and Bud excelled.

Theresa was eventually able to start seeing clients in her home again. By chance, she happened to have a string of troubled children who exhibited quite violent behavior: yelling, screaming, throwing a tantrum and stomping on the floor, or throwing things across the room. After one particularly intense and loud incident, with an object being thrown against the door to the back room where Bud was housed, Theresa realized that Bud was surprisingly quiet. A few months later, while they were walking down the street a loud firecracker went off near them. Theresa and Bud both jumped back and were startled, but Bud did not bark or growl. Today, Theresa uses Bud to socialize with many of her pediatric clients. Some of these kids yell or make other sudden noises, at which point Bud just moves to the other room. He no longer demonstrates aggressive behavior around loud noises. Theresa estimates that Bud hears loud and surprising noises three or four times each month, but for the last two years he has had no aggressive reactions to those sounds other than to look toward them and move away.

Further investigation needed

I have worked with dozens and dozens of aggressive dogs. The most impressive changes have occurred with dogs that have had a lengthy break from exposure to triggers combined with lots of fun, advanced training as part of a stable program. When that advanced training is not part of the equation, most of the dogs I've worked with continue to have aggression challenges.

In the cases I have presented, the aggression problems diminished because of a combination of factors: a good initial treatment protocol, a stable loving home, a long break from the triggers, a positive-reinforcement training environment, ongoing daily training, advanced training, and the passage of time. It is impossible to separate each of these components. As I compare the cases above with similar cases that did not include the advanced training element, I can't help but make the connection. The advanced training alone did not solve the aggression problem, but did it stretch the dogs' abilities and help them become more adaptable, confident, and accepting of changes? It is a question that I think requires further investigation

Creating the Thinking Dog

One of the many benefits of training is that it helps you and your dog communicate better. Training creates rules that set clearer expectations about behavior in various situations. Once your dog is exposed to training on a regular basis, those rules become generalized, and he learns to apply them in new but similar conditions and settings. That ability gives your dog the confidence to experiment. Suddenly, you realize that your dog is thinking and problem solving: he has learned to be creative. Each of the articles in this chapter shows how training enhances communication with your dog and makes him a truly creative training partner.

101 Things to Do with a Box 324
by Karen Pryor

When Animals Train Us 328
by Lori Chamberland

Carnivorous Chairs and the Cone of Shame: Creativity in Action ... 331
by Alena Van Arendonk

The Unexpected Benefits of Training 336
by Ken Ramirez

101 Things to Do with a Box
by Karen Pryor

This training game derived from a dolphin research project in which I and others participated, "The creative porpoise: training for novel behavior," published in the *Journal of Experimental Analysis of Behavior* in 1969. It has become a favorite with dog trainers. It's especially good for "crossover" dogs with a long history of correction-based training, since it encourages mental and physical flexibility and gives the dog courage to try something on its own.

Step one

Take an ordinary cardboard box, any size. Cut the sides down to about three inches, and put the box on the floor. Click the dog for looking at the box. Treat. If the dog goes near or past the box, even by accident, click. Next, after you click, toss the treat near or in the box. If the dog steps toward the box to get the treat, click the step and toss another treat. If he steps into the box, great. Click again, even if he is eating his previous treats, and offer him another treat in your hand.

Sometimes you can cook up a lot of "box action" in a hurry this way: click for stepping toward or into the box. Alternately toss the treat into the box and hold the treat out in your hand so the dog has to come back to you. If the dog is reluctant to step into the box and so doesn't eat that treat, it doesn't matter: he knows he got it. If treats accumulate in the box, fine. When he does step into the box, he'll get a jackpot. If you decide to stop the session before that happens, fine. Pick up the treats in the box, and put them away for a later session. Remember, never treat without clicking first, and always click for a reason: for some action of the dog's.

If you need more behavior to click, you can move yourself to different parts of the room so the box is between you and the dog, increasing the likelihood of steps in the direction of the box. Don't call the dog, don't pat the box, don't chat, don't encourage the dog, and don't "help" him. All of that stuff may just make him more suspicious. Click foot movements toward

Chapter 9 – Creating the Thinking Dog

the box, never mind from how far away, and then treat. If you get in five or six good clicks for moving in the direction or near or past the box, and then the dog "loses interest" and goes away, fine. You can always play "box" again later. In between sessions, the reinforcements you did get in will do their work for you; each little session will make things livelier the next time.

You are, after all, teaching your dog new rules to a new game. If you have already trained your dog by conventional methods, the dog may be respecting the general rule, "Wait to be told what to do." So the first rule of this new game, "Do something on your own, and I will click," is a toughie. In that case, the box game is especially valuable, and the first tiny steps are especially exciting—although they would be invisible to an onlooker, and may right now seem invisible to you.

End the first session with a "click for nothing" and a jackpot consisting of either a handful of treats, or a free grab at the whole bowl. Hmm. That'll get him thinking. The next time that cardboard box comes out, he will be alert to new possibilities. Clicks. Treats. Jackpots.

"That cardboard box makes my person behave strangely, but on the whole, I like this new strangeness. Box? Something I can do, myself? With that box?"

Those are new ideas, but they will come.

If your dog is very suspicious, you may need to do the first exercise over again once, or twice, or several times, until he "believes" something a human might phrase thus: "All that is going on here is that the click sound means my person gives me delicious food. And the box is not a trap, the box is a signal that click and treat time is here, if I can just find out how to make my person click."

Step two

Whether these things occur in the same session or several sessions later, here are some behaviors to click. Click the dog for stepping in the box, for pushing the box, pawing the box, mouthing the box, smelling the box, dragging the box, picking up the box, thumping the box—in short, for anything the dog does with the box.

Remember to click *while* the behavior is going on, not after the dog stops. As soon as you click, the dog will stop, of course, to get his treat. But because the click marked the behavior, the dog will do that behavior again, or some version of it, to try to get you to click again. You do not lose the behavior by interrupting it with a click.

You may end up in a wild flurry of box-related behavior. Great! Your dog is already learning to problem-solve in a creative way. If you get swamped and can't decide which thing to click, just jackpot and end the session. Now you have something to think about between sessions.

On the other hand, you may get a more methodical, slow, careful testing by the dog: the dog carefully repeats just what was clicked before. One paw in the box, say. Fine—but right away *you* need to become flexible about what you click, or you will end up as a matched pair of behavioral bookends. Paw, click. Paw, click. Paw, click. That is not the way to win this game.

So, when the dog begins to offer the behavior the same way, repeatedly, withhold your click. He puts the paw out, you wait. Your behavior has changed; the dog's behavior will change, too. The dog might keep the paw there longer. Fine, that's something new to click. He might pull it out; you could click that, once or twice. He might put the other paw in, too—fine, click that. Now he may try something new.

And? Where do we go from here? Well, once your dog has discovered that messing around with the box is apparently the point of this game, you will have enough behavior to select from, so that you can now begin to click only for certain behaviors, behaviors that aim toward a plan. It's as if you have a whole box of Scrabble letters, and you are going to start selecting letters that spell a word. This process is part of "shaping."

Step three

Variations and final products: What could you shape from cardboard box behaviors?

Behavior: Get in the box and stay there

Initial behavior: Dog puts paw in box. Click, toss treats. Then don't click, just wait and see. Maybe you'll get two paws in box. Click. Now get four paws in box. Get dog in box. Options: Sitting or lying in box; staying in box until clicked; staying in box until called, then clicked for coming.

Chapter 9 – Creating the Thinking Dog

Uses: Put the dog to bed. Put the dog in its crate. Let children amuse themselves and make friends with the dog by clicking the dog for hopping into a box and out again (works with cats, too). One third-grade teacher takes her papillon to school on special events days, in a picnic basket. When the basket is opened, the dog hops out, plays with the children, and then hops back in again.

Behavior: Carry the box

Initial behavior: Dog grabs the edge of the box in its teeth and lifts it off the floor.

Uses: Millions. Carry a box. Carry a basket. Put things away: magazines back on the pile, toys in the toy box. A dog that has learned the generalized or generic rule, "Lifting things in my mouth is reinforceable," can learn many additional skills.

Behavior: Tip the box over onto yourself

I don't know what good this is, but it's not hard to get; it crops up often in the "101 Things to Do with a Box" game. If the dog paws the near edge of the box hard enough, it will flip. My Border terrier, Skookum, discovered that he could tip the living-room wastebasket (wicker, bowl-shaped, empty) over on himself, so that he was hidden inside it. Then he scooted around in there, making the wastebasket move mysteriously across the floor. It was without a doubt the funniest thing any of our dinner guests had ever seen a dog do. Since terriers love being laughed with (but never at), clicks and treats were not necessary to maintain the behavior once he had discovered it—and he learned to wait until he was invited to do it, usually when we had company.

When Animals Train Us
by Lori Chamberland

Adolescent Border collies are excellent trainers.

Blink, my third dog, was the first one to train me to give him water on request. One day as we stood in the kitchen together, he pawed his empty water bowl deliberately. The sound of his nails hitting the ceramic made it go "ding!" Then he looked me right in the eye. I did what any well-trained animal would do: I responded to my cue promptly and I filled his bowl with water. Weeks went by and it happened again in the kitchen. "Ding!" I again filled the water bowl. More time went by and this time I was in the living room, but Blink was in the kitchen. "Ding!" Again, I filled the water bowl.

Was I teaching Blink that dinging his bowl meant he was going to get some water? Or was he teaching me that my cue to get him water was "ding"? In fact, he was training me.

By filling his bowl every time, I was positively reinforcing the behavior of Blink dinging the bowl. By wagging his tail, drinking happily, and (to be anthropomorphic) appearing appreciative, he was positively reinforcing my behavior of filling his bowl.

I am sure that, just like our dogs, during the early phase of my training I was not yet aware of what I was being trained to do. At some point during my admittedly quick learning process, I became cognizant that I should get water for the dog. Then, at some other point, I recognized clearly that I now had a discriminative stimulus (a cue) that meant one thing and one thing only: get me water now.

Along the way Blink made some deliberate decisions. He chose the cue, not me. And he put some reasoning into his choice. He could have chosen to whine, bark, paw at me, and so on. But he chose a cue that involved an object (the bowl) where he usually finds water present. His cue is also an auditory cue, a sound that is not an intrinsic or typical noise dogs make (like

Chapter 9 – Creating the Thinking Dog

barking or whining). It required him to use his paw to strike an object in a particular way.

Once I was fluent in my water-fetching behavior, Blink shopped the cue around, testing it for stimulus control. He tried the "ding!" cue on a different person in the household. He transferred it to the water bowl in my office. He even transferred it to a different house, with a different water bowl and a different person. One time when my co-worker was dog-sitting for me, Blink let her know he was out of water by dinging his bowl and waiting. When she also responded promptly to the cue, I'm sure Blink was very pleased with himself—and with her!

The four quadrants

Although I think he's quite a clever boy, Blink is not an unusually gifted member of his species in figuring out how to train me to get him water. Dogs train humans to do things like that for them all the time: feed me, let me outside, take me on a walk, scratch my belly, pick me up, pet me, throw this for me, and so on. And we train them to do things that benefit us: sit quietly, walk beside me, search out the bad guy or the missing child, retrieve objects, and so on.

Dogs have never heard of Pavlov and Skinner. Nobody ever sat them down and schooled them on the four quadrants of operant conditioning and the laws of learning. Yet, they are skilled trainers. They don't stick to positive reinforcement, though! Animals train us quite effectively using all four quadrants. Here are a few examples; I'll bet you can come up with dozens more:

Positive punishment:

Human: (usually an "all dogs *love* me!"-type stranger) insists on trying to approach a fearful dog

Dog: Licks lips, turns head away, hides behind owner, then finally lunges and barks.

Result: Human backs off. The behavior of trying to approach that dog has been positively punished.

Negative punishment:

Human: Pets the dog on the top of the head (pat-pat-pat).

Dog: Moves away immediately and goes to lie down.

Result: Human learns that dog doesn't like being petted on the top of the head and stops doing that. The behavior of petting the dog on top of the head has been negatively punished.

Negative reinforcement:

Human: Sits at the desk, ignoring the dog.

Dog: Paw-paw-paw, scratch-scratch-scratch.

Result: Human relents and gives some type of attention to the dog to make the pawing and scratching stop. The behavior of giving attention to the dog has been negatively reinforced.

Positive reinforcement:

Human: Looks at dog and smiles

Dog: Comes closer to human and offers soft, prolonged eye contact

Result: The behavior of smiling at the dog has been positively reinforced.

While we humans frequently botch our timing (especially with punishment), dogs' timing is impeccable—without any formal training! Humans yell at their dogs for shredding the couch pillows hours after the "crime" occurs. The only thing we're "punishing" is the dog coming to say hello to us after we've been gone all day. On the other hand, when dogs deliver a punisher it's usually a punisher with perfect timing and razor-sharp precision. A well-timed air snap that comes this close to your flesh doesn't injure you in the slightest but is usually enough to scare you away in one single event. Show me a human who can accomplish that with zero training.

You've almost certainly heard that "Dogs are always learning." That's very true. And I think we can add to that, "Dogs are always teaching." A good training session is a conversation between trainer and trainee. The more we realize that the role of trainer is fluid and that sometimes we're the trainee, the better off our relationships with our animals will be.

Chapter 9 – Creating the Thinking Dog

Carnivorous Chairs and the Cone of Shame: Creativity in Action
by Alena Van Arendonk

In training circles, we *love* to talk about the added benefits of clicker training—engaging the dog's mind, the respondent conditioning of a positive emotional state, the fostering of creativity in both trainer and trainee.

Creativity? Is that a good thing?

Several years ago, on a large training-community mailing list, one person posed a very honest question: "Why should I want my dog to be creative?" The question merits some consideration. Aside from the giddy elation that overcomes behavior nerds (like myself) when we see a training subject acquire a new skill or thought process, how useful or desirable is it to have a creative animal? After all, the more you teach the dog to problem-solve, the more trouble the dog can get into. If I train my dog to open doors, can't he escape the house, or steal food out of the refrigerator? If he learns to manipulate objects in his environment, won't he figure out how to open the crate door or knock the lid off the trash can?

Leaving aside for the moment the question of sloppy training (good stimulus control and proactive training will prevent most of these hypothetical problems), let's look at some of the advantages of producing a creative dog.

Confidence-building

My blue Doberman, Lucrezia, was the most clicker-savvy dog I have ever owned. She was also by far the most fearful dog I have ever owned. Among her various phobias, Lucrezia was terrified of things being over her head. If a treat rolled under a table or chair, she ducked away in fear rather than put her nose in the shadow of the object to find the treat. She eyed the furniture warily, as if the chair would collapse on her head and devour her.

Around this time I was teaching training classes in a big-box store, and Lucrezia was my demo dog. One of the things we did to kill time on slow days was a variability exercise, or the "show me something new" game, in which the dog offers a completely novel behavior for each successive click. Lucrezia loved this game, and invented all sorts of new ways to poke, touch, grab, bite, sit on, or move around an object. Since our training area included a row of chairs, I sometimes had her "show me something new" with a chair. One day, after exhausting all manner of nose-pokes and chin-rests and paw-whacks, Lucrezia came up with wrapping her paw around the metal chair leg. Click and treat. Next, she offered the new behavior of dragging the chair a few inches with her paw. Click and treat again; move on to the next trick. When we were finished with the session, I put the chair back in the row and set up for the next class.

Some time later, I tossed Lucrezia a piece of food that hit the concrete floor and rolled, ending up against the wall behind the row of chairs. When she saw that her treat was under a chair, Lucrezia balked and backed up, looking helplessly from me to the chair, too frightened to stretch her neck under the chair to get the treat. After a few moments of conflict, suddenly Lucrezia perked up. She walked up to the chair, hooked her paw around the leg, dragged the chair out of the way, and ate her treat. Then she pranced over to me, head high: "Look, Mommy, I outsmarted that scary, dog-eating chair!"

I found this astonishing at the time. Now that I have a better grasp of behavior science, it blows me away that a young, fairly novice dog (she'd been with me about a year) was able to recall a one-repetition behavior and apply it in what was clearly a stressful situation.

Back to creativity. That particular behavior, grabbing and dragging the chair, was 100%-invented by the dog. I did not teach her to move the chair. Apart from the single click and treat during our game, I had never reinforced her for moving the chair. I had not counter-conditioned her to regard chairs as non-scary objects. In fact, for the rest of her life Lucrezia remained hesitant to eat treats from beneath furniture. The original and underlying fear issue was still there. But, encouraged to develop her own creative problem-solving skills, the dog could approach and deal with something that frightened her. What Lucrezia invented was not only a means of getting to a treat. It was, in effect, a coping mechanism.

Contingency plans

Even if confidence is not an issue, there are times when it is beneficial for a dog to find another approach, one that does not rely on the same old routine.

Chapter 9 – Creating the Thinking Dog

When things go wrong (and they will!), it's nice to be able to invent another option on the fly.

A few months ago, my Doberman, Valenzia, was attacked by another dog and badly injured. To protect the hundreds of stitches and staples and drains and other insults that were embedded in her, Valenzia had to wear an Elizabethan collar, what we now call, thanks to the writers of the Pixar film *Up*, "the cone of shame."

I could write an entire creativity article just about Valenzia and medical collars. She has demonstrated her creativity by inventing a way to remove every kind of protective medical collar I've ever put on her! But this anecdote involves a collar she hadn't yet removed (if only because she was too sore and swollen to twist out of it).

The door into my fenced backyard exits from a walk-out basement, which is accessible from the house only via a steep, narrow stairway. Because of the injuries to her legs, Valenzia was convalescing in a pen in the basement where she could be walked outside to relieve herself without taking any stairs. Valenzia is used to sleeping in my bedroom, and she's a very clingy dog even when she's feeling at her best. You can imagine how she felt about being confined alone downstairs! She was determined to get upstairs, and she didn't care how many stitches she ripped out doing it. I had to keep a baby gate across the stairs from the basement to prevent her from dashing up to the house.

One day I failed to block the stairs completely when I let her out of the pen, and Valenzia bolted up the steps toward the main floor. She made it about halfway before the plastic cone around her neck sagged low enough to hook on a step, jolting her to an abrupt (and probably painful) halt. She tried to push forward a couple of times, but the collar blocked her. She was stuck.

I called her from the base of the steps, but she glanced back at me with an eloquent look that distinctly translated to, "I'm *not* going back in that pen." Valenzia paused for a moment, looking down at the steps. Then, with astonishing athleticism and flexibility for a dog in her condition, she launched her hind end into the air and pivoted 180 degrees on the narrow stairs so that she was facing me at the bottom. Carefully, she lifted one hind foot and felt for the step behind her, then the next step. She began backing up the stairs, lifting her head to let the edge of the cone bump up each step in her wake.

I was too stunned to stop her as she backed to the top of the stairs, pivoted again, and dashed into the house to run laps and make a mess of my floors. *I had never taught Valenzia to back up the stairs.* Anyone who has ever trained a dog to back through ladder rungs or up steps knows that dogs aren't instinctively aware of their back feet. It usually takes time and practice to develop hind-end awareness and control. Yet, here was my dog inventing it on her own because going up the stairs front-first wasn't working very well.

Individually, all of the component behaviors make sense. With Valenzia, I've done a lot of free-shaping (a simple form of cognitive problem-solving) and enough kinetic behaviors (jumping, targeting to platforms, and so on) for her to be able to move her body consciously and with intention. The 180-degree pivot is something she can do mid-air (another behavior she invented), so doing it with her front feet on the ground is a reasonable variation. Valenzia knows how to find a platform and step up onto it, so it's not surprising that she possesses the mechanics of finding and stepping up on the stairs. What is so impressive to me is that she was able to recognize the cause of the problem (the low-hanging cone around her neck), figure out what would remove the obstacle (turning it the other way), and chain separate behaviors together as a response.

Man, clever animals are neat!

On the small scale, a dog figuring out the stairs is not necessarily a useful behavior. In this case, it caused me some additional hassle—I had to catch the dog, get her back in her pen, and scrub the blood off the floors. But apply this same thought process to a dog performing a function that is valuable to humans:

- A search dog's path is cut off by debris, and he needs to find an alternate route back to his handler.
- A service dog's harness fails, and she needs to maintain physical contact with her person.
- A police dog sent to search a building has to surmount obstacles such as fences, closed doors, and furniture to reach the suspect in hiding.

Of course animals are trained for as many contingencies as possible in situations like these, but there are many instances where something unforeseeable

Chapter 9 – Creating the Thinking Dog

may go wrong. If the dog can perform the required job some other way than Plan A, it can be very helpful, or even life-saving.

Training options

As a trainer, I *love* building creativity in my dogs because it makes it so much easier to teach new behaviors. Not every dog follows the exact same training plan. Some dogs learn faster with capturing, others with targeting, others with adducting known behaviors, others with free shaping. But the more creativity and analytical thinking you foster in your animal, the more options you have available to train new or complex behaviors. If you have a creative dog, you may even be able to skip steps in your training plan.

When I wanted Valenzia to put her front feet on an overturned bowl and bow, I was able to shape the position in just a few minutes because she began offering me various behaviors immediately—targeting, foot movement, head movement, joint flexion, variations of one or two feet, with or without nose touch. She tried every possible combination, just to see what would work. I was presented with a wide range of behaviors to select from, instead of having to coax the dog along one muscle movement at a time to build the position I wanted. Could I have shaped a novice dog to do the exact same behavior? Certainly! But without the dog offering me everything she could think of, it would have taken more training steps and significantly more time.

Much of the speed and the offering of behavior can be attributed to experience—what we call having a clicker-savvy dog, or a dog that has learned to move until he/she hears the click and to repeat the marked behavior. But the experimentation, the offering of new variations, is a form of creativity that results from being reinforced consistently for trying new things and inventing new combinations.

The creative advantage

I am convinced that the benefits of producing a creative animal far outstrip the potential downsides. Sure, you may have a dog that figures out how to open the cabinets or go up the stairs when you don't want him to. You might experience a few inconveniences, at least until you use your own clicker creativity to train something more desirable. In the end, the benefits to your dog, the time you'll save in training, and the potential new behaviors your dog might invent are worth a hypothetical hassle or two.

The Unexpected Benefits of Training
by Ken Ramirez

We discuss the benefits of training and the advantages of focusing on positive reinforcement quite frequently, but I have long believed that training does far more than we realize. Positive reinforcement training expands animals' repertoires, makes them better problem-solvers, increases their resilience to change and, dare I say it, boosts their intelligence. The evidence of these benefits is anecdotal, but I would suggest that the examples below present a compelling case for supporting these claims.

Escape from predation

A friend and colleague of mine, Ilana Bram, shared a story from a local co-op where she trains goats to do various husbandry behaviors. The co-op also has chickens living on site, and Ilana began training one hen in particular named Chickie. Chickie really took to the training and was an eager learner, developing a small but solid repertoire of behaviors.

Sadly, raccoons got into the enclosure and killed almost all of the chicken population. Only four birds survived the attack, and Chickie was one of them. Ilana asked if I thought Chickie's exposure to training contributed to her ability to escape the attack. She accurately pointed out that training had expanded Chickie's behavioral repertoire, which included climbing on objects, flying short distances, and exposure to new areas within the enclosure. Ilana said that Chickie's personality seemed to change after the training; she was more daring and exploratory, venturing farther out than the other chickens, and boldly soliciting treats from people. Might these new traits have given her a survival advantage?

I immediately responded, "Yes!" I have long believed that training gives animals new skills and makes them better problem-solvers. We will never know for sure whether those skills made a difference to Chickie on that terrible night, but I believe they did. This incident brought to mind other examples of well-trained animals showing resilience and accomplishing incredible things.

Chapter 9 – Creating the Thinking Dog

Earthquake survival

I spent several years as the trainer for a group of more than 200 birds in a park in Mexico City. The population included several species of parrots, ravens, toucans, birds of prey, and a variety of songbirds. These birds lived in social groups in large free-flight aviaries. We did basic training with all the birds, but we focused most of our attention and advanced training on the birds that were part of our daily shows. The complexity of training varied from species to species, but included flying on cue, medical behaviors, tactile behaviors, vocalizations, and lots of socialization and desensitization to new people and places.

Early one morning, Mexico City experienced a devastating earthquake that registered 8.0 on the Richter scale and created widespread damage in the area. When I arrived at the park, I found that although three of the aviaries were still standing, two of the aviaries had sustained serious damage. A large building next to the enclosures had collapsed, and huge slabs of concrete and shards of glass had torn holes in the aviary and crushed or buried sections of the birds' homes.

As we inspected the area, what we found was heartbreaking. Most of the 62 birds who lived in the damaged aviaries had died, primarily from inhaling smoke and dust created by the collapsed building. Words cannot describe the pain we experienced over the wonderfully bright lives that were lost that morning.

But something miraculous also happened; we discovered 17 birds that had somehow survived and made their way to safety. The birds were hanging out in three different places. They had found their way to the trainer's office, the flight training area, and the show stage. Of the 17 birds that lived, 14 were birds from our show. They included five macaws, three ravens, two Amazon parrots, two cockatoos, and two toucans. Only two birds from our show failed to escape the disaster.

Given the variety of species involved, their escape from two different aviaries, the unusual routes and extraordinary effort to get to where we found them, and the large number of similar species living in the same space that did not survive, it seems more than a coincidence that it was primarily the well-trained birds that found their way to safety. All of the birds had spent time in the training locations and had access to those spaces; the only difference was that they had not had the same complex and extensive training. We could not find any other logical explanation.

Late-night fishing

On a lighter note, I would like to share the story of a California sea lion named Jones that I worked with in Texas. We were doing some renovations to one of our sea lion habitats, so we relocated Jones and six other males in a temporary home located right next to a large lake. Jones was an older, well-trained, very experienced animal. The other six animals were rescued animals that we had recently adopted, and although they were part of our training program, they were still in the early stages of training.

The sea lions had been living in their temporary habitat for about six weeks when we began to notice that Jones was starting his mornings very slowly. He was healthy and bright-eyed, but he behaved as though he had just eaten a huge meal. We knew this wasn't the case because his last meal had been the night before. Sea lions have voracious appetites, and Jones would still eat his morning meal, but he ate slowly and seemed full. The veterinarian found no signs of illness, and we were baffled.

This unusual behavior had gone on for almost two weeks when in the wee hours of the morning I received a phone call from one of our night security officers. He claimed that he saw a large animal in the lake. I knew that the only animals living in the lake were fish, nothing large like our security guard was describing, so I went into the park to investigate.

It was still dark at 4:00 am when I arrived to check out the mysterious report. In the moonlight, I could see a large body break the surface of the water, then quickly disappear below the surface. It took me several minutes to recognize the distinct form of a sea lion! But how was that possible? I dashed over to the sea lion habitats in alarm.

When I arrived at the habitat next to the lake, I immediately noticed there were six instead of seven animals. Jones was missing. That must be him in the lake! I carefully inspected the habitat. No open doors; they were all locked. No holes, gaps or openings in the fence or wall. How did he get out? Had he really been fishing in the lake like this for the past two weeks? It didn't make sense.

Chapter 9 – Creating the Thinking Dog

I decided not to call him over nor alert him to my presence. I found a comfortable spot to sit and observe out of sight. At 5:45 a.m., as the sun began to rise, Jones made his way out of the lake. He paused in the shallow beach water, and seemed to be looking around, as if to make sure nobody was looking (am I being anthropomorphic, or what!). Then he waddled over to his habitat, approached the shortest part of the fence, and stood up on his rear flippers. This is not a natural behavior, but one that I had taught him years before. He was barely able to place his chin on the top of the fence. Then, with a Herculean effort, he used his chin to pull himself up, while using his front and rear flippers to walk up the wall. None of this was typical sea lion behavior. After a 5-minute struggle, he pulled his 550-pound frame to the top of the fence, and plopped to the ground on the inside of his habitat. He proceeded to get comfortable in his favorite sleeping spot, exactly where we find him every morning!

The next evening, I watched Jones again from my hiding spot. About an hour after closing, Jones woke up from his slumber, paced the entire exhibit as if looking to make sure nobody was watching (yes, anthropomorphic again). Then he carefully reversed the process, climbing out of the exhibit, just as I had watched him climb back in that morning. It was obviously difficult and required some balancing skill, strength, and determination, but he eventually made it over the fence and went straight for the lake where he foraged for fish all night long, returning back home at sunrise, just as he had done the night before.

I feel certain that Jones' 10-year training experience, regular exercise of his neck and flipper muscles, and his trained repertoire of climbing and standing, made his fishing expedition possible. Was his impeccable timing of climbing in and out when he could not be observed related to his expanded problem-solving ability? Could his desire to come back every morning be a sign that he clearly enjoyed interactions with his trainers? It didn't seem as if he returned just to get a free breakfast; he showed little interest in eating from us when he returned! I believe this story demonstrates a variety of ways that training gives animals a wider repertoire of skills.

So many other examples

These three stories just scratch the surface; I have worked with many animals that demonstrated unique and untrained problem-solving skills. There was a dolphin, Misty, who learned to collect trash and hide it away in a drain like a bank account so that she could cash it in for fish when she felt the need. Ranbir the gibbon, upon seeing a wild snake enter his habitat, figured out how to hide in a restraint box and lock himself in so that he was safely out of harm's way. Service dog Lambo, faced with a fire and an unconscious owner, took the initiative to grab the sleeping baby by the onesie and carry it to the neighbor's house. Lambo's action resulted in getting the owner help in time, and ultimately saving the lives of all involved. We see examples in the service and guide dog world all the time of dogs that go far beyond what they were trained to do and accomplish the improbable.

Final thoughts

Training expands animals' views of their world and enables them to accomplish tasks that had not been specifically trained. Positive reinforcement opens up learners' thinking and allows them to explore and grow with greater confidence. Animals trained with punishment tend to have the opposite happen; their worldview shrinks and they are hesitant to try new things. The more I am exposed to the power and benefits of positive training, the more impressed I am by the possibilities and the remarkable ways that animals benefit.

Training Terms

Aversive: Any circumstance or event that causes pain, fear, or emotional discomfort.

Back-chaining: A training strategy in which you train the last behavior in a chain first, then train the next-to-last behavior, then the behavior before that, and so on. Back-chaining takes advantage of the Premack principle, which reinforces performing a less-desired activity with the opportunity to perform a more-desired activity.

Balanced training: A euphemism used to describe a mix of traditional or punishment-based training and other training techniques, such as clicker training.

Behavior: Any observable action an animal does.

Behavior chain: A series of behaviors linked together in a continuous sequence by cues and maintained by a reinforcer at the end of the chain. Each cue serves as the marker and the reinforcer for the previous behavior, and the cue for the next behavior.

Bridging stimulus: An event marker that identifies the desired response and "bridges" the time between the response and the delivery of the primary reinforcer. The clicker is a bridging stimulus.

Calming signals: Subtle body signals dogs use to indicate stress and to avoid or diffuse confrontation and aggression.

Chaining: The process of combining multiple behaviors into a continuous sequence linked together by cues and maintained by a reinforcer at the end of the chain. Each cue serves as the marker and the reinforcer for the previous behavior, and the cue for the next behavior.

Classical conditioning: The process of associating a neutral stimulus with an involuntary response until the stimulus elicits the response. A famous example was Ivan Pavlov's discovery that dogs drooled when they heard a bell that was previously paired with food. Also called respondent conditioning.

Clicker: A toy noisemaker. Animal trainers use the clicker as an event marker to mark a desired response. The sound of the clicker is an excellent marker because it is unique, quick, and consistent.

Clicker training: A system of teaching that uses positive reinforcement in combination with an event marker.

ClickerExpo: A clicker training conference organized by Karen Pryor Clicker Training that features lectures, hands-on labs, performances, and networking events. For more information, visit ClickerExpo.com.

Compulsion training: The traditional style of dog training, where the dog is compelled to perform a behavior and physically corrected for noncompliance.

Conditioned punisher: A conditioned stimulus that signifies that an aversive is coming and that is used to deter or interrupt behavior. If the behavior stops or changes, the aversive may be avoided. For example, a trainer who says "ack" to interrupt a behavior or gives the warning beep of a shock collar when a dog gets too close to the boundary of an electric fence is using a conditioned punisher.

Conditioned reinforcer: A neutral stimulus paired with a primary reinforcer until the neutral stimulus takes on the reinforcing properties of the primary reinforcer. A clicker, after repeatedly being associated with a food treat or other reinforcer, becomes a conditioned reinforcer.

Conditioned stimulus: Any stimulus that has preceded a particular behavior or event sufficiently often to provoke awareness or response. Clicks and cues are both examples of conditioned stimuli.

Consequence: The result of an action. Consequences frequently, but not always, affect future behavior, making the behavior more or less likely to occur. *The five principles of operant conditioning* describe the potential results.

Continuous reinforcement: The simplest schedule of reinforcement. Every desired response is reinforced.

Correction: A euphemism for applying a physical aversive, which is intended to communicate that the dog did something wrong. In some cases, the trainer then guides the dog through the desired behavior. When the aversive is followed by the desired behavior, the aversive is considered instructive, thus the euphemism "correction."

Counter-conditioning: Pairing one stimulus that evokes one response with another that evokes an opposite response, so that the first stimulus comes to evoke the second response. For example, for a dog that is afraid of men wearing hats, the trainer repeatedly feeds the dog his favorite food when a man wearing a hat approaches. The goal is to replace the animal's apprehension with the pleasure—and anticipation—elicited by the food. You must proceed with counter-conditioning gradually, however; if the process is rushed, the favorite food may take on the fear association instead.

Criteria: The specific, trainer-defined characteristics of a desired response in a training session. The trainer clicks at the instant the animal achieves each criterion. Criteria can include not only the physical behavior, but elements like latency, duration, and distance.

Crossover dog: A dog that has previously been trained by a non-clicker method and now is being clicker trained.

Crossover trainer: A trainer who previously used non-clicker methods to train animals and is now clicker training.

Cue: A stimulus that elicits a behavior. Cues may be verbal, physical (for instance, a hand signal), or environmental (for instance, a curb may become a cue to sit if the dog is always cued to sit before crossing a road).

Desensitization: The process of increasing an animal's tolerance of a particular stimulus by gradually increasing the presence of the stimulus, for instance, by making a noise louder or more frequent.

Differential reinforcement: A reinforcement method in which some responses are rewarded and others aren't. For example, a trainer wanting tucked sits would reward tucked sits and ignore all others. Differential reinforcement is not a schedule of reinforcement.

Environmental reinforcer: Anything in the environment that your dog wants. Trainers can use access to these items or activities as powerful reinforcers for desired behavior. For example, say your dog wants to greet an approaching dog. You can ask for a behavior you want first and then let your dog's compliance (or noncompliance) determine whether he gets to meet and greet.

Event marker: A signal used to mark desired behavior at the instant it occurs. The clicker is an event marker.

Extinction: The weakening—and eventual disappearance—of behavior through nonreinforcement or "ignoring" the behavior. In extinction, nothing is added or removed from the environment. For example, a dog may repeatedly reach his paw under a fence to try to get a treat on the other side. If he cannot reach the treat (reaching for the treat doesn't work because it isn't reinforced through success), the dog will eventually quit pawing at the fenceline.

Extinction burst: A characteristic of extinction. If a previously reinforced behavior is no longer reinforced, the animal may increase the intensity or frequency of the behavior to try to earn the reinforcement again. If the behavior still is not reinforced, it will diminish again after an extinction burst.

Five principles of operant conditioning: A reference to the possible consequences of behavior. See *positive punishment, negative punishment, positive reinforcement, negative reinforcement,* and *extinction.*

Fixed interval: Describes a schedule of reinforcement in which the trainer reinforces a desired behavior after a specific period of time—for example, every minute.

Fixed ratio: Describes a schedule of reinforcement in which the trainer reinforces a desired behavior after a specific number of responses—for example, a trainer reinforcing after every two correct responses or after every three correct responses.

Four quadrants of operant conditioning: A reference to a popular chart illustrating the concepts of reinforcement and punishment. Some trainers feel that this description is misleading in two ways: It neglects to mention extinction, and it is sometimes perceived to imply that all the principles of operant conditioning are of equal value in a training program.

Habituation: The ability to get used to and stop reacting to meaningless stimuli.

Head halter: Similar to a horse's halter, a dog's head halter gives the trainer control of the dog's head, making it easier to manage a dog on leash until the dog has been taught to walk at the handler's side or to act calmly in exciting or scary situations.

Interval reinforcement: Describes a schedule of reinforcement in which the trainer reinforces the desired response after a specific period of time—for example, every minute. In variable interval reinforcement, the trainer reinforces after varying periods of time within a certain timeframe.

Jackpot: A large or high-value surprise reinforcer given after a particularly exceptional effort.

Keep-going signal (KGS): A signal, verbal or otherwise, given in the middle of a behavior to tell the dog he is doing the behavior correctly and should keep doing what he's doing. Keep-going signals are not discussed in the scientific literature but are a practical development that is controversial in some circles because of disagreements about their value in training.

Latency: The time between the cue and the response. Ideally, that time is zero—or as close to immediate as possible.

Luring: A hands-off method of guiding the dog through a behavior. For example, a food lure can be used to guide a dog from a sit into a down. This is a common method of getting more complex behaviors. Lures are usually food, but can be anything the dog finds reinforcing, such as a toy. Trainers must take care to fade the lure early so the dog will not become dependent on the lure.

Marker: A signal used to mark desired behavior at the instant it occurs. The clicker is a marker.

Modeling: A technique used in traditional training to get behavior. At the outset, the dog is physically guided, or otherwise compelled, to do the behavior. Pushing a dog's rear into a sit is modeling. Clicker trainers don't generally use modeling because they want dogs to be active participants in the training process, using their brains to figure out what will earn them clicks. This technique is sometimes referred to as *molding*.

Negative punishment (P-): The act of taking away something the animal will work for in order to suppress (lessen the frequency of) a behavior. For example, a dog jumps on you to get attention. By turning your back or leaving the room, you apply P- by removing the attention he wants.

Negative reinforcement (R-): The act of removing something the animal will work to avoid in order to strengthen (increase the frequency of) a behavior. Heeling is traditionally taught through R-. The dog receives a correction when he walks anywhere except in heel position. Walking in heel position increases, because that is the only "safe" place to walk—because that removes the threat of correction. The key to R- is that the trainer must first apply or threaten an aversive for it to be removed.

No Reward Marker (NRM): Intended to be a signal to say, "No, that isn't what I want. Try again." An NRM is a conditioned punisher, which serves just the opposite role of a clicker (which is a conditioned reinforcer). It marks the moment the dog makes a wrong move or initiates an undesirable action. Like all punishers, an NRM when used properly will decrease the frequency of the behavior it follows, but can also cause frustration in the learner.

Operant conditioning (OC): The process of changing an animal's response to a certain stimulus by manipulating the consequences that immediately follow the response. B.F. Skinner developed the five principles of operant conditioning. Clicker training is a subset of operant conditioning, using only positive reinforcement, extinction, and, to a lesser extent, negative punishment.

Permanent criteria: Criteria that are found in the final behavior. Permanent criteria should be trained to a higher level of reliability than temporary criteria.

Poison(ed): No longer reinforcing for the dog, for instance, a cue that has accidentally become associated with a punishment.

Positive punishment (P+): The act of adding something the animal will work to avoid in order to suppress (lessen the frequency of) a behavior. For example, jerking on the leash to stop a dog from jumping on someone is P+ used to suppress the behavior of jumping. Other common examples of P+ include yelling, nose taps, spanking, electric shock, and assorted "booby traps."

Positive reinforcement (R+): The act of adding something the animal will work for in order to strengthen (increase the frequency of) a behavior. For example, giving the dog a treat for sitting is R+ used to increase the probability that the dog will sit again.

Training Terms

Premack principle: A theory stating that a stronger response or a preferred response will reinforce a weaker response; in other words, a higher-probability behavior can be used to reinforce a lower-probability behavior. Parents use this principle all the time: "Eat your broccoli and then you can have ice cream." A dog trainer may ask the dog to lie on his mat quietly and then reinforce that by allowing the dog to go outside.

Primary reinforcer: A reinforcer that the animal is born needing. Food, water, and sex are examples of primary reinforcers. Contrast with *secondary*—or *conditioned*—*reinforcer.*

Proofing: Teaching a dog to perform a behavior in the presence of distractions.

Punishment: In operant conditioning, a consequence to a behavior in which something is added to or removed from the situation to make the behavior less likely to occur in the future.

Rate of reinforcement: The number of reinforcers given for desired responses in a specific period of time. A high rate of reinforcement is critical to training success.

Reinforcement: In operant conditioning, a consequence to a behavior in which something is added to or removed from the situation to make the behavior more likely to occur in the future.

Reinforcement ratio: A schedule of reinforcement in which the trainer reinforces desired behavior based on the number of responses. In a fixed-ratio reinforcement schedule, the trainer reinforces after a pre-determined number of "correct" responses. In a variable-ratio reinforcement schedule, the trainer reinforces after a random number of correct responses. These schedules are generally used in research settings to study animal learning; they are not usually used for day-to-day practical training.

Reinforcer: Anything a dog will work to obtain. In operant conditioning, it increases the frequency of the behavior it follows.

Release word (release cue): A word (or cue) that signals the end of a behavior. After a behavior is strong and on cue, trainers sometimes replace the clicker with a release word.

Respondent conditioning: The process of associating a neutral stimulus with an involuntary response until the stimulus elicits the response. A famous example was Ivan Pavlov's discovery that dogs drooled when they heard a bell that was previously paired with food. Also called *classical conditioning*.

Secondary reinforcer: A learned reinforcer, one that the animal is not born needing. A secondary reinforcer may be as, or even more, powerful than a primary reinforcer. A properly trained clicker is a conditioned reinforcer. See *conditioned reinforcer*.

Shaping: Building new behavior by selectively reinforcing variations in existing behavior, during the action rather than after completion, to increase or strengthen the behavior in a specific manner or direction.

Spontaneous recovery: A characteristic of extinction in which a behavior that was thought to be extinct reappears unexpectedly. If the trainer ensures that the behavior is not reinforced, it will quickly disappear again.

Stimulus: A change in the environment. If the stimulus has no effect on the animal, it is a neutral stimulus. A stimulus that stands out in the environment, that the animal notices more than other environmental stimuli, is a salient stimulus. A stimulus that causes a change of state in the animal, that causes him to perform a specific behavior, for example, is a discriminative stimulus. A properly trained cue is a discriminative stimulus.

Stimulus control: A conditioned stimulus becomes a discriminative stimulus (or cue) when it is followed by a specific learned behavior or reaction. A response is said to be "under stimulus control" when presentation of the particular stimulus fulfills these four conditions: the behavior is always offered when that cue is presented; the behavior is not offered in the absence of that cue; the behavior is not offered in response to some other cue; and no other behavior occurs in response to that cue.

Successive approximation: The process of increasing or altering a behavior incrementally by repeatedly changing the environment to amplify or extend the behavior. For example, increasing the weight of a load or the height of a jump by small increments will amplify the effort to pull a load or jump an obstacle. Often referred to as the small steps that are used to build a behavior.

Target: Something the animal is taught to touch with some part of his body.

Training Terms

Target stick: A mobile target the animal is taught to follow. Trainers often use target sticks as guides to shape behavior.

Temporary criteria: Criteria that are stepping stones to a final behavior that won't be present, in their current form, in the final behavior. Temporary criteria should be trained only to about 80% reliability before "making it harder." If a temporary criterion is reinforced for too long, the animal may be reluctant to change its behavior.

Timing: Refers to the timing of the click. Ideally, the click should occur at exactly the same instant the target criterion is achieved. Timing is a mechanical skill that requires practice. The trainer must be able to recognize the behaviors that precede the target behavior in order to click at the very moment the target behavior occurs.

Traditional training: Compulsion training. Traditional training is sometimes characterized by modeling or luring to get the behavior, and by the use of negative reinforcement and positive punishment to proof it.

Training period: A pre-set period of time scheduled for training. A training period may be composed of multiple training sessions.

Training session: A period of time devoted solely to training. The trainer can decide either the duration of the session or number of repetitions in advance. Criteria should remain constant during a single session. At the end of a training session, the trainer evaluates the animal's progress and decides whether to make the next session harder or stay with the same criteria.

Variable ratio: A schedule of reinforcement in which the trainer reinforces desired behavior after varying numbers of "correct" responses.

Variable schedule of reinforcement (VSR): Technically, either a variable interval or a variable-ratio schedule of reinforcement. Most trainers, however, use VSR to mean a variable-ratio reinforcement schedule.

BETTER TOGETHER

Author Biographies

Melissa Alexander

Melissa C. Alexander is the author of *Click for Joy! Questions and Answers from Clicker Trainers and their Dogs*. She is also the owner of the popular ClickerSolutions mailing list and website. Melissa lives on a farmlette in the Cascade Mountains outside of Seattle with her husband, dogs, and occasionally a horse or two. She dreams of relocating her menagerie (minus the horses) to a sailboat for a trip around the world. In her spare time, Melissa writes fiction and spends far too much time on the Internet.

Alena Van Arendonk

Alena Van Arendonk is a trainer at Canines In Action, Inc. She has been training professionally since 2000 and specializes in working with fearful and fear-aggressive dogs. Alena also juggles the hats of fine artist, actress, costumer, writer, and all-around geek.

Nan Arthur

Nan Arthur, KPA CTP, KPA faculty member, CDBC, CPDT-KSA, has been involved in the behavior and training of dogs for more than 22 years. She is the author of *Chill Out Fido! How to Calm Your Dog* and is a member of PPG and IAABC. Nan owns Nan Arthur's Whole Dog Training, providing private training and group classes throughout San Diego County.

Laura VanArendonk Baugh

Laura VanArendonk Baugh, KPA CTP, CPDT, started playing with animals at an early age and never grew out of it. After 13 years of traditional dog training she discovered clicker training, and she has never looked back. Laura operates Canines In Action, Inc., in Indianapolis and is also a Karen Pryor Academy faculty member.

Aidan Bindoff

Aidan Bindoff is a professional dog trainer who specializes in helping reactive and aggressive dogs through his business, www.everydog.com.au, in

Tasmania, Australia. He also works in statistics and applied mathematics, with projects ranging from marine predator tracking to neuroscience, where he has been able to combine his passion for animals, psychology, science, and data.

Irith Bloom

Irith Bloom, KPA CTP, CPDT-KSA, CDBC, Victoria Stilwell Positively Dog Trainer (VSPDT), and Certified Behavior Adjustment Training Instructor (CBATI), has been training animals since the 1980s. She is the owner of The Sophisticated Dog, LLC, in Los Angeles, a faculty member at Victoria Stilwell Academy, chair of the Education Committee of the Association of Professional Dog Trainers (APDT), and a volunteer for National English Shepherd Rescue.

Hannah Branigan

Hannah Branigan, KPA faculty member, strives to train in a criticism-free environment. Her commitment and success are evident in group classes and in-home training lessons, as well as in areas of special interest that include conformation, obedience, Schutzhund, agility, and rally.

Lori Chamberland

Lori Chamberland is the Director of Karen Pryor Academy. She also provides limited in-home dog training in the Hudson, MA, area. A canine sports enthusiast, Lori and her dogs have competed in agility, K9 Nose Work, and Treibball.

Aaron Clayton

Aaron Clayton is the Chief Executive Officer of Karen Pryor Clicker Training (KPCT). In 2001, Aaron joined training icon Karen Pryor to launch KPCT. Through clickertraining.com, Karen Pryor Academy, and ClickerExpo, as well as through innovative training products and publications, the company has shown thousands of people how better training and teaching produces better relationships. Aaron is a frequent contributor to the company's blogs.

Sarah Dixon

Sarah Dixon, CDBC, KPA CTP, works as a dog trainer and behavior specialist for Instinct Dog Behavior & Training, LLC, in New York City.

Author Biographies

Sarah has trained animals her entire life and has experience working with dogs, cats, horses, parrots, and various small animals. She is dedicated to continuing education, and has completed multiple courses in dog training and animal behavior. Sarah is particularly interested in helping puppies, newly adopted dogs, and dogs that have behavioral issues.

Terrie Hayward

Terrie Hayward holds a master's degree in bilingual special education. She is a KPA faculty member, a KPA CTP, and a CPDT. Additionally, Terrie is certified as a Canine Separation Anxiety Trainer (CSAT) and is an Associate Member of the International Association of Animal Behavior Consultants (IAABC). A member of the Pet Professional Guild, Terrie has authored articles on training for *BARK* magazine, *Pet Business,* and *Grooming Business* magazine, and is the author of the pocket guide to working with deaf dogs, *A Deaf Dog Joins the Family*.

Colleen Koch

The veterinary practice of Colleen Koch, DVM, KPA CTP, aspires to improve a patient's emotional state at every clinic visit. For years, Colleen has been offering treats to pets during vaccinations and other unpleasant treatments, easing pets of all ages into acceptance of medical care via positive association. Currently, she limits her cases to patients with behavior problems, seeing those animals at the University of Missouri Veterinary Health Center in Wentzville, Missouri, MO, and at Lincoln Land Animal Clinic, Ltd, in Jacksonville, Illinois. Colleen completed her American College of Veterinary Behaviorist non-conforming residency recently; she hopes to sit for the board exam in 2017.

Casey Lomonaco

Casey Lomonaco lives in upstate New York, where she offers editorial, writing, and behavior consulting services through her company Rewarding Behaviors Dog Training. When she is not working with or writing about dogs, she is knitting, reading, or hiking in a forest—with dogs.

Laurie Luck

Laurie Luck, KPA CTP, KPA faculty member, is the founder of Smart Dog University. She has been involved with many pet-dog trainer certification initiatives, all based on humane training practices and the latest scientific knowledge. Laurie also participates in service dog training, and she and her Tango are a pet-therapy team. Through her work with dogs and owners, Laurie has developed many happy canine and human friendships.

Rebecca Lynch

Rebecca Lynch, KPA CTP, is an experienced dog trainer, veterinary technician, and K9 Search and Rescue officer. She is the owner of Elzy Acres Rescue and Resort, and is one of the founding members of Force Free Tennessee, an association of credentialed, positive animal professionals. Rebecca's goal is to strengthen the bond between humans and animals through positive training and communication.

Debbie Martin

Debbie Martin, LVT, KPA CTP, KPA faculty member emeritus, Veterinary Technician Specialist in Behavior, and Kenneth Martin, DVM, Diplomate of the American College of Veterinary Behaviorists, work together at Veterinary Behavior Consultations, LLC. They provide behavior consultations, behavior modification, and training. Debbie and Kenneth Martin are also the co-owners of TEAM Education in Animal Behavior and provide continuing education seminars and webinars pertinent to animal behavior and training.

The Martins are the authors of *Puppy Start Right: Foundation Training for the Companion Dog,* on which the Puppy Start Right for Instructors course at Karen Pryor Academy is based. Debbie and Ken Martin are contributing authors, and Debbie is the co-editor, of the textbook *Canine and Feline Behavior for Veterinary Technicians and Nurses.*

Clint Matthews

Clint Matthews, husband, father to two sons, and owner of three German shorthaired pointers (GSP), trains all of his dogs with clicker training. Gus, age 7, having mastered his fear of the truck, is being trained as a gundog and is a great hunting partner. Jett, age 6, took third place in the 2011 National Futurity Field Trial Stake German Shorthair Pointer Club of America, and has earned his AKC Field Champion title. Emma, age 3, is on her way toward her own Field Champion title with eight placements. These three family dogs are showing terrific results from positive training!

Author Biographies

Joan Orr

Joan Orr is a co-founder of TAGteach International. She is also the producer of the award-winning *Clicker Puppy* DVD, co-founder of the nonprofit Doggone Safe, co-creator of the board game Doggone Crazy!, and co-author of *Getting Started: Clicking with Your Rabbit*. Part of the first advisory board that established Karen Pryor Academy for Animal Training & Behavior, Joan was also a ClickerExpo faculty member for nine years.

Emma Parsons

Emma Parsons is a Canine Behavior Consultant for SureFire Dogs in Westborough, MA, and Masterpeace Dog Training in Franklin, MA. She is also the acclaimed author of *Click to Calm: Healing the Aggressive Dog* and *Teaching the Reactive Dog Class: Leading the Journey from Reactivity to Reliability*. Emma lives with her husband Greg, and is owned by four clicker-trained dogs: Lizzie-Taylor, Austyn-Roque, Kayden-Blue, and Wylie-Rae. All of her dogs are serious competitors in both agility and obedience.

Gale Pryor

Gale Pryor is a healthcare journalist and senior writer for athenaInsight, an online daily media hub about health systems and reform in the U.S. Her writing credits include *Parenting Magazine*, *National Public Radio*, and two bestselling books on breastfeeding.

Karen Pryor

Karen Pryor is a scientist, a writer, and a pioneer in modern positive training for both animals and people. Her most popular book, *Don't Shoot the Dog!*, has been translated into 17 languages and is considered to be the "bible" on positive behavioral training. Karen is the founder of Karen Pryor Clicker Training and Karen Pryor Academy. Currently, she mentors graduate students at Hunter College and is using positive clicker training methods to teach surgical skills to interns and residents at Montefiore Hospital in New York.

Ken Ramirez

Ken Ramirez is the Executive Vice President and Chief Training Officer at Karen Pryor Clicker Training. A trainer and consultant for nearly 40 years, Ken previously served as the Executive Vice President, Animal Care and Training, at Chicago's world-famous Shedd Aquarium. He is the author of several books and DVDs, including *ANIMAL TRAINING: Successful Animal Management Through Positive Reinforcement*, which has become required reading for many trainers in the zoological field.

Kathy Sdao

An applied animal behaviorist and a fulltime animal trainer for 30 years, Kathy Sdao worked first with marine mammals and now works with dogs and their people. Kathy co-founded Tacoma's first dog daycare facility and began teaching clicker-training classes. Since 1998, she has owned Bright Spot Dog Training, providing family consultations about challenging dogs, teaching private lessons, and mentoring professional trainers. An original faculty member, Kathy has led courses at 30 ClickerExpo conferences. She has traveled extensively—across the United States, Canada, and Europe, and to Australia, Israel, Japan, and Mexico. In 2012, Kathy published her first book, *Plenty in Life Is Free: Reflections on Dogs, Training and Finding Grace*.

Kellie Snider

Kellie Snider, MS, studied behavior analysis at the University of North Texas. She conducted her thesis research on the Constructional Aggression Treatment, under the direction of Jesús Rosales-Ruiz. Since 2008, Kellie has been the Animal Behavior Programs Manager at the SPCA of Texas, a major animal welfare organization that manages two adoptions shelters, one rescue shelter, and three wellness clinics in north Texas. Kellie is a Certified Fear Free Pet Professional. Currently, she is writing a book on Constructional Aggression Treatment for Lumina Media Publishing.

Sarah Stoycos

Sarah Stoycos, KPA CTP, is the owner/trainer for Laughing Dog Academy in the Washington, DC, area. She offers in-home training and behavior modification. Sarah also teaches classes at Your Dog's Friend, an award-winning non-profit in Rockville, MD, with a mission to help keep dogs out of shelters by educating and supporting their humans. She is the founder and director of the Foster Dog Alliance, a low-cost program that assists people who foster dogs for rescues and shelters, helping them make their foster dogs more adoptable through positive training. In addition to dogs, Sarah has worked with rescued, rehabilitated, and injured seals and abandoned seal pups; she has cared for sanctuary chimps and monkeys, too. A former college professor who loves to teach, Sarah enjoys meeting new people and showing them ways to communicate better with their dogs.

Alice Tong

Alice Tong, KPA CTP, LCSW, provides private training services through her business Choose Positive Dog Training. A licensed clinical social worker, Alice is skilled at reading and assisting humans and dogs of all personalities. Her focus is always on positive methods, respectful communication, and high-quality service.

Laura Monaco Torelli

Laura Monaco Torelli began her career as a professional trainer at the Shedd Aquarium. She worked as a supervisory keeper at San Diego and Brookfield zoos before founding Animal Behavior Training Concepts in Chicago, Illinois. Laura currently serves as a KPA faculty member; she collaborates with veterinary behaviorist John Ciribassi at Animal Behavior Partners; and she is a staff trainer with Dr. Ciribassi's practice, Chicagoland Veterinary Behavior Consultants.

Kiki Yablon

Kiki Yablon, KPA CTP, CPDT-KA, offers in-home dog training in Chicago. She also serves as training manager for Animal Behavior Training Concepts and helps teach behavior analysis to animal professionals as a co-instructor for Dr. Susan Friedman's Living and Learning with Animals course. Kiki is a former editor of *Outside, Chicago Magazine,* and the *Chicago Reader.* More of her writing can be found at kikiyablondogtraining.com.

Made in the USA
Middletown, DE
06 January 2017